"I found JUDAISM BEYOND GOD *interesting, provocative, annoying, fascinating, argumentative, dogmatic, funny, earnest....In short, I found in the book many of the qualities I have found in Sherwin Wine over the years. That, of course, makes the book worth reading and the text an example of Wine's integrity....*

"Wine's focus on the human features of [the Humanistic Jewish movement] — anger, skepticism, humor, and self-reliance — make his book important to Humanists and not simply to Jewish Humanists or Humanistic Jews."

HOWARD B. RADEST
Director, The Ethical Culture Schools
President, International Humanist and
Ethical Union

"This is a highly controversial book that challenges some of the most revered 'truths' of Jewish historical interpretation, including those held by many secularists, past and present. For example: the worship of one God did not come from Jewish experience. It was an attempt to deny it....

"At the same time, this book explains to modern Jews the sources of many of their confusions. Meeting head-on a complex and an endlessly written about subject, it bristles with staccato sentences and a sophisticated sense of humor. Even if you disagree with Wine's conclusions, you can't fault his clarity of expression."

MAX ROSENFELD
Yiddish translator, and
leader within the secular Jewish movement

JUDAISM
BEYOND
GOD

JUDAISM
BEYOND
GOD

A Radical New Way to Be Jewish

Sherwin T. Wine

Society for Humanistic Judaism
Farmington Hills, Michigan

Published by
Society for Humanistic Judaism
28611 West Twelve Mile Road
Farmington Hills, Michigan 48018
(313) 478-7610

Library of Congress Catalogue Card Number
85-61942

ISBN 0-912645-08-3

Printed in the United States of America

CONTENTS

FOREWORD

Judaism is no single religion or philosophy of life. It embraces that spectrum of alternatives that find significance and value in Jewish identity.

Judaism without God is an important existing alternative among Jewish people throughout the world. Most secular and humanistic Jews have never bothered to deal with the philosophic and historic foundations of their commitment. Many of them suffer from the disability of not feeling legitimately Jewish. Others do not even know that such an option exists.

This book was written to serve the needs of these people and to explain the humanistic option to the wider public, both Jewish and non-Jewish. It would not have been possible without the generous help of good friends: Ronald Milan, Chairman of the Publications Committee of the Society for Humanistic Judaism; Bonnie Cousens, Co-Editor of the journal *Humanistic Judaism*; and Miriam Jerris, Executive Director of the Society for Humanistic Judaism.

A secular Judaism is the *real* alternative to the existing theistic varieties that dominate the American scene. It may be *your* alternative.

CHAPTER I

The Jew

What is a Jew?

The question is an obsessive one for Jews. While their enemies seem to have no trouble dealing with the question, Jews never seem to get enough of it. Over and over, they invent discussions and classes to explore the issue. Over and over, they listen to the answers. Over and over, they find them wanting. Dissatisfied, they begin their futile effort once again.

Why is it so hard for Jews to answer the question? Do Muslims run around all the time asking "What is a Muslim?" Do Greeks devote their adult education projects to exploring "What is a Greek?" What makes Jews so compulsive about defining themselves?

Part of the reason is that Jews do not like the answers their enemies invent. Part of the reason is that the conventional categories of *race, nation,* and *religion* do not fit the Jews easily. But the chief cause is that most Jews do not really want an answer to the question. Confusion allows them to choose the definition that is convenient for the moment. It also allows them to postpone dealing with the discomfort they feel about being Jewish.

Jewish identity is a controversial status. It rarely arouses indifference. Even those who plead that they never have experienced anti-Semitism often plead too hard. And those who complain about Jewish oversensitivity are correct about the unattractiveness of victims but wrong about the provocations.

In the century of the Holocaust, valuing Jewish identity requires special effort and determination. People who are always talking about how "proud" they are to be what they are have more doubts than they are willing to admit. Comfortable identity rarely needs affirmation — or definition.

Being Jewish is an involuntary condition for most Jews. Some people choose Jewish identity. But most discover that they have it. It is an inheritance, which they can either enjoy or not enjoy, indulge or not indulge. Jewishness does not start with a theological decision. It begins in the womb. Membership precedes conviction.

The question for most Jews is not "Should I or should I not be Jewish?" Destiny has already decided that issue. The question is "How do I respond to my Jewish identity?" or "What should I do about it?"

Some Jews respond to the question with active resentment. If they had their choice, they would have chosen another identity. They are annoyed by what the fates have dished out. They work very hard at removing all public signs of their Jewish condition. They avoid the company of Jews. They separate their family from their friends. They suffer anti-Semitic jokes because they agree with them.

But active resentment may take another course. Guilt, embarrassment, and the futility of denial may prevent withdrawal. Forced to identify themselves as Jews, the resenters now make distinctions between socially acceptable Jews and the socially unacceptable. They boast of being Jewish and simultaneously avoid stereotyped Jewish behavior. They support and join conventional Jewish organizations because they do not want any more controversy. Above all, they fight anti-Semitism because it is the mirror image of their own guilty objection.

Many Jews respond to their Jewish identity with passive resentment. They accept their Jewish condition but do not wish to do anything about it. They are interested in neither active denial nor affirmation. If you ask them what their feelings are, they will describe them as indifference — although Jewish identity in the Western world is too controversial to sponsor a yawn. If they are very passive, they will be recruited for Jewish organizational life. But they will secretly prefer that Jewish activity be boring enough to justify avoidance.

Some resenters are sufficiently intellectual to need an ideology of resentment. They argue that universalism is incompatible with Jewishness. The preservation of Jewish identity becomes a moral offense because it maintains unnecessary barriers between people. In order not to appear self-hating, they deplore all forms of group identity. They officially dream of people without labels.

In former years, thousands of Jewish intellectuals became the champions of a cosmopolitan union. Socialists like Marx and Trotsky predicted the eventual disappearance of national enthusiasm and its replacement by human solidarity. Cultivating Jewish identity was a reactionary enterprise, a futile resistance to the laws of history. Whether their perception was a genuine plunge into idealism or a cover-up for self-hate, we shall never know. Most likely, it was a combination of both. Certainly, it was a clever retaliation to maintain that if Jewish identity was dispensable, so were all others.

Yet resentment, active or passive, is not where most Jews are. Despite all the negative involuntary aspects of Jewish identity, they value it in a positive way and would be reluctant to give it up, even if they could. Their ambivalence is a union of discomfort and attachment. They feel guilty about the discomfort and vaguely noble about the attachment. They would like to do something constructive with their Jewish identity. They would like to make it a comfortable part of their life. They would like to attach their deepest convictions and strongest values to it. They would even like the approval of their ancestors for what they choose to do with their existence. But they do not know quite what to do.

For traditional Jews, making Jewish identity a significant part of their lives is fairly easy. Since they are comfortable with the religious behavior of the past, they have no difficulty integrating their Jewishness with their philosophy of life. The union of Jewish identity with the theology of Torah and the Talmud gives them no problem. They are believers. They can do conventional Jewish things with conviction. The official group tradition and their own perception of reality coincide.

But many Jews who value their Jewishness, however ambivalently, are less comfortable. The historic procedures for expressing their membership in the Jewish people rub against their personal integrity. They feel Jewish but not religious. Or they feel religious but not the way the rabbis prescribe.

God bothers them. After the Holocaust, they are not sure that he really exists. And if he does, they are not sure they want to talk to him.

Tradition bothers them. It is very authoritarian, always talking about divine commands and leaving little room for more than timid feedback. Its emphasis on pious reverence seems to go against the grain of what it means to be Jewish. Laughter and creative *hutspa* are not welcome in its presence. The religious image is annoying. Most of the heroes are prophets, priests, and rabbis. The secular side of modern Jewish life seems to find no echo in the Jewish past. Either they turn these ancient teachers into early day contemporary philosophers or they have to disown their founding fathers.

The telling of Jewish history presents its problems. The official version is so filled with stories of miracles, supernatural events, and divine guidance that it is too unbelievable to explain anything. It simply becomes a half-hearted exercise for Sunday school children or a ceremonial drama around the Passover table.

The portrayal of the Jewish personality leaves much to be desired. If Jews are the "People of the Book," it is hard to prove it from Jewish behavior. Most modern Jews read a lot of books. But the Bible is not one of them. Deploring the discrepancy does not change the reality. The reading Jewish public is more intellectual than it is pious. But it finds no real approval for its choices.

The passionate exclusiveness of Jewish authorities is embarrassing. On the one hand, the Jews are featured as the inventors of love, brotherhood, and morality. On the other hand, they are warned against too much social intercourse with Gentiles and the sin of intermarriage. The conflict between group survival and decent openness turns the Jewish establishment into an example of the very moral hypocrisy it claims to abhor.

In the face of all these problems, valuing Jewish identity is not enough. Jewish identity needs to find some way to express itself that does not violate other values that are equally important or more important. It needs to promote personal integrity. It needs to deal honestly with the issue of God. It needs to challenge the exclusive claims of the religious tradition. It needs to present a realistic version of Jewish history to the Jewish masses and to incorporate it into Jewish celebration. It needs to revise the vision of the ideal Jew and to let it conform with the real moral and intellectual aspirations of contemporary Jews. It needs to challenge the parochialism of the past and to provide a more compassionate answer.

For those Jews who regard their Jewish identity as an unwelcome intrusion, a negative condition, a disability worthy of resentment, none of these tasks is relevant. The less comfortable Jewishness is, the more easily it will be rejected or avoided.

For those Jews who are sincerely traditional, none of these tasks is relevant either. They have what they need.

For those Jews who see their Jewishness as something positive but who do not see any real connection between Jewish identity and their own personal philosophy of life, maintaining two separate compartments will be quite enough. They will do their Jewishness in conventional institutions and their personal commitments elsewhere.

But for those Jews who are not traditional, who want to integrate their Jewish identity with their personal convictions, the challenge is important.

If you are one of these Jews, this book is for you.

CHAPTER II

The Yahveh Story

On a pragmatic level, historic Judaism is a doctrine about the value of Jewish identity. It seeks to justify Jewish attachment and to encourage Jewish connections. It explains why Jews should choose to remain Jews.

Judaism is different from Christianity in many ways. Its ethnic base is national rather than imperial.[1] Its cultural roots are Hebrew, not Greek and Roman. Its history is more an experience of appeasement than power. But especially different is the fact that Jews existed before Judaism. The Jewish nation was a political and ethnic reality long before the priestly and rabbinic religious establishments became the rulers of the Jews and invented Judaism.

Christianity did not provide reasons for saving an old identity; it invented a new one. But the creators of Judaism started out as Jews. And as Jews, they found new reasons for remaining Jews. Threatened by ethnic and linguistic assimilation, they found religious justification for the preservation of Jewish identity. Theology did not precede Jewish identity and mold it. It started with the Jewish people and catered to its needs.[2]

The defeat and conquest of the Jews by foreign powers — Chaldeans and Persians — made Judaism possible. It made Jewish identity vulnerable, and it brought to power ambitious clergymen. These priests and rabbis developed a system of affirmations about the world and the Jewish people to

motivate the Jews to retain their national identity. The amaz-
ing product of their work, in its final form, is rabbinic
Judaism. Given the continuing power of the religious
establishment, it became traditional Judaism.

Rabbinic Judaism was created out of priestly Judaism by
an ambitious scholar class that promised more than the
priests offered. Rabbinic rewards included political independence and personal immortality. The rabbis also claimed that the written priestly Torah was incomplete. God's instructions to Israel, they said, were especially present in an
oral tradition of laws and stories which had never been
recorded. The Oral Torah was just as important as the Written Torah. And only the rabbis knew what it was and how to
interpret it. Ultimately, this oral tradition was written
down; the Talmud became the basic anthology of rabbinic
Judaism.

The rabbinic fathers speak out of the pages of the Talmud.
As the rulers of the Jews, they provide grand reasons for
Jews to remain Jews. As strong believers in the existence
and power of a god named Yahveh, they make him the center
of their motivational system.

The story of Yahveh is a matter of controversy. Traditional Jews see him as a real being, the supreme ruler of the
universe, who existed long before the Jewish people came on
the scene. Others see him as the personal creation of the
Jewish people, a useful fiction serving the emotional needs of
the nation.

Whatever the truth, the rabbinic message made the Jews
want to stay Jewish. It offered theological goodies that many
Jews found irresistible.

The official rabbinic story goes something like this:

Yahveh is the god of the whole world. There are no other
gods. If indeed there are other godlike beings, they are so inferior, they can best be described as angels. Yahveh is all-

powerful: there is nothing he cannot do. He is also all-knowing: there is nothing of which he is unaware.

Although Yahveh manufactured men and women, he was not pleased with his creation. The first people disappointed him. And he has often been tempted to dispose of them entirely.[3]

Frustrated, he chose quality over quantity. He chose Abraham to be the ancestor of his special people and made a treaty with him.[4] If the descendants of Abraham would follow his instructions and strive to become more godlike, he would reward them with special gifts and special consideration. Jerusalem, the capital of the Jews, would become his earthly residence. And the Jews would have the privilege of living closest to his earthly palace and his earthly presence.[5]

Ultimately, Yahveh will turn the earth into what he wants it to be. Before the establishment of Paradise, there will be the Final Judgment. The dead will rise from their graves and be assigned to either Paradise or Hell.[6] And before the Final Judgment, the living wicked will be defeated by the Messiah, the deputy of Yahveh.[7]

Because of their special status, the Jews will fare better than all the other nations on Judgment Day.[8] The Messiah will establish the capital of the world in Jerusalem.[9] And the faithful Jews will find it easier to enter Paradise than the less virtuous members of other nations. They will also have the pleasure of seeing their enemies humiliated and crushed.

The price of these rewards is the halakha, a way of life described by the spokesmen of Yahveh in the Torah and the Talmud.[10] The halakha is a time-consuming set of behaviors that includes regular acts of worship, the avoidance of certain foods and substances, the maintenance of the patriarchal family, a special concern with the Sabbath and male circumcision, and separation from the contaminating influence of pagan lifestyles.

Another price is special punishment, the counterpart to special reward. Since the Jews will be receiving unusual benefits, they will have to accept unusual surveillance. Yahveh expects more of them than he expects of others. He will punish them more harshly when they fail to live up to their side of the bargain. The suffering of the Jews is, therefore, not a sign of Jewish degradation. It is a sign of their special status, the power of Yahveh, and the hard work necessary for final salvation.

But Jewish privilege is not confined to those who are born Jews. It is also open to those who want to become Jews and to enjoy the special awards. Foreigners are welcome to join the Jewish nation so long as they assume the discipline of the halakha and repudiate their former connections. No Gentile is excluded from salvation who desires it.[11]

Above all, Yahveh is both universal and particular. He is a universal god, but he has a particular name. Monotheists who want to call him Zeus, Jupiter, Mazda — or simply God — are missing the boat. He is a universal god, but he has given special privileges to a particular nation. Greeks, Romans, and Persians are not as close to him as the Jews. He is a universal god, but he recommends a particular discipline. Cultural pluralism is fine for philosophers, but it is unacceptable to him.

This story about Yahveh is a powerful motivating story. Although it appears to be an epic about Yahveh, it is, in reality, an epic about the Jews. It explains clearly and unequivocally why staying Jewish is important and why becoming Jewish is attractive.

So long as Jews believed it, they had a compelling reason to remain Jewish. Non-Jews who believed it also had a compelling reason to become Jewish. Rabbinic Judaism provided a way not only for maintaining Jewish numbers but also for increasing them.

Whether you regard the Yahveh story as truth or mythology, you have to admit that the epic makes Jewish identity a valuable identity. If your connection with Abraham and the halakha will guarantee you the highest eternal rewards, even persecution and the inconvenience of the ritual are worth enduring.

The rabbis gave Jews a reason for preserving Jewish identity even when they no longer lived in a Jewish land, no longer spoke a Jewish language, and no longer enjoyed a Jewish government. Only the Greeks, with their strong conviction in the superiority of their language and culture, were as arrogant as the Jews. But the Judaism of the rabbis proved to be a tough rival. It gave Hellenism a run for its money. When large numbers of Jews left Israel and were dispersed throughout the Greek-speaking world, they possessed a good reason for remaining Jews.

Rabbinic Judaism had no real competition among Jews for many centuries. In a world where gods, angels, and demons were as "real" as mountains and rivers, the Yahveh story was believable. And, as long as it was believable, it dominated the Jewish world.

Of course, the epic had its problems. The obsession of Yahveh with a particular name and a particular people did seem a bit odd for a world god. And the tale was more than vague about what would happen to Gentiles, especially the righteous ones, on Judgment Day. But these defects were trivial for people who wanted to believe and who found it convenient to do so.

Christianity, in time, offered an equally compelling myth. But its inherent anti-Semitism made it uncomfortable for Jews. Christians claimed to be the divine replacement for the Jews. They provided reasons for the Syrians, Greeks, and Romans to lord it over their Hebrew competitors. Ultimately, the Christian story proved more appealing to the Gentiles than the Jewish one. Because of Christian competition and hostility, Judaism ceased to expand and retained its identification with Hebrew ethnicity.

The Muslim challenge was equally unconvincing to Jews. Islam started out as an Arab religion. But through Arab conquest and through its own motivating story, Islam Arabized many other nations. As a competing Semitic myth, it outdistanced Judaism and restricted the expansion of Judaism in Western Asia and North Africa. But Islam was unsuccessful in motivating Jews to forego Jewish identity. Despite the appeal of Arab political success and the luxury of the Muslim Paradise, most Jews found the rabbinic system more satisfying. The rabbis had turned Jewish defeat and humiliation into a positive sign of divine favor, a penance in the present for the rewards of the future. With an ideology that successfully explained disaster as the prelude to victory, change was unnecessary.

Until modern times, the Yahveh story convinced most Jews to remain Jews. Although they had opportunities to become Christians or Muslims and to abandon Jewish identity, they refused to give up their Jewishness. From time to time, racial prejudice prevented assimilation. (The Marranos tried and failed.) But, on the whole, Jewish identity was rejectable and, therefore, voluntary.

Even the physical assault on the Jews in the Christian Middle Ages did not undermine the rabbinic faith and its sense of a special destiny for the Jews. Suffering became a badge of honor.[12]

CHAPTER III

The Secular Revolution

Today, the Yahveh story has lost most of its believing public. Bands of the faithful survive. But they are small in number and desperate. The chief sign of their desperation is their militancy.

But another sign of their desperation is the way they sell the Yahveh story. Lubavitcher missionaries push the Jewish survival value of the story in order to make it acceptable. Without this rationale, the Jews will disappear, they plead. Without some formal adherence to this divine epic, the behavior patterns that keep the Jews separate and distinct will lose their meaning. The hidden agenda lies exposed. In calmer times, you believed because the tale was believable. And Jewish survival was the consequence of your belief. Today, you *try* to believe because the formal act of "believing" is good for Jewish survival. And conviction may follow.

The truth is that, in this day and age, the story is not very believable. Guilt has replaced conviction. Jews are threatened with extinction if the story is rejected. But, then, religion becomes the enemy of integrity.[1]

Who is to blame for the subversion of this sustaining myth?

No one person in particular is to blame. But a whole movement of people, most of them not Jewish, who lived in Western Europe during the past four centuries, were responsible. They were the devotees of the Enlightenment, the Age of Reason, the Era of Science. They were the creators of the Secular Revolution.

The Secular Revolution did exactly what its name suggests. It made the world more secular. It undermined the two pillars of a religious society — a strong belief in the world of the supernatural and the popularity of worship. It turned religious epics into myths and made public acts of reverence, even directed to human rulers, an uncomfortable experience.

The Secular Revolution was not an explosive event although it had explosive moments, like the American War of Independence and the storming of the Bastille. It was a gradual transformation of thinking and behavior. Its beginnings were imperceptible and its development, long.

Secularism did not begin as a bold rejection of religious ideas and religious behavior. It started out as a new awareness of human power and strength. As people grew more confident in their own ability to solve their problems and to control their environment, they felt less of a need to turn to supernatural help and to rely on worship. Religion gradually became less important. And the teachers of religion became less powerful. In time, much of religion, itself, became secularized.

Economic development in the thirteenth, fourteenth, and fifteenth centuries was responsible for this new sense of human achievement. The new prosperity, centered in Italy and the Netherlands, transformed cities from fortresses into busy places of trade and manufacturing. An ambitious new merchant class emerged. Money became more plentiful. Leisure became more commonplace. And new professions of learning arose to rival the clergy and to challenge the preeminence of their religious information.

The challenge to the clergy was not direct or assaultive. It was much more subtle. Its vehicle was the revival of the secular literature of the Greeks and Romans that we call the

Renaissance. In time, the secular art forms of the past were also revived and imitated. A new class developed — scholars who became experts in this classical tradition and teachers of a new education.

What appeared to be old was really new. The ideas of the Classical Tradition emerged as an alternative authority to the doctrines of the Church. The challengers of Church authority did not denounce traditional religion. Such a procedure was politically and emotionally unacceptable. They simply devoted more and more time to secular and classical studies, using the old literature in new ways. The effect of their work was an increasing uninterest in the propaganda of the Church. The middle and upper classes became more secular without having to give up the religious practices to which they were attached.

The Protestant Reformation served the future of the secular revolution, although without conscious intent. While it was certainly an expression of popular religious fervor, it undermined the authority of the professional clergy that gave religion power. It also made the reading of the Bible its chief sacrament, thus promoting the very literacy that would be its own undoing. Once you can read religious books, you can also read secular ones.

Secularism became bolder in the seventeenth century and produced the Enlightenment. The new scholar class no longer hid behind the garments of ancient writers. They composed their own secular philosophies, which paid scant respect to Christian authority. Bacon, Descartes, Hobbes, and Spinoza discarded religious faith as an essential path to truth and publicly embraced secular reason. The hidden agenda of the Renaissance now showed its face. Christian doctrine and the Christian clergy were dispensable.

The Enlightenment kept God for ceremonial purposes but castrated him. By the time we get to Newton and Voltaire, he has been retired from active duty. He is only allowed to design and manufacture the world. Once the laws of nature are in place, he cannot even change his mind. He remains a helpless spectator, an unemployed deity, unable to intervene in the daily affairs of the world. If the gods have nursing homes, he is in one of them.

In the nineteenth century, atheism is safely proclaimed. But it never becomes terribly popular. For most secular scholars, the new God of the liberals was too boring to fight. They preferred to pursue secular studies, to establish secular universities, and to undertake scientific research. As long as the religious establishment did not interfere with their secular work, there was no need for confrontation. Only where the conservative clergy offered active resistance, as in Latin and Slavic countries, did militant atheistic anticlerical movements arise to promote the secular point of view.

By the twentieth century, even the establishment churches of the Protestant world were too intimidated to teach the old Christian epic. The education of the Protestant clergy became a secular enterprise. The Resurrection, the after-life, and the supernatural faded out of Protestant sermons. Self-fulfillment and social action became "religious" themes. And the Bible was interpreted to accommodate any new secular fashion. Genesis was available to endorse both evolution and female equality. For liberal Christians, the forms remained, but the substance was gone.

The Secular Revolution subverted all the reigning epic stories that motivated religious behavior and supported religious identity. The hero of these stories was God, however named. When Kant demonstrated at the end of the eighteenth century that it was impossible to prove either the existence or the non-existence of God, he was giving intellectual expression to a social experience. In increasing numbers, people no longer cared whether God existed or not. They had found alternative secular sources for strength and meaning.

Science was not as personal as God. But it did promise more reliable power than prayer.

The new epics of the secular age shifted their attention from God to people. They became more humanistic. People were seen less as the creatures of God and more as the masters of their own story. Even if they were limited by the laws of nature, by the weakness of their own power, they had no conscious rivals to direct their lives and to interfere with their own plans. People were no longer the supporting actors in their own drama. They were the leading characters.

Any new motivating story about group identity would have to take this change into account.

Secular humanism is the philosophic consequence of the Secular Revolution. It is a set of ideas about the world and its people that pervades Western society, especially its educated and managerial classes. Since the conquest of the world by Western culture coincided with the Secular Revolution, it is a powerful force in all countries and nations.

While the surviving institution of the old religious culture is the church or synagogue, the "temples" of secular humanism are the schools of secular studies. And its "clergy" are the teachers and professionals who use them and graduate from them.

Most secular humanists do not know that they are what they are and do not choose to use the label. Having never been united as a group with a strong group identity, they often have a clearer idea of what they do not believe than of what they do believe. If they are asked to define themselves with regard to conventional religion, they will tend to pick a conventional label like "Jewish" or "Christian" and then add, "but I'm not very religious." A few will say, "none."

When the leaders of the religious Radical Right describe secular humanism as a powerful threat, they are telling the truth. While the forces of secular humanism are very weak, the ideas of secular humanism are very strong. The militancy of the Moral Majority is a testimony to the power of these beliefs.

What is the nature of these powerful ideas?

For the secular humanist, there are two major commitments. Each one is an answer to the two basic questions of any philosophy of life. The first is the question of truth and reality: What *is* the world like? The second is the question of value and morality: What *ought* the world to be like?

CHAPTER IV

Faith and Reason

Faith and Obedience. These are the traditional answers to the *two* questions any philosophy of life must answer: What is the nature of reality? How do we respond to that reality?

Rabbis, sheikhs, and Christian priests all agreed that faith and obedience were marvelous, even though they disagreed about the content of faith and the rules of obedience. Virtue and piety went together.

Faith is a procedure for answering the question: What *is* the world like? It prescribes a method for discovering the truth. In every old culture, it recommends that people trust the advice of their ancestors. It insists that the wisdom of the past is still true and that the authority of the past is still reliable.

For most of human history, people had no reason to question the information they received from their ancestors. Since very little changed, the old statements about life and people did not challenge experience. And since any new idea could easily be made to appear old (there were so few of them), faith was comfortable. Farming and religion used faith all the time. Imitating the past seemed the sensible thing to do.

Jews were no exception. Since the people of the past seemed smarter than the people of the present, they deserved respect. Prophets and the rabbinic sages were superior to the sages of the present. Some of them had spoken to God. And God knew everything.

As for obedience, it was equally credible. It was a procedure for answering the question: How *ought* we to behave? In a social setting where the patriarchal family predominated, obeying fathers did not have to be explained. God was the natural extension of paternal authority. He might promise rewards and threaten punishments, but his ultimate moral authority lay in the vulnerable childhood experience of every human being.

Faith reassured the masses that God really commanded what tradition said he commanded. And obedience was the natural response to that information. Of course, people often tried to obey and failed. The will was not always strong enough to do what was right. But guilt made them uncomfortable enough to remember the importance of obedience.

In the Jewish world of faith and conformity, scholarship was memorizing the rules. Every old rule had to come from a legitimate chain of command. And every new rule had to be derived from some old rule. The genius of the rabbis was devoted to making texts mean what they did not seem to mean. Nevertheless, the rabbis seemed to enjoy their work. They loved the challenge of squeezing ethical juice from ritual lemons. Letting rules stand on their own merit would have undermined their professional skills.

The Secular Revolution encountered faith and obedience and found them wanting. What had appeared so comfortable for so many generations was now awkward, badly suited to the age of science and industry.

The emerging secular world was a place of change. New ideas were being proposed. New inventions were being created. The people were on the move. Cities were growing. Trade and technology were changing the face of life. In such a turmoil, respect for the past was less convincing than before. Trusting ancestors seemed a bit silly, especially when one was in the process of repudiating them. Faith kept bumping into new discoveries and finding them hostile.

Obedience also fell on hard times. As interest in God began to wane, following his instructions became less urgent. People simply talked more and more about their own needs and less and less about his. In an age of revolution, defying fathers, even divine ones, was more fashionable and earned public support. For citizens of a secular democratic state, pious reverence seemed out of date.

But what were the substitutes? The old questions still needed answers, even if they were new answers.

Reason and dignity moved in to fill the gap. They became the ideological twins of the secular age. The call to reason and the defense of human dignity rallied the new intellectuals. A new "religion" was emerging that was different from every one that came before.

This new humanism found its authority in these two alternatives — and it still does. After three centuries of triumph, trouble, and regret, the philosophy of the secular age rests on their merits.

Reason is a dignified word. Too dignified for some people, it is confusing to others, even to those who claim they like it. It has been around for so long that both its defenders and its detractors tend to talk about it without understanding it.

Reason pre-dated the Age of Reason. The hunter who improved the stone tool, the peasant who perfected the plow, the anonymous hero who invented the wheel — all used reason even though they gave it no name. The common-sensical procedure of solving problems by testing ideas against the evidence of daily experience is the beginning of rational thinking. In every culture, ordinary and extraordinary people were using it all the time, even while they were using faith and revering their ancestors. As practical wisdom, reason has been around for a long time, even in societies that gave all honor to priests.

But its formal evolution to recognized status was left to the Greeks. Not to all the Greeks, because most of them were very pious, just like their neighbors. But to a rising scholar class of secular philosopher teachers who taught the children of the leisure class. Athens became their headquarters. New schools became their training ground. Reason became the dramatized symbol of their resistance to tradition.

In the hands of Plato, reason became a romantic idol, a new divinity. Aristotle was a more modest user. So were Protagoras, Democritus, and Epicurus.[1] Falling in love with reason became fashionable in their circles. And the new propaganda for reason often became as pretentious and as silly as the vocabulary of lovemaking.

Nevertheless, an important first step had been taken. Faith and obedience had been challenged. The human mind had been invited to question ancestral tradition and to judge ideas and morals on their own secular merits. While the social and economic development of the ancient world did not allow the Athenian challenge to take deep root, it lingered in the underground of the Christian, Muslim, and Jewish worlds as a theme worth reviving. The philosophers were premature, but they were not irrelevant.

All through the pious centuries of the Middle Ages, the admirers of reason studied the words of the secular Greeks and tried to make them religiously respectable. Both Plato and Aristotle found their establishment devotees and were elevated to philosophic sainthood. Aquinas, Avicenna, and Maimonides made reason legitimate, even though inferior to faith.

But the advent of the Secular Revolution made the voices of reason bolder. Descartes and Spinoza dismissed faith and gave reason first place. Newton, Locke, and Kant, each in his own way, advanced the primacy of rational thinking. By the nineteenth century, among respectable philosophers, faith was no longer a credible competitor. If there were arguments, they were either disputes about the nature of reason or challenges from personal intuition.

In the twentieth century, no major intellectual figure advocates faith. While the masses struggle to retain their traditional commitments, the educated elite gives them very little help. Many contemporary thinkers and philosophers bemoan the deficiencies of reason, but they have not provided a more convincing challenger.

The triumph of reason is no mere accident. It rests on the spreading economy of an urban and industrial world. The age of science is the twin of the age of technology. The city environment of capitalism undermines the old family structure that makes faith possible. The militancy of religious fundamentalists in our contemporary society is not a sign of their confidence. It reflects their desperation.

The age of capitalism became the first triumphant age of reason. The ancient Greek humanists lived in a primitive economic world that was not able to sustain their insights. Modern times are unique. They are very different from the past. If people are having difficulty in finding their place in the life of reason, it is because the life of reason is very new and very frightening. Our old skills for survival no longer work. And we have not yet developed all the new skills we need.

Because of their intimate involvement with capitalism, Jews were especially affected by the triumph of reason. An open competitive society was not a friend of faith. But it was good for Jews. Secular thinking and secular professions became avenues for Jewish advancement and were openly embraced. The Jew and Reason discovered that their personal agendas coincided.

WHAT IS REASON?

The word *reason* is often confusing because it refers to two different thinking processes. The first is best called *formal* reason. The second is called *practical* reason.

Formal reason is logic. It is the enemy of confusion and contradiction. It views paradox with suspicion. It prefers clarity. It explores the meaning of what we say and tries to make our communication more precise and more effective. It loves implication, drawing out from ideas their hidden connections. If "all men are primates," and "Moses is a man," then "Moses is a primate." The problem with formal reason is that it is essentially sterile. It is not interested in whether its statements correspond to reality. It simply focuses on the connection between premises and conclusions. If your premises are absurd, so will your conclusions be. If "God is all-powerful," and "Yahveh is God," then "Yahveh is all-powerful." As you can see, formal reason — all by itself — has limited value. Absurd premises yield absurd conclusions.

Some philosophers have tried to make formal reason do more than it can. They are the writers who love to spell *reason* with a capital *R*. They want to turn logic into an instrument of interesting truth. Plato imagined that formal ideas preceded experience, and Descartes maintained that pure logic could demonstrate the existence of God. But, in the end, their pretensions remained pretentious. An honest manipulation of words does not describe reality. It only trains us to describe what is real.

Practical reason is different from formal reason. It is less precise and less neat. Because it is dealing with reality more than words, it is restrained by facts. The events of the real world are messier than formal reason can tolerate and often refuse to fit the words that are available. The science laboratory is not as neat as the mathematics classroom, but it is closer to reality. And mathematics is only useful when it becomes an assistant to science.

Practical reason, on the popular level, is generally called *commonsense*. In its more refined state, it is called the *scientific method*. In the world of philosophy, it is known as *empiricism*. English philosophers like Francis Bacon, John Locke, and John Stuart Mill were its special champions.

Pragmatic thinkers start with the world we experience. The basic stuff of this world is *events*, otherwise known as *facts*. Events do not appear in some random fashion. They follow uniform patterns. Or they seem to, most of the time. These *patterns*, pretentiously labeled the *laws of nature* (as though they were the official decrees of some divine supervisor), are the directors of the universal drama. Since they are compulsive and relentless, they produce the theater of *cause and effect*. Master students of the patterns have become the prophets of modern times. From one event, they can predict another. The triumph of secular science lies in this prophetic power.

Commonsensical people do not make statements about the world without paying attention to facts and patterns. Since the world is the setting for their survival and for the satisfaction of their basic desires, they need to be in touch with what the world *is* and not with what they want the world to be.

A responsibility to facts is the humble basis of true science. An observation is made. The observation prompts a statement, the hypothesis. The facts necessary to prove the statement true are listed, the plan of verification. An experiment to find the facts is conducted. If they are found, the statement is declared to be true. If some of them are found, the statement is "maybe." If none of them is found, the statement is presumed to be false.

All facts are measurable in some way. Otherwise, we would not be able to distinguish one fact from another. There are differences of size, shape, structure, and movement. Some facts are hidden. Our senses cannot experience them directly. We know about them from their effects. Some facts are private. Like personal thoughts and feelings, they can only be known directly by one person. But other people may sense them through their external consequences.

Practical reason is not always incompatible with faith. Many faith traditions contain practical wisdom. But there are major differences. Faith starts with a presumption of truth. Truth may be reenforced by the facts, but it does not depend on them. For the fundamentalists, creationism is true even if no facts can be found to support their argument. For the God-believers, God is real before they look for the evidence. But reason starts with no commitment to conclusions. It allows the facts to be the judge.[2]

Faith prefers certainty. The ancestral tradition is not *maybe* true; it *is* true. Most faith traditions are ultimately attributed to the gods or God. If gods are the authors, there can be no error. They know all and see all. Absolute conviction is appropriate to divine information. But reason needs to be more humble. The facts are less accommodating than God. They dribble in one by one. The "true" statement of today may be refuted by the evidence of tomorrow. Knowledge is change. Judgments are tentative, waiting for new confirmation. Although we may arrive at strong conclusions in the face of overwhelming evidence, there are no fixed conclusions. The earth is round — until the facts change.[3]

Faith encourages reverence. Since there is no reason to doubt God's word, challenge is unnecessary. Eternal truth does not need testing. But reason knows how fragile most statements about reality really are. It is always testing and re-testing. It is never satisfied. Truth has to keep proving its truthfulness.

Faith is parochial. It only has meaning for the people who are attached to its particular tradition. It cannot talk to people who are feeling no connection. Christian faith is different from Muslim faith. Muslim faith is different from Hindu faith. They cannot really communicate. There is no way of comparing apples and oranges. Each faith rests in its own ancestral bed. You either believe or you do not believe. But reason is universal. Facts do not belong to any nation. They are not possessed by any tradition. They simply *are*. Reason is the only procedure for the discovery of truth which crosses cultural boundaries and still makes sense. The facts are as Chinese as they are American. Science can do what a thousand interfaith banquets never really do.

Faith is easily intimidated. Exploration of the unknown is rarely encouraged. The faithful view the universe as a place that only God can fully comprehend. Ancestral tradition is only a glimpse of a total perspective that is not available to human beings. The word *mystery* describes the way the faithful perceive reality. It is impenetrable. The best you can do with the "mystery" is worship it. But reason has *hutspa*. For the reasonable person, exploring is the essence of existence. All facts are fair game. No corner of the universe, if it can be reached, can put up a sign "do not touch, I am a mystery." Even God, if he exists, should be interviewed before he is worshipped.

Faith wants to believe. It is uncomfortable with uncertainty. What is unknown is, at least, known by God. What is known must be believed fervently. To treat ancestral tradition as tentative judgments is to insult your ancestors and to undermine the structure that gives you the shelter of so much approval. The faithful are always dividing people into *believers* and *non-believers*. But reason is less eager to believe. It waits for the facts.[4] It is more comfortable with uncertainty. It prefers no answer to just any old answer that makes you feel good. It even makes decisions when the conse-

quences cannot easily be known because it is necessary to
make decisions. Reasonable people are frequently *agnostic*
(saying, "I don't know") about many things. They are more
willing to endure the anxiety of waiting for answers than the
indignity of settling for comfortable fiction. They want the
truth, not comfort.

Faith and reason are different. They are not compatible.
The discoveries of practical reason can be incorporated into
faith. But the spirit of reason cannot. The essence of reason is
the power of the living human mind to understand, to predict,
and to control. For the truly faithful, that power belongs to
the dead — and to the voice of the dead, tradition.

From the very beginning, the faithful have given reason a
bad press. They have accused it of "crimes" it does not commit. They claim that reason is "cold," the enemy of emotion.
Faith, they claim, is "warm," a fuzzy friend in a world of hard
surfaces. The rational and the emotional are portrayed as
opposites. Thinking and feeling are treated as contrasts. Of
course, the charge is false. After all, no human response is
unemotional. Even coldness is an emotion. And the content
of faith is not always warm. Threats of divine punishment can
hardly be called affirmative stroking.

Reasonable people are very emotional. If they were not,
they would have no motivation to use their reason. They
passionately desire to survive, to protect their young, to have
pleasure, to defend their dignity, to be happy. But they make
an important distinction. They use their feelings to respond
to reality. They do not use their feelings to "find" reality.
Nor do they confine legitimate emotion to nostalgia. The love
and fear of ancestors is only one of many emotional responses
in the human repertory. Creative defiance is just as
emotional and just as legitimate. For those who value it, the
pleasure of self-esteem is as strong a feeling as the longing
for tradition. Although reason is a more confronting posture

than faith and therefore initially "colder," it warms up with time, as we feel stronger and more self-confident. Faith is a more appeasing posture and therefore initially "warmer." But it gets colder as we come face to face with judgmental gods. The rewards of faith are not always "warm fuzzies."

Some people accuse reason of being the enemy of intuition. Intuition is immediate knowing. It is the assurance that a statement is true even before the facts have been checked. Intuition is different from faith. It may be totally personal, totally opposed to the conclusions of tradition. Many modern mystics, intrigued by the spiritual possibilities of self-exploration, reject faith as much as reason. They hew their own personal path out of their own personal perception. The "aquarian conspiracy"[5] is no friend of establishment religion. Intuitionists may be as confronting to faith as the rationalists.

In the nineteenth century, the Secular Revolution featured a romantic opposition to triumphant science. The romantics wanted no part of the old religion, but they were equally suspicious of the new technology and the materialistic world of uniformity it seemed to be creating. Nietzsche[6] was their most successful spokesman. And the existentialists of the twentieth century continued this protest. What was personal, individual, and subjective became, in their ideology, superior to what was collective and "objective." Science produced arrogant experts, just like the old religion, and diminished the value of the individual mind. The masters of fact were as threatening as the masters of tradition. The elevation of *intuition* became the best defense against the past and the future.

Intuition is very appealing as the arbiter of truth. It is easy to use, requiring little homework. It is free, obliged to no one but the intuitionists, themselves. It is spontaneous, resisting the plodding caution of rationalist ideas. Many rebels against the religious past have found intuition irresistible. They have used their intuition to produce a wide range of "outrageous" world views. They can turn out an adventurous atheist just as easily as a competitive mystic.

Reasonable people find intuition attractive in many ways. The progress of science begins with bold intuition. Creative thinkers first sense that something is true even before they go out to look for the facts. Without intuition, there would be no hypotheses to investigate. The process of recall is also aided by intuition. Our brain stores the conclusions of commonsense in the unconscious and feeds them back to us as intuition so that we do not have to repeat the reasoning process. The reality of evolutionary memory is also expressed in intuition. Information about the world may be transmitted genetically and appear in our mind as a hard-to-resist conclusion. Intuition may also be a welcome reply to the fact-finders who always see the parts but never the whole. Figuring out how to put the pieces together may be more spontaneous than the act of cutting them out.

But reason also finds intuition dangerous. If all intuitions lead to truth, how do you decide between two intuitions that conflict? Some arguments can be handled by simply allowing people to act out whatever they perceive to be true. But some arguments have social consequences that cannot be dealt with by avoiding the issue. What do we say to an "aquarian" mother who believes that she has the spiritual power to heal her sick child without medicine? What do we say to the male chauvinist legislator who just knows that women prefer to be dominated? What do we say to the young person who believes that an invasion from outer space is imminent and is contemplating suicide? Do we simply thank them for their observations and announce that all truth is subjective and that all intuitions are equally valid?

All intuitions are not equally valid. Some intuitions are

true and useful. Some intuitions are false and harmless. Some intuitions are false and dangerous. But how do we decide which ones are which? Intuition alone is useless because it has no universal criterion for evaluating intuitions. Faith is useless because it is almost as arbitrary as intuition. Only reason works. In the end, intuitions have to be tested by an appeal to fact. Scientists know this. They start out with intuition and move on to experiment. Business people know this. They act on their hunches and face the consequences. Free people know this. They are only as free as the facts will allow them to be.[7]

Masters of fact are annoying. They rub against our egalitarian wishes. In rebelling against the masters of tradition, we often want to dispose of all masters. Intuition becomes our deadly weapon. It becomes the excuse for pretension and self-indulgence. But it is no substitute for education. Smug experts with closed minds and narrow vision deserve our contempt. But conscientious masters who never stop testing and changing their conclusions deserve our respectful listening.

In the age of science, the Secular Revolution features a "rational faith." It is different from the old faith. It has nothing to do with ancestral tradition. It avoids arrogant intuition. It prefers competence. Reasonable people trust the advice of experts in their lives who have proven their competence. The family physician who heals us, the family lawyer who successfully defends our freedom, the neighborhood plumber who knows how to keep the house pipes working — all of them are masters of facts we do not have time to master. And we, in turn, derive our dignity from our own competence. "Rational faith" is always conditional. It goes only as far as the facts allow. Incompetent doctors do not deserve it. Incompetent educators do not deserve it. Even incompetent gods can expect no devotion.

GOD

As a method for approaching reality, reason is not very significant if we never use it. The conclusions are more interesting than the procedure. The Secular Revolution produced a new belief system which challenged the old one and made its adherents respond with anger. The attention to facts, and not to tradition, created an upheaval in belief. A new view of reality emerged.

God was the central figure in the world of tradition. The universe was his creation. He could do with it whatever he wanted. As an all-powerful, demanding, intervening super-father, he dwarfed the rest of reality. God was part of a supernatural world of angels and demons who did not have to obey the laws of nature and who possessed extraordinary powers that natural creatures did not have and could not understand. The world of faith was a frightening place, loaded with natural disaster and supernatural terror.

God was an unchallenged given. In the age of faith, you might argue about the nature of his personality and desires, but you never challenged his existence. Jews, Christians, and Muslims disputed endlessly. But atheists were never part of the discussion. To question the reality of God was to question the validity of faith.

The need to prove the existence of God is the beginning of his end. It means that people are starting to doubt. An organization where the employees begin to doubt the existence of their employer is in deep trouble. As reason grew in strength, more and more religious philosophers became embarrassed with their divine superstar and his behavior. Why does an all-powerful God allow the suffering he can certainly prevent? Why does an all-knowing God hold people responsible for behavior he already knows they will perform?

Why is a God of the whole universe interested in the daily behavior of an insignificant peasant?

Answers were not easy to come by. Ultimately, God was turned into a vague abstract retired superstar who was so distant and mysterious that nothing positive could be said about him. Any atheist could almost be comfortable with the God of Maimonides.[8] But then why bother with God at all?

As modern science revealed the vastness of the universe, a divine father figure with a personal interest in planet Earth became less believable. The world of Copernicus, Galileo, and Newton made people too small to be noticeable and God too big to be approachable. For many thoughtful people, having him around was pragmatically the same as not having him around. Since he had lost his power to intimidate, God became a perfunctory sweet frosting on the natural cake of the world.

Ultimately, Immanuel Kant, the philosopher of Koenigsberg, a mild and unpretentious man, did God in. He demonstrated that the existence of a supreme being was problematical and that reason could neither prove his reality nor disprove it.[9] This unseemly slaughter transformed theology. The main question shifted from "Does God really exist?" to "Do people need God?" Theology became a department of psychology. The issue was no longer whether God was really there, only whether people needed God to be there. How humiliating! By the twentieth century, the religious experience — which, at least, is open to study and investigation — became the new focus of theology. Believing in God became a new form of psychotherapy.[10]

The age of reason did not kill God through angry disbelief. It disposed of him in a much more deadly fashion. It made him too vague to be interesting. Theology passed from the excitement of hell, fire, and brimstone to the boredom of abstraction with capital letters. The "All," the "One," the

"Ground of Being" are like the emperor's clothing. You are not even sure they are there. And if they are, who cares? Ultimately, the masters of contemporary religion refused to admit to any God that was meaningful. He lingered on as a word of reverence. Most people believed — but there was nothing to believe in.[11]

In a world without God, people's attention turned to the natural world. Theology was replaced by physics, chemistry, biology, and geology. These new sciences changed our view of the world. The planet Earth became a small satellite spinning around a small star. The earth grew older and older. And humanity discovered that it was the cousin of the ape.

Divine creation was out. Evolution was in.

Evolution is the monumental epic story of the secular age. It is more than the story of the development of life. It includes the entire universe — from the moment of the Big Bang to the present. It starts with electrons and photons, gravitons and gluons. It moves on to atoms, stars, and galaxies. It features explosions, transformations, and glorious fires. It encompasses the birth and death of millions of suns, the formation of billions of moons. Nothing ever stops changing, always turning from one thing into another.

The stuff of evolution is not the divine word. It is elusive energy. Everything is a disguise for energy. Comets and leopards, rocks and people — all share the same little particles, the same little flashes of substance. The evolution of earthly life is only a small chapter in the saga of a changing universe.

Bible stories cannot match the grandeur of this unfolding epic. Boiling rocks and flying reptiles are only two of a trillion wonders. Instead of emerging neatly packaged and classified for human use, the universe moves on its messy way in cruel indifference to human desire.

The Garden of Eden has been replaced by East African gorges. Adam and Eve walk upright, but they have sloping foreheads and jutting jaws. Our roots are not in heaven. They are in water holes and swamps. And our embryonic bodies cannot hide the fact that fish and frogs are part of our family tree.

Reason has presented us with a new setting. The world we live in is both messy and orderly. All units of energy under the same conditions behave in the same way, no matter where they are or when they are.

Since the universe is a collection of events, not a thing, it was not "manufactured" or "created." Energy changes form and association. It may squeeze together or thinly spread. It may contract and explode. But its universal drama has no beginning and no end.

Events in the universe have causes. But the universe, as a whole, has no cause. The question, "Who made the World?" is naive. Even if we incorrectly assume that the world is a manufactured object, the conventional answer, "God," is unsatisfying. For if one can legitimately ask, "Who made the world?" one can, with equal justice, ask, "Who made God?" The logical answer, "Super-God," leads us down a trail of regression that provides no enlightenment. If we can imagine a God without a beginning, we can much more easily imagine a world without a beginning.[12]

The age of reason is the age without God. While nostalgia preserves him in the vocabulary of the powerful, he has lost his substance. The terrifying heavenly superfather has been replaced by a dispensable philosophical abstraction. He has lost his ability to intimidate and to attract. The world he supposedly created is now more interesting than he is. Science has replaced theology as the intellectual commitment of modern times. If science and modern theology appear compatible, it is hardly a tribute to religion. Liberal religion has produced a God too vacuous to be taken seriously. Fundamentalist religion, as the surviving popular resistance to the age of reason, may be rude and assaultive. But, at least, its

God is worth noticing. The God of the fundamentalists can enforce what he commands.

The problem in the contemporary world is not the power of God. It is the power of people. The technology that is born of science has given humanity the intimidating force that was formerly reserved for divinity. In a time of biological engineering and computer slaves, new "deities" of knowledge and power have emerged. The natural world, all by itself, provides us with access to overwhelming might.

In the age of science, the leaders of humanity are faced with the question only gods used to ask: "How do we use the terrifying power we possess?" The tricks of old Yahveh on mountaintops are now easily duplicated by run of the mill military establishments. And the non-traditional electric switch has turned "Let there be light" into a routine human experience.

No redefining the word *God* will change the reality we now perceive. The world that reason has revealed to us may give us more anxiety than we want. Or it may fill us with the pleasant anticipation of new adventure and opportunity. But its new face cannot be easily denied.

CHAPTER V

Ethics and Dignity

Is and *ought* are usually far apart. They describe the tension between reality and desire. The world that is does not always correspond to the world we want.

Values are different from facts. In the world of values, facts are not only discovered. They are also judged. Some are *good*. Some are *bad*. Some are *right*. Some are *wrong*.

For many people, reality is very unpleasant. They do not like the facts. They are uncomfortable with the truth they encounter. If they can change it, they will. But if they cannot, they will often use fantasy to remake reality. Facts become the victims of values. They become the mirror image of human desire.

For the fantasy prone, hate can be made to appear as love. Disaster can pose as victory. Death can be turned into an illusion. What is unacceptable is no longer real. "I believe" emerges as "I need to believe."

Many people do not like the strange and unfamiliar world that science presents. They prefer familiar settings, even if they are filled with terrifying gods and harsh punishments. The devil is more acceptable than evolution. Supernatural power is more desirable than electromagnetism. Many people like the world that faith portrays. They prefer to be scared in traditional ways.

The scientific world-view yields some annoying facts. The earth is not the center of the universe. The laws of nature do not change when we talk to them. Minds cannot exist without brains. Our genes determine much of our behavior.

These facts are annoying because they cannot really be changed. Despite our new "divine" power, they remind us of our limitations. Liking them or not liking them is an academic exercise. They will remain even if we hate them, even if we think them unfair, inappropriate, or ugly. Denouncing the law of gravity is more than frustrating. It is the beginning of insanity.

Values are interesting only when they relate to what we can reasonably change. As human power expands, the boundaries of this changeable world will also expand. Personal death is unavoidable in the twentieth century. It may become avoidable in the twenty-second. If it does, immortality will become an appropriate issue for value judgment. "Should we or should we not choose to live forever?" Right now, spending time with the question is an idle exercise. Coping with inevitable death is a more practical project.

Values tend to deal with a much smaller part of the universe than truth. Reason travels far and wide, poking its nose into every corner of the universe and revealing all the facts we cannot presently change. But values stick close to the earth, close to the human species, close to human behavior. Human activity and human relations may be insignificant from the perspective of the universe. But, at least, we can do something about them. What we "disapprove" of, we can change.

The study of what people are is called anthropology. But the study of what people ought to be is called *ethics*. From the beginning of human self-awareness, men and women have been struggling with the question, "How should I behave?" When it comes to human behavior, we tend to be very judgmental. We have a whole set of encouraging words to support certain behavior — "right," "fair," "just," "moral." We have a whole set of intimidating words to condemn other behavior — "wrong," "unfair," "unjust," "immoral." Parents and authority figures use them to command. Children and servants use them to protest.

The Secular Revolution not only changed the way we describe the world. It also changed the way we evaluate it — especially the way we evaluate human behavior.

Traditional morality is authoritarian. It is the counterpart of faith. In a world where parents and ancestors were the most reliable support system, they had authority, the power to command and to be obeyed. So powerful were they that the threat of physical violence was unnecessary. The threat of disapproval was enough.

Authoritarian morality looks for the *authors* of commands. It wants to know *who* the people are who are giving the orders. If they are power figures familiar to the world of family and religion, they are legitimate. Gods, priests, prophets, and ancestors have the best qualifications. But if they are free-lance individuals from the world of science and city-slicking, they are illegitimate. Their voices have no roots.

In an authoritarian system, morality is memory. The experts are familiar with the chain of command. They are always able to trace back the legitimate command to the legitimate commander. If Moses said it, if Jesus said it, if Mohammed said it — then no more discussion is required. An order is an order, especially if the right person ordered it. Faith handles *ought* as easily as it handles *is*.

Authoritarian ethics prosper in a village environment of strong extended families where change and diversity are absent. God is the echo of ancestral tradition. Obedience is effortless. Challenge is useless. If there are moral alternatives, no one is interested.

The primary virtue of an authoritarian society is humility. Humility is a combination of obedience and resignation. It is the emotional and behavioral response to membership in a large stable continuous family. Humble people do not assume that they are masters of their lives. They assume that others are. And they do not consciously resent this subjection. Father, forefathers, and God are part of a stable structure that gives them security and shelters them from dangerous intrusion. Survival is harsh. Solidarity is necessary. Visions of individual dignity are irrelevant.

Religious ethics, whether Christian, Muslim, or Jewish, has its roots in this environment. Even the development of fortress and market cities does not disrupt this moral tranquility. The countryside is so close and so pervasive, the trade and craft establishment so small, that the family compound is as convenient for merchants as it is for farmers.

The subversion of the authoritarian system goes hand in hand with the subversion of village life. The age of science and capitalism destroys village tranquillity, disperses families, and fosters enterprises too big for family relationships. In the urban industrial world of capitalism, the extended family becomes an economic drag, an inefficient unit of production. A mobile society prefers a mobile work force. It prefers money to land, personal skills to tribal attachments, flexibility to tradition. In such a world, the individual becomes the most convenient work unit. Individuals can be moved from place to place and can be attached to strangers for cooperative effort. The work team of the factory or the office replaces the family.

The age of faith looks to the past. But the age of science looks to the future. The wisdom of ancestors and elders is questionable. Today's usefulness may become tomorrow's obsolescence. The young may know more than the old. Change undermines tradition. Reverence for tradition becomes an effort and has to be defended.

When the Secular Revolution took over, humility became a difficult virtue. Ancestors were far away, in family plots long forgotten. Schools replaced parents as teachers and educators. New knowledge made the young more competent than the old. The individual and the nuclear family fended for themselves. The big city featured many cultures and competing traditions. What was once a sacred inheritance became an option in a free consumer society. Obedience became selective in a world of many commanders. Resignation became inappropriate in a society that encouraged ambition.

In the marketplace of many options, authoritarian ethics collapsed. Religion remained an inheritance. But its maintenance became a choice. Ethics was still dictated. But people were selective, picking from the past what was convenient. As individual self-awareness increased, a new moral standard evolved pragmatically. Most people were unaware that they were embracing it. They often imagined that they were still traditional. But some new criterion for determining right and wrong was now necessary — especially in an environment of choice.

We call this new standard *consequentialism*. While authoritarianism is concerned with the author of a command, consequentialism deals with the consequences of following it. "What will happen if I do it?" replaces "Who said it?" The consequentialist deals with the rivalry of competing prophets — each of whom claims to be speaking for God and tradition — by saying, "I do not care who is the author of the command. I am only interested in what will happen to me and to others if we choose to obey it. If it produces good consequences, it is right. If it produces bad consequences, it is wrong. And *good* and *bad* are equally independent of any authority figure."[1]

Consequentialism, like reason, has deep roots in human history. Long before anybody gave it a name, it was there. It was often a backup system for authoritarian models. In the Bible, two incentives are offered for obedience to God.

The first is authoritarian. It simply finishes off a command with "I am Yahveh, your God." The second is consequential (just in case the first one does not work). It promises rewards for good behavior and punishments for bad behavior. The second system does what a consequential appeal generally does. It responds to some human desire or fear. It seeks to motivate conformity by promising the satisfaction of human needs.[2]

Throughout human history, where tradition did not forbid it, most practical advice was consequential. The needs of the client would be assessed. And a procedure for fulfilling them would be recommended. Money, love, power, prestige, and survival were the familiar goals. Even new religions used it to secure adherents, promising everything from youth to eternal life.

For most consequentialists, a good consequence is the satisfaction of basic human needs; a bad consequence is the frustration of basic human needs. The human being replaces God as the focus of ethics. If God continues to exist, he is only morally relevant as the creator of these needs. Morality ceases to be theistic, God-oriented. It becomes humanistic, people-oriented.[3]

But what human needs?

As Freud pointed out, what may promote our survival may not promote our pleasure.[4] And what may promote our pleasure may not promote our dignity. Equally important, what may advance my survival may not advance yours.

If the problem of authoritarianism is competing authorities, the problem of consequentialism is competing human needs. The philosophers of the Secular Revolution have argued endlessly over *which* need is primary. Thomas Hobbes and Ayn Rand opted for survival.[5] Jeremy Bentham and John Stuart Mill preferred pleasure.[6] Friedrich Nietzsche and Albert Camus elevated dignity.[7] Bertrand Russell tried to include them all by referring to a harmony of desires that he called "happiness."

In the end, *happiness* proved too vague to resolve conflict. *Pleasure* always seemed trivial in comparison to other needs. Even John Stuart Mill had to distinguish between higher and lower pleasures, making pleasure inferior to some higher standard. *Survival* turned selfishness into a virtue and did not jibe with the biological history of parents and children. *Dignity* or self-esteem seemed to have fewer difficulties than the others. But what exactly did it mean?

The Secular Revolution as a moral revolution is tied up with the concept of human dignity. As an emotional and behavioral experience, dignity is the polar opposite of humility. Neither obedience nor resignation is the stuff out of which dignity is made.

Historically, dignity was an aristocratic virtue. It was the privilege of rulers. Gods, kings, and nobles monopolized it. It suggested space, privacy, grandeur, and autonomy. It conferred the power of mastery over one's own life. People of dignity did not bow or scrape. They might choose understatement and modesty. But they did not cultivate humility.

Ultimate dignity was divine. God was subordinate to no one, the total master of his own existence. On earth, there were imitators of God, "divinely approved" rulers who enjoyed immense freedom and immune power. Beneath them were the masses who aspired to no dignity. Humility was their cup of tea. As loyal servants, they humbly accepted the designation of "subjects."

Dignity has deep evolutionary roots. It may be the oldest organic strategy. Even the most primitive organisms define their space and their territory as a means of assuring survival. Long before living creatures banded together for mutual defense, they sought their individual niche. And even when they learned to share space and to support each other, they displayed ambivalence. Anger is the defense of dignity and personal "space." It is older than love and keeps it from turning into self-effacing subjection.[8]

In human terms, dignity is the freedom and power to run your own life. It is the experience of autonomy, competence, and personal choice. It is the refusal to act out the role of obedient servant. It is the willingness to make decisions and to take responsibility for them. Although dignity began as a strategy for survival, like many evolutionary novelties, it ultimately turned into an end in itself. For those who experience dignity as a supreme value, there are times when both survival and pleasure will be sacrificed to sustain it. In other words, a life without pleasure is sustainable. But a life without dignity is not worth living.

Dignity is scarce in a survival culture. Self-awareness remains undeveloped when eking out a living is the agenda for the day. Poverty and dependence inhibit a sense of individuality and encourage people to huddle and cringe.

The Secular Revolution made dignity available to the masses. As science and technology liberated most people from the drudgery of daily survival, the new affluence and the new leisure gave them aristocratic aspirations. Egalitarian behavior is the sign of modern times. Even the richest and most powerful can no longer behave like the nobles of earlier centuries. The poorest and most destitute victims of our industrial age demand their dignity. The reverence of the lower classes for the upper classes is gone.

In the contemporary world of individual agendas, the demand for dignity continues to increase. Traditional hierarchical structures are collapsing. Women demand equality with men. Blacks demand equality with whites. The young demand equality with the old. Even children speak of their right to freedom. As for God, he is no longer presented in educated circles as a lord and master. The new egalitarian theology prefers him to be a cosmic friend.

Dignity has emerged as the primary value of the secular age. Personal liberation movements and national liberation movements (including the Jews) derive their energy from it. No successful political movement, however dictatorial, can dismiss it. In fact, it becomes the justification in the Communist world for allowing "temporary" tyranny. Money and love can be denounced. Religion and piety can be condemned. But never dignity.

The morality of the secular age embraces the satisfaction of all human needs. But it subordinates them all to the requirement of dignity. Even love has its limits. The traditional mother and wife whose selfless caring and unconditional loyalty often yielded personal humiliation is ethically suspect in the new world.

If personal dignity is the secular answer to religious humility, what does it mean to lead a life of dignity? How is this new ethical commitment expressed in personal style and day to day behavior?

Dignity means *autonomy*. It encourages all people to be the masters of their own lives. In the old political setting, the ruled were the subjects of their rulers. In the new political setting, they are citizens, self-governing social entities. If there are authorities, as there must be, they derive their power from their election to office. Since we are mutually dependent, we surrender part of our autonomy to shared protectors, especially the government. And since we are often ignorant, we discipline freedom so that we can learn from those who have more knowledge than we do. We do not serve authority. Authority, including ancestral tradition, serves us.

Dignity means *responsibility*. If we have assumed authority over our own lives, we cannot turn the responsibility for our decisions over to others. We cannot pretend to be helpless when it is convenient to do so. The style of dignity is very hard to learn. Many aspirants want all of its privileges but none of its liabilities. People who always see themselves as

victims of circumstances discard their dignity. They give it all
to destiny or God.

Dignity means *individuality*. As social beings, we need
groups, we find ourselves in groups, and we join groups. As
primates with a very long childhood, we do not separate from
parents easily. But we are individual beings, unique and distinct from all others. Groups give us protection and recognition. But they do not give us identity. In the pre-industrial
world where family connection was all-pervasive, it was very
difficult for us to see ourselves as separate persons. But in
the urban world of many connections, individuality defines
the continuity that carries us from one group to another,
from one relationship to another.

Dignity means *courage*. Reality is not always what we
want it to be. We are not as strong as we want to be. We are
not as smart as we want to be. We do not live as long as we
want to live. Death is a painful fact we would prefer to avoid.
Believing that we are immortal is an understandable temp-
tation. But believing because we need to believe is without
dignity. Self-respect requires the courage to face the facts
and to live with them. If we wish to be the rulers of our own
lives, we cannot plead the weakness of traditional followers
who prefer to be sheltered from the truth.[9]

Dignity means *sensitivity*. We have many needs to
satisfy. The pursuit of dignity does not preclude the pursuit
of pleasure or the pursuit of love or the pursuit of safety. The
satisfaction of human needs is the criterion for good and bad,
right and wrong. But while no need equals in importance the
drive for dignity, all the others are still important. Reasonable people come to terms with all their needs. They are
sensitive to their diversity and do not try to diminish them.
The pursuit of self-esteem is only one of many projects, even
if it is the most compelling.

Dignity means *mutuality*. The defense of my dignity is
also the defense of yours. Traditional societies accorded

dignity to very few and reduced the rest to servility. Master and servant were social complements and depended on each other for their identity. But the humiliation of others limits our generosity and makes us grow tall by keeping others short. In a pre-industrial society of subsistence living, such a strategy for dignity might be understandable. But in the contemporary world of technological plenty and machine slaves, dignity for everybody makes society more just.

Dignity means *control*. In an urban setting of constant stimulation, mere spontaneity is dangerous. Uncontrolled anger, jealousy, love, or fear may undermine our sense of being in charge of our lives and subvert our self-esteem. In the end, we must be able not only to experience our emotions. We must also be able to use them constructively. Self-discipline does not make us "cold." It simply enables us to use our "heat" to warm our dignity.

Dignity means *democracy*. The right to advise comes from competence. But the right to rule comes from the people who are governed. Political authority does not travel down. It travels up. If citizens are masters, the government is the servant. Elites are inevitable. But they must be responsible to the people who choose them and use them.

Dignity means *hutspa*. *Hutspa* is that untranslatable Hebrew and Yiddish word that suggests outrageous defiance. People of dignity respect legitimate authority. But they do not worship it. No ruler is infallible. No institution is unquestionably good. Reverence suggests more than any authority can possibly deliver. Citizens do not bow. They confront the ruler eye to eye. They challenge and question. They offer conditional loyalty. If God indeed exists, people of dignity do not make him a king. They find worship obsequious and prayer a fawning experience. God needs to explain his behavior like everybody else.[10]

The Secular Revolution is the age of human dignity. Even though most people never get it, they dream of it. Even though rulers often deny it to their masses, they praise it and pretend to value it. Even the harshest dictator no longer speaks of masters and servants. People want dignity — even if it is an illusion.

ETHICAL RULES

There is no distinction, in principle, between personal ethics and social ethics. The criterion of dignity applies to both areas. The distinction is pragmatic. Personal ethics applies to that area of life where it is easy to motivate people to be moral. Social ethics applies to that area of life where it is difficult to motivate people to be moral. For most of our human evolution, we lived in small intimate groups. Our moral "intuitions" are derived from this experience. Relating ethically to large anonymous masses is a new and difficult experience for which we are not well prepared. Social ethics, if it is meaningful, does not invent a different set of operating principles. It searches for ways to persuade the individual to be concerned with the dignity of distant strangers.

The ethics of dignity is governed by three operating principles.

The first operating principle is: *I have a moral obligation to strive for greater mastery and control over my own life.*

Many secularists fail to make a distinction between freedom and dignity. They elevate personal autonomy and liberty to first place. They assume that the highest virtue is the right of individuals to do with their lives as they see fit. If they want to abandon work, if they want to take drugs, if they want to smoke themselves into lung cancer, if they want to drop out of school and training for social usefulness, if they want to eat themselves into grotesque obesity — all these wants are legitimate and individuals have the perfect right to indulge them. As masters of their own lives, they can do with them as they please, even terminating their lives at any time they so desire. They have no obligation to make their life style conform to any criterion other than their own personal will. "I do not have the right to tell you what to do with your life. And you do not have the right to tell me what to do with my life," says the secular libertarian.

It is quite obvious from this description that absolute freedom and dignity are incompatible. People may freely choose to diminish their own powers and to reduce the capacity they possess to be masters of their own destinies. Such self-destructive behavior is clearly opposed to long-term autonomy and self-esteem. Other people may not choose to compel them to reverse their self-destructive course. But that reluctance does not mean that individuals do not have the ethical obligation to abstain from ruinous behavior.

The right of parents to guide the development of their children arises from this concern for dignity. Children may be rightfully compelled to study certain subjects, to practice certain useful skills, and to abstain from harmful substances. As children grow up and, by virtue of their training, assume more and more responsibility for their own lives, they are granted more and more freedom. Their freedom is subordinate to their preparation for dignity.

When children turn into adults, their dignity is incompatible with intensive restraint. Their increasing freedom is part of their training for self-esteem. But the dilemma remains. Adults may use their freedom immorally by choosing to reduce their self-control.

However, there may be times when the intrusions of government and public opinion have greater value than the freedom lost. Forbidding smoking and the use of hallucinogenic drugs, requiring the citizen to master useful scientific information, and insisting on the observance of health precautions may be appropriate restrictions in a world where their opposites may be dangerous to personal welfare.

Even when no restraints are imposed, the individual who pursues self-destruction may justifiably be condemned by family and friends for immoral behavior. Dignity is no license to choose any path. It is an achievement which requires enormous discipline. The discipline is just as important as the freedom.

The discipline of self-esteem includes the earnest attempt to learn more and more about ourselves and our environment and to use that information to determine more and more of our own future.

The second operating principle is: *I have a moral obligation to be reliable and trustworthy.*

Every society rests on a social contract — not a formal contract which was signed by its members at sometime in the past, but an implicit contract which every citizen consents to by participating in the benefits of social life. This "contract" guarantees the survival and security of its individual endorsers and includes at least one stipulation: a promise to keep promises. Where people are unreliable, no society is possible. Only predictability makes security a reality.

A society that provides for the safety of its members includes the following promises, whether or not they are formally articulated: a promise to abstain from all physical violence except in self-defense; a promise to protect the publicly recognized possessions of another person; a promise to avoid dependency on the support of others until self-reliance is exhausted; a promise to be responsible for the survival and training of one's own children; a promise to tell the truth where the truth is good for others.

Trustworthiness promotes both security and dignity. People who know that they have the power to be reliable have a greater sense of self-control than opportunists.

All personal relations involve implicit promises to be supportive. Publicly declared marriages and friendships include a commitment to assistance and loyalty. Lovers and spouses have a right to insist on exclusive sexual relations with their partners. Friends have a right to expect help in distress. Co-workers have a right to expect conscientious cooperation.

The third operating principle is: *I have a moral obligation to be generous.*

People who seek to be the masters of their own lives do not cling to their possessions desperately. Such attachments are signs of weakness and limit the boldness which is necessary to self-esteem. The discipline of dignity often trains us to handle adversity with periodic renunciation.[11]

Sharing with others is more than an act of compassion. In personal relations, it is an act of self-interest, reenforcing the bonds of friendship and family that are indispensable to safety and personal happiness. It is also an expression of personal dignity, dramatizing our desire to avoid fearful pettiness.[12] Many of the people in our personal world will receive more than they give us. But that imbalance is the test of generosity.

GOOD HUMOR

The ethics of dignity needs the tempering of good humor. Too many secular utopians and social reformers prefer Messianic fantasies to the reality of human existence. Many Marxists and libertarians have inappropriate expectations about the human possibility.[13]

If we are good-humored, we admit that ethical rules are not absolute guidelines. They are useful summaries of past wisdom. If we wish to teach people (especially children) how to defend their dignity and the dignity of others, we need to convey the experience of the past in the easiest possible way. Rules, or operating principles, serve that purpose. Since they are too brief to be all-inclusive, they are bound to have exceptions. Telling all the truth to dumb and ugly people may not be the best way to protect their dignity.

If we are good-humored, we acknowledge that it is impossible to motivate people to satisfy needs that are not their own. Parents nurture children and friends help each other because they unconsciously do not distinguish between their own needs and the needs of their families and loved ones. If they did, they would not help them. Whether individuals are seduced by the rewards of love, status, or security is less important than the fact that they need to be seduced. Human drives are individual. And so are satisfactions. Phrases like "the general will" or "the general welfare" conjure up social monsters that do not really exist. An effective ethic is able to motivate individuals to serve the needs of others as though they were their very own.

If we are good-humored, we recognize that there are few actions which an individual may choose to indulge that do not affect the lives of others. The vision of a large realm of activity that only affects the welfare of the individual doing it is an illusion. The famous liberal prescription that grants individuals the right to be the total masters of their own lives in those areas of their existence that do not touch the interests of others sounds good on paper. But it does not work very well in reality. In an overcrowded world, almost every personal activity involves somebody else. Sex, the color of one's house, smoking, and the noise level of one's stereo are "private" activities that have social consequences. Even the personal failure to take care of one's own health may create an intolerable social burden. John Stuart Mill was wrong when he imagined that each person was capable of a private world which was of no concern to others.[14]

If we are good-humored, we refuse to make behavioral demands on ourselves and other people that we are, by nature, unable to fulfill. Asking people to dismiss all anger, hate, and jealousy when these dispositions are intrinsic to human nature is an exercise in futility. There is a human nature. The human potential is not unlimited. Nor is the human personality infinitely malleable. To dismiss what is not dismissable is to program human beings for failure. Morality is not always easy. But it is attached to realizable goals. A rational ethic may tame anger, hate, and jealousy in the same way that it tames love. However, it does not seek to arrange what reality cannot arrange.

If we are good-humored, we make a distinction between behavior and motivation. Some people are devotees of the cult of intentions. They are always concerned with why people do what they do. They are absorbed with inner thoughts and feelings over which the individual has absolutely no control. If love is primarily a feeling, it is absurd to demand it. If love is a behavior, it is something we can choose to do, even if we do not feel it. Most ethical people have large amounts of anti-social thoughts and feelings. For that reason, morality requires a great deal of discipline. In the end, from the ethical point of view, people are their behavior.

CONCLUSION

The ethics of the Secular Revolution is a revolutionary departure from the style of traditional morality. The vision of a strong, self-reliant, trustworthy, generous person who strives to remain consistent in the face of an indifferent universe is quite different from the ideal of a humble obedient servant who relies on the justice of destiny.[15] This vision of human dignity is the ultimate criterion for decision-making in the "new" morality.

CHAPTER VI

The Rejectionists

The life of reason and dignity is called humanism. It is the philosophy that flows naturally from the Secular Revolution. Shifting attention from the supernatural to the natural, from the divine to the human, is the humanistic perspective. When it was fresh, two hundred years ago, it was a startling change.

For Jews, it was as traumatic as it was for Christians. Rabbinic Judaism was tied to the life of faith and humility. It was God-centered, long-suffering, and eager to push the world to come. Through its eyes, the Yahveh connection gave Jewish identity its significance. On a planet without Yahveh, there seemed to be little reason to preserve Jewishness.

In Western Europe and North America, the Secular Revolution removed the political disabilities from which Jews suffered.[1] Secular citizenship in a secular state was now available. Religion was separated from government. Privilege was separated from pedigree. Work was freed from inherited status. If Jews no longer desired to be Jewish, they did not have to become Christian. They could be comfortably unaffiliated and never be bothered. The secular alternative removed the taint of treason and the pain of guilt.

As emancipation spread, the Jews found themselves in a world they had never before experienced. The government had decreed that religion and ethnicity were private matters. Indulging them was a matter of personal choice. In the secular state, reason would provide the basis of public morality. And dignity would turn group identity into an individual option. You are what you choose, no less and no more. If compulsion and prejudice lingered, education would untimately drive them away.

Many Jews embraced the Secular Revolution. Secularists and Jews shared a common enemy, the Christian Church. Whatever weakened the church was good for both the humanists and the Jews. A force that undermined the power of the Christian clergy could not easily be ignored. But the unholy alliance took its Jewish toll. Convenience turned into conviction. And the weapons that were invented to assault Christianity were now turned on Judaism. Yahveh and Christ faced similar unemployment.

For the Western Jews, the new world of science and capitalism opened up new opportunities. In the vocabulary of Darwinian natural selection, Jewish talent had found its ideal environment. All the social traits that the Middle Ages despised, the capitalistic society adored. All the survival skills the Jews had acquired for defense in an agricultural milieu were now the very stuff out of which successful enterprise was made. Pushiness, planning, mobility, and money management were acts of desperation in a village culture. In an urban environment, they were the keys to wealth and prosperity. The new secular world made the individual Jew freer and more powerful than at any time in the history of the Jewish people. But for Jewish identity, the change spelled trouble, especially since the new opportunities were economically so seductive.

Humanism undermined all the old reasons for valuing and preserving Jewish identity. God was no longer personal or interesting. The afterlife was questionable. Supernatural power was the embarrassing product of superstition. Chosen peoplehood was a parochial arrogance. The rabbis knew less about the world than the new scholar class of scientists and academicians. And all of the new ideas were packaged in the rewards of economic advantage and political equality.

In the new world of free enterprise and consumer choice, the rabbis were at a disadvantage. They were not accustomed to selling their product. Even in a hostile Christian environment, they had depended on government support for tradition. The language of persuasion was less familiar to them than the language of command. Competition was not a familiar game. Trained to enunciate faith, they did not know how to speak with the voice of reason. Familiar with people who practiced humility, they did not know how to deal with people who insisted on dignity.

Three Jewish responses emerged in the confrontation. The first response was *rejectionist*. The Rejectionists despised the Secular Revolution and its consequences. They sought to keep rabbinic Judaism intact and to protect it from intrusion. The second response was *ambivalent*. The Ambivalents enjoyed both the new world and the old. They were unwilling to forego either the comforts of tradition or the benefits of secular achievement. The third response was *enthusiastic*. The Enthusiasts welcomed the changes and encouraged Jews to embrace them.

In both the Jewish and Christian worlds, and later in the Muslim world, large numbers of people did not like what history had dished out to them. The new industrial society, with its cities and machines, with its family decline and personal freedom, was an ugly, cruel, and immoral place in which to live. A culture that mocked tradition and made ancestors obsolete seemed to threaten the stability of the social order and to promote chaos.

Religious fundamentalists are the legacy of the Rejectionists. Whether Jewish, Christian, or Muslim, they are a persistent minority in the modern world. They are very uncomfortable in the setting of science and the consumer culture. Although they generally learn to survive or prosper in the new economic and social environment, they denounce the present and hanker after the past.

But preserving the past in the present is different from maintaining the past in the past. The existence of a new rival establishment culture produces a siege mentality. Traditionalists see themselves in hostile territory surrounded by aggressive enemies. Secularism is a successful "devil" and has put God on the defensive. The serenity of the old village way of life is now replaced by a new militancy. Anger becomes a dominant emotional theme. Hate for the secular challengers and fear of their victory becomes an obsession. Fundamentalism is different from the old life of faith and humility. It is always defending itself and assaulting its enemies.

Rabbinic Judaism in the contemporary milieu, no matter how intensely rejectionist, has to be different from what it was before — simply because so much of its time is spent avoiding the temptations of the secular world. It needs to be more intolerant and less generous. Otherwise it will not survive.

The very word *orthodoxy* is a strident challenge. It means "the right way" — as opposed to all the "wrong" ways. Before the Secular Revolution, it was unnecessary in the Jewish world. Rabbinic Judaism was so pervasive that it simply *was* Judaism. It needed no qualifying adjectives. But modern times has reduced all religion to a consumer choice. And the competitive world persuades us to overpraise our virtues and to overstate the faults of our enemies.

The center of Jewish resistance to the Secular Revolution was Poland. The old Polish kingdom, including Lithuania and West Russia, contained the largest Jewish community in the world. Not only was it religiously separate from the Polish Catholic population, it was also ethnically distinct. Yiddish made Ashkenazic Jews a unique nation.

The Secular Revolution took a while to get to Poland. England, Holland, France, and Germany were better candidates for its activity. When it did arrive, it encountered a Jewish world of poverty and small towns where rabbinical seminaries flourished and rabbinical scholarship was the test of status. Economic survival was still too precarious for secular conversions to occur easily.

Ironically, a movement that began in southern Poland in defiance of the rabbinic establishment became the most effective defender of tradition. The Hasidim found fault with Orthodoxy, not because it had too much faith and too much humility, but because it had too little. Starting in Podolia with an illiterate miracle worker, the Hasidic resistance spread like wildfire through Poland and West Russia. It was a religious revival with many faces. Ecstatic dancing, faith healing, and a renewed interest in the supernatural reflected its indictment of the Talmudic scholar class. In their poverty, the new devotees needed a more available God than the rabbis were willing to provide. The scholar class of the Secular Revolution would have satisfied them even less.

Although the Hasidim fought the rabbis, they did not reject rabbinic Judaism. They accepted the authority of the Halakha. They dreamed of the world to come. They expected the Messiah. Their holy roller frenzies were a supplement, not a substitute. And their mystical interpretation of the Torah was an addition, not an alternative. Had the secular challenge not emerged, they might have separated themselves from official Orthodoxy and become a rival folk religion. But the presence of the secular foe brought the two movements together again.

The Hasidic movement was what the old-time religion really needed. The boring God of Maimonides, the darling of the rabbinic intellectual establishment, was turned into a passionate dabbler in supernatural power. No longer dispassionate, he was really interested in saving the Jews and would do it soon. No longer distant and aloof, he was now readily available in personal experience and in the extraordinary power of the Hasidic gurus. Humble trust in the protection of God and the guru produced the "born-again" Jew, a person to whom divinity was an experience, not a routine.

Without knowing it, Hasidism created the best form of religious resistance to the secular age. In a secular society where old hierarchies crumble and egalitarian ideals circulate, a God who behaves like a distant king offends the democratic sensibilities of the ambitious masses. The people of faith and humility want a God who is intimidating enough to be interesting but who is friendly enough to make them feel important. Priests and rabbis who have scholar temperaments and who keep God as their own personal exclusive contact interfere with these expectations. The most successful rejectionist religions in a democratic age are fundamentalist charismatic anti-intellectual movements that pay strong allegience to the old traditions and also depict God as a love-the-ordinary-man democratic politician. The clergy of establishment groups, even the conservative ones, suffers from either too much secular education or too much attachment to old monarchical forms of government to serve the masses. Ironically, the secular revolution reenforced the power of anticlerical folk religions.

The Misnagdim, the opponents of the Hasidim, also denounced the Secular Revolution. But they lacked the supernatural fervor and the democratic vocabulary to be convincing. Their rabbinic leadership had already been corrupted by "rational theology," and they would ultimately find themselves more comfortable talking to secular intellectuals than to ecstatic faith healers. In time, most of the children of the Misnagdim drifted away from Orthodoxy to more secular outlooks. The Hasidim were more successful in hanging on to their descendants and in recruiting new devotees.

In 1912, the return of the Hasidim to the Orthodox fold was dramatized by the organization of the *Agudat Yisrael* in Poland. This coalition (called simply the *Aguda*) was created to fight the overwhelming threat of the new secularism in Jewish life. All the major leaders of the Jewish Rejectionist world, Hasidic and non-Hasidic, formed a united front against their common enemy.[2] Internal disputes were less important than resistance to the insidious humanism.

The program of the *Aguda* was the defense of rabbinic Judaism against the agents of secularism — whether they called themselves Modern Orthodox, Conservative, Reform, Zionist, or Bundist. There was to be no compromise with the secular age. It was not the job of tradition to accommodate itself to the demands of the new urban world of science and technology. It was the job of this new world to return to tradition.

From the very beginning, the fuel of the *Aguda* was Hasidic fervor. When the Holocaust destroyed the Polish center of this "Rejectionist Front," its refugees made their way to North America and Israel where most Jews had embraced the life style of the Secular Revolution. While the Misnaged refugees created protective islands of tradition, ghettos within ghettos, some of the Hasidim turned to active missionizing in "enemy" territory. The Lubavitchers (followers of the Hasidic guru dynasty from Lubavitch in West Russia), in particular, went out recruiting among the young, the malcontent misfits of the secular age. They have experienced considerable success.

The Jewish Rejectionists of today are not the old decaying Misnaged scholars of former years. They are often very young people who have repudiated the secular commitments and interests of the Jewish establishment and its ambivalent verbal attachment to "tradition" and who have become "born-again" Jews. With Hasidic fervor, they have become

militant and aggressive. And being children of secular education and secular skills, they combine their hostility to the
world of humanism with a clever use of its techniques of promotion, advertising, and democratic persuasion. But in the
end, the Rejectionists cannot reject everything.

The new recruits join for many reasons, personal and
ideological. One of the main motivations is the ease with
which rejectionism helps them deal with their Jewish identity. Stung by anti-Semitism and open to answers with which
the secular temperament is uncomfortable, they see in the old
piety a clear, visible, and public way to affirm their Jewish
pride. Because they view themselves as struggling in a hostile
Jewish environment, they often lack the grace and good
humor of their pious ancestors. They are awkward, having to
be both defensive and offensive at the same time. Selling in
the consumer culture is never easy.

The major problem with the Rejectionists — other than an
attempt to reject a world that they cannot fully disown — is
their fierce internal competition. The issue is not money. The
issue is piety. Scholars and recruits compete with each other
for the status of superpietists. The favorite game is for one
devotee to accuse another of being less pious than he ought to
be. The internal world of *yeshiva* politics is a mean world of
accusation and counter-accusation, constant surveillance,
and the fear of losing religious status. If the secular threat
were not there, they would be nicer to each other. But the
presence of the non-believing enemy creates a wartime
mentality. Any concession is a form of treason. And self-
righteousness becomes a favorite pastime.

CHAPTER VII

The Ambivalents

The Ambivalents make up the Jewish establishment in North America. They come in two main varieties, Conservative and Reform. While they endorse the Secular Revolution in most of their daily activities, they reject its implications for Jewish identity. They have one foot in the world of faith and humility and one foot in the world of reason and dignity. Since the two worlds are not compatible with each other, they have difficulty finding a secure stance. It is often more comfortable just to stand on one foot for a while and then to shift to the other.

Ambivalents are experts in avoidance activity. They seek to avoid painful confrontations. They wish to disown neither faith nor reason. They want to have both. They want the motivation system of faith and the information system of reason. They want the humility of prayer and the dignity of personal freedom. They fantasize that if Moses and Einstein met each other, they would have a friendly conversation.

The dividing line between conservatives and reformers is the issue of the Halakha, the rabbinic law. Conservatives want to keep it or, at least, pretend to keep it. Reformers are willing to dispense with it.

Conservatives are broader than the official Conservative Movement. They include (in an ascending order of deviation) the Modern Orthodox, the self-proclaimed Conservatives, and the Reconstructionists. All three praise the Halakha and wish to preserve it.[1] If they contemplate changes, they want to find Halakhic reasons for making them. While their stated philosophies may be very naturalistic and very secular, their recommended behavior is very traditional. They have a great need to preserve the appearance of rabbinic Judaism if not its substance.[2]

All three are into worship. The form and content of their prayers are virtually identical with the requirements of the traditional rabbis. All three are into the rabbinic dietary laws, the behavioral restrictions of the Sabbath and the holidays, and the historic requirements for marriage and divorce.

MODERN ORTHODOXY

Modern Orthodoxy is the establishment Judaism of Western Europe. It is sedate and decorous. It is traditional and secular. Its leaders receive a good secular education and train in modern seminaries. Its members participate in all the professions of an urban society. Appearance-wise, they are indistinguishable from all the other citizens of the secular state. What is unique about their behavior is mainly evident in their homes and synagogues. These institutions become the focus of their traditional attachments. Since most of the unique behavior patterns of the rabbinic lifestyle are incongruous with secular existence, they are praised but rarely observed. Female segregation, ritual purity, and the dress code do not find any real community support and are not enforced by public opinion.[3]

While it is important to the Modern Orthodox to be designated "Orthodox," they are despised and denounced by the Rejectionists. Separate seating for the sexes in the synagogue is hardly a substitute for traditional belief. An "orthodoxy" that avoids discussing divine rewards and punishments, the salvation of the Messiah, the resurrection of the dead, and the importance of the world to come undermines the motivation of the Halakha and subverts the traditional justification for preserving Jewish identity. Proving that the dietary laws are good for health and hygiene (true or not) turns the argument into a rational consequential one and deprives the rabbinic tradition of the supernatural context out of which it arose.

The Rejectionists are right. Modern Orthodoxy sometimes looks like Orthodoxy. But it tastes different. And most of its adherents are more comfortable spending time with their secular friends than with pious Hasidim.

CONSERVATISM

The Conservative Movement is made of much the same stuff as Modern Orthodoxy. But it is bolder. Spawned in Germany in the middle of the nineteenth century, it found its most comfortable home in North America. Identified with three rabbinical seminaries in Breslau, Budapest, and New York, it was explained and defended by scholar luminaries like Zacharias Frankel, Heinrich Graetz, and Solomon Schechter.[4]

Initially united with the reformers in an alliance against the Rejectionists, its leaders split early from the coalition on the issue of the Halakha. Developing a "positive historical"

approach to the problem of Jewish behavior and Jewish identity, they adopted a pragmatic stance: free philosophic inquiry together with moderate ritual conformity. The mind
would be reasonable, but the body would be traditional. Since
most people settle for appearances, it was an appealing compromise. Secularized Jews could feel traditional without having to be assaulted by traditional ideas.

All Conservatives agreed that nothing should be done to
destroy the appearance of tradition — at least, in synagogue
behavior and holiday observance. Musical instruments might
be tried for Sabbath worship. The sexes might be mixed for
synagogue services. Protestant style sermons might be added for public edification. But little was done to shatter the
"look" of tradition. And nothing was done for which a
Talmudic justification was not found.

As time makes innovation seem traditional, creeping
change never destroys the illusion. When the Conservatives
ultimately ordain their women rabbis, they will dress them up
in the symbols of the old male chauvinism and find a Talmudic
quotation to justify their action.[5]

The Conservative Movement in America has been the
most successful of all the modern Jewish "denominations"
because it allows the Jews to have their cake and eat it
simultaneously. Like Modern Orthodoxy, it chooses to offend
no one — or, at least, very few. Since it deals primarily with
appearances, it has difficulty dealing with the substance of
belief and integrity. Speaking the ideas of reason and dignity
while wearing the costume of faith and humility is precarious
theater. It gives all moral power to the Rejectionists who, at
least, believe in what they do.

Here is the problem: having to prove that you are what
you are not undermines your dignity. Many Conservative
rabbis suffer from a guilty reverence of pious authority. They
admire teachers who despise them.

RECONSTRUCTIONISM

Reconstructionism is the third style of the Jewish Ambivalent. It arose out of Conservative Judaism and is emotionally allied with it. In fact, Reconstructionism fits very neatly into its pragmatic operating procedure — free philosophic inquiry and Halakhic behavior.

Mordecai Kaplan, who was the founder of the Reconstructionist Movement and its reigning guru, was a graduate and teacher of the Jewish Theological Seminary, the New York school for Conservative Judaism. He was born in Lithuania over a hundred years ago and came to America at an early age. He organized his own congregation on the west side of Manhattan, which he called the Society for the Advancement of Judaism and which became the pioneer congregation of his new movement.

Kaplan was the emotional child of Europe and of the traditional lifestyle of the Litvak Jew. But he was the intellectual child of two secular humanists, John Dewey and Emile Durkheim. Dewey, the philosopher, maintained that religion could have a humanistic meaning. It was the celebration of all those powers in the universe that help us stay alive and solve our problems. "God" is the symbol of that power.[6] Durkheim, the sociologist, maintained that religion was a social enterprise, a ritual glue that kept everybody together. The heart of religion was sacred behavior, the untouchable and unchangeable set of actions by which any group affirmed its unity.[7] If one takes Dewey and Durkheim, mixes them up, and adds a large dose of Litvak loyalty, one gets Reconstructionism.

Kaplan tried to wed humanism and Halakha. He claimed that Judaism was not a specific combination of theological beliefs. It was a religious civilization and could accommodate many different systems of thought. He claimed that *God* could be redefined as the creative energy of the universe that enables individuals and communities to survive. And salvation was fulfillment in the here and now. Above all, he pleaded for the *reconstruction* of the Jewish community to allow for diversity in unity.

The unity for Kaplan was the *folk*, the Jewish people. And the sign of that unity was an adherence to the three folk sancta: God, Israel, and Torah — in other words, the Halakha, or a slightly amended reasonable facsimile of it designated folk-religion.[8] In the end, it was the same old Conservative package: act traditional and think humanist; use all the words of faith and humility and make them mean reason and dignity. The official Reconstructionist prayer book is hardly distinguishable from the Conservative one.

Reconstructionism differs from Conservatism in its refusal to endorse the idea of the Chosen People. For Kaplan, this concept was a violation of the humanistic respect for the value of all cultures and civilizations. But its removal from the vocabulary of the prayerbook (which was a small change) seemed bizarre. Why bother to change one little item in the service when the whole concept of a worship experience where people talk to God for three hours is inconsistent with an impersonal deity? How can any reasonable person talk to creative energy?

There is a humorless edge to Kaplan. If you want to combine Halakha and humanism, do not be fastidious. Nothing really fits anyway. In that respect, conventional Conservatism is superior to Reconstructionism. It never tried to be profound. It lets the absurdity stand because it is emotionally satisfying. Ambivalence should never insist on consistency.

Modern Orthodoxy, Conservatism, and Reconstructionism are best described by the Yiddish phrase: *nisht a hin, nisht a her* — neither here nor there. They may work for some people. But they do not take reason and dignity seriously enough. A humanism that is dressed up to look like rabbinic Judaism is ashamed of what it is.

REFORM

Reform — at least in the beginning — chose a bolder format. It broke with rabbinic Judaism and rejected the Halakha. Living in Northern Europe, the early Reformers were influenced by Protestant culture and by its attachment to the Bible. Fearful of proclaiming reason alone as the source of truth, they searched for a more traditional authority. Faith in the Bible was so respectable in their environment that it seemed a natural alternative. Some of them began to assault Orthodoxy with denunciations of Talmudic superstition and with appeals for a return to the purity of the Bible.

But the Bible was hardly the anthology for teaching the Secular Revolution. In many respects, it was more "primitive" and less reasonable than the Talmud. Its view of the universe, nature, and society was not compatible with modern science. Its description of the rights of husbands, wives, and foreigners seemed a bit awkward as a preface to human dignity and universalism. And it was loaded with all kinds of laws about sacrifice, ritual purity, and dietary practices that the Reformers were eager to discard on rational grounds. Although they hesitated to give up such a powerful weapon, something else was clearly needed.

In the 1840s, there appeared a German duo of renegade rabbis, Abraham Geiger and Samuel Holdheim, who provided Reform with a presentable ideology. Unlike the Conservatives who were stuck with the theological formulations of the

Halakha and who (with the exception of the Reconstructionists) never really attempted to deal with an alternative value for Jewish identity, the Reform renegades
sought to find a justification for Jewish identity in the age of
reason.

Their new formulation took account of the consequences
of the Secular Revolution on Jewish life. In Western Europe,
they had lost their national culture. Neither language nor folk
customs separated them from other Europeans in their
region. Emancipation meant secular citizenship and secular
education and the opportunity to sign up for the new secular
nationalism of England, France, and Germany. As for the
Halakha, it had been discarded by many secularized Jews as a
burdensome interference with social integration.

The Reform ideologues, for obvious reasons, discarded
ethnicity and nationality as motivating values.[9] They seemed
to have no future. Personal Messiahs and supernatural
rewards were also rejected. They offended reason. Rabbinic
law was irrelevant. It rubbed against the higher values of secular existence.[10]

Only theological ideas remained. But which one? The ideologues selected monotheism. But what is uniquely Jewish
about monotheism? Millions of non-Jews worship one God.
Here the Reformers picked up on the traditional idea of the
Chosen People (which Kaplan was later to discard) and
transformed it. While it was true that many Gentiles were
already monotheists, the Jews were the divinely appointed
missionaries of ethical monotheism. The special job of the
Jews was to be the role model advertisers of the one God.[11]

Jewish history was a "progressive revelation" of the existence and nature of the Supreme Being. While the Bible and
Talmud were expressions of this revelation, they were
imperfect and open to emendation by future events. The age
of reason was only one more step in the development of that

disclosure. Ultimately, the nature of God would be totally revealed. The Messianic age of peace and love would follow. And the Jews could retire from their age-old job.

The Reform overhaul of the meaning and value of Jewish identity was bold and clear. Its only problem was that it was ludicrous. Why are Jewish monotheists more divinely-appointed than Muslim monotheists? It would seem that it is the job of every sincere monotheist to be a missionary for the cause. How can any people designate themselves as ethical role models without ceasing to be exactly what they want to be? Self-righteousness is morally offensive. In what way does Jewish history reveal the existence of a nice single God? Jewish suffering suggests that he is either not so nice or that he is nice but limited. But, above all, what does ethical monotheism have to do with the age of reason or the Secular Revolution? The modern urban industrial world is hardly the setting for divine enthusiasts among the educated elite. Why would a bunch of Jewish "not-quite agnostics," with a perfunctory formal belief in a perfunctory God, be chosen for such a missionary task? Yahveh must be as confused as his army of converters.

The one positive aspect of this theological travesty was that Reform Jews never took this formal ideology seriously. Like the Conservatives, they just limped along on the inertia of old identities. And like the Conservatives, they preferred the consolation of traditional endorsement. They really wanted "kosherizing" by the Bible. But which part? Their non-observance made the endorsement of most of it very difficult.

Enter Prophetic Judaism. Many of the Reform leaders latched on to the Yahveh prophets who are praised by the editors of the Bible. Elijah, Amos, Hosea, Isaiah, Jeremiah, and Micah suddenly emerged as Reform heroes. The new scientific criticism of the Bible indicated that it was more complex and less unified than faith and tradition had described it.[12] It had different authors from the writers the rabbis had designated. There were many internal contradictions. Individual books were patchwork creations from many separate documents. And much of the prophetic message was older than the Torah and was distorted by it.

The Prophets became the comfortable heroes of the Reform layperson. Since they were old, traditional, and Biblical, they were more understandable than Geiger's "spirit of the age." No matter that the prophets were devotees of ecstatic visions and supernatural intrusion. No matter that they were profoundly opposed to urbanization and the breakdown of the shepherd economy. No matter that their devotion to Yahveh was accompanied by a violent hostility to the worshipers of other gods. No matter that they were absolutely certain of the truth of their own personal revelation and intensely intolerant of disagreement. No matter that their love of the "good" and their hatred of "evil" did not mean a society of dignity and personal freedom.[13] They had become the unlikely heroes of the age of reason. Yahveh would have had a fit.

The Reform Movement ended with slogans. Its formal ideology and its informal heroes had very little to do with Reform behavior.[14] For a while, its Protestant format and its hostility to Jewish nationalism gave its adherents a form of social security. But they did not do very much to make Jewish identity interesting or worthwhile.

CONCLUSION

None of the Ambivalents had come up with a doctrine of Jewish identity that could match the power of the

Rejectionist story. Since they sought their authority in Rejectionist literature and in Rejectionist heroes, they ended up with pale variations on Rejectionist themes. Modern Orthodoxy formally acknowledged the old story but was too secularized to use it. Conservatism saw itself as the defender of tradition but was uncomfortable with the traditional reasons for it. Reform latched on to the morality of the prophets but never wanted to deal with their religion. Reconstructionism talked a lot about the primacy of the Jewish people but then vetoed their right to dispose of God and the Torah.

The Ambivalents were ultimately rescued by an experience they would have chosen to avoid and by a movement they did not invent.

The experience was the rise of anti-Semitism. A new secular anti-Semitism emerged in Europe that found less fault with Jewish belief than with Jews. The Jews were portrayed as the "devils" of the modern world, the chosen people in reverse. In the secular age, their historic hostility to Christ was less important than their supposed sinister manipulation of both capitalism and communism to immoral ends. Jewish success made them vulnerable and opened them to the hatred of the people who were less successful. Ironically, the anti-Semite found Jewish identity very significant, more significant than many Jews did.

Zionism was the movement and the ideology that grew up in response to anti-Semitism. Its founders were neither Rejectionists nor Ambivalents. Most of them were Enthusiasts for the secular age. Jewish secular nationalism was the child of the new world and initially aroused the hostility of all Rejectionists and many Ambivalents.

But it rescued the Ambivalents by giving them an attached fuel system for Jewish identity. All of the Ambivalents ultimately plugged into Zionist energy to keep their own sluggish enterprises going. After the state of Israel was established, caution vanished. Every Ambivalent institution got its Zionist "fix" daily.

Conservatism was the first to plug into the enterprise. Modern Orthodoxy followed. Reconstructionism made a serious attempt to reconcile secular nationalism with "traditional" religion. Even Reform, with its historic opposition to Jewish nationalism, ultimately succumbed.

The price of their rescue is eternal dependence. The Ambivalents need Zionism. But Zionism does not really need the Ambivalents.

CHAPTER VIII

The Enthusiasts

Rejectionists hated the Secular Revolution. Ambivalents loved and hated it. But Enthusiasts loved it unashamedly.

Many Jewish Enthusiasts no longer found any value in Jewish identity. They just became secular. They had no reason to bother with their ethnic origins. They had no need to be religious. Either the local form of nationalism or utopian universalism suited them perfectly. Most of them saw no purpose in turning Christian. Christianity was as offensive to them as rabbinic Judaism. In a secular state, they could be comfortably French or German without having to pretend to be religious.

ETHICAL CULTURE

Some Enthusiasts were influenced by the Reform Movement and came to believe (because they wanted to believe) that Jewishness was a voluntary religious identity. Since they no longer believed in the existence of God or were not sure about his existence, they imagined that they were no longer Jews (even though their Gentile neighbors knew better). Eager to identify with a religion that was neither Jewish nor Christian, they were attracted to the efforts of the new Ethical Culture.

The Ethical Movement does not identify itself as a Jewish movement, but many outsiders do. For many years, the overwhelming majority of its members were Jews. And bourgeois Jewish secularists who were neither nationalistic nor Zionistic found a home there. While the movement did nothing positive to develop Jewish self-awareness, the organization enabled Jews to spend time with Jews, especially in the New York area. It was a haven for many Jews who could find no comfortable place in establishment institutions.

Founded in 1876 in New York City by Felix Adler, the son of a radical Reform rabbi, it was dominated for many years by the culture and style of the German Jewish elite. Although Adler denied that Judaism was anything more than a religion and maintained that Jewish identity was a religious identity distinct from Ethical Culture, he functioned as an agnostic rabbi who served the cultural community with which he was familiar.

Adler was a devotee of Kant. Like Kant, he believed that the existence of God could be neither demonstrated nor disproved and that ethical laws did not derive from revealed religion. They came from the imperative of intuitive reason — a fancy reformulation of the Golden Rule. Although Adler insisted that his ethical philosophy was a religion, God and prayer were excluded from his Sunday meetings. It was the kind of setting in which a secularist or an atheist would feel very comfortable.

The Ethical Movement was the result of the need of assimilated Western Jews to define themselves religiously for political safety.[1] Cultural pluralism was anathema to the German Jewish bourgeoisie. Conversion to Christianity was intellectually unacceptable and emotionally guilt-producing. Ethical Culture was a suitable compromise, granting philosophic integrity and Jewish association. In New York City, it became an important presence in Jewish life.

The decline of the movement set in after the First World War. The aging and shrinking of the German Jewish population reduced the possibilities of recruitment. Russian Jewish secularists were not sufficiently bourgeois and did not need religious identity for respectability. They turned to socialism and Yiddish culture, preferring political and ethnic associations to religious ones. Above all, rising anti-Semitism and Hitler's Holocaust drove many universalists back to Jewish identity. Both disillusionment and guilt made them alter their ideological commitment.

YIDDISH NATIONALISM

But Ethical Culture was a minor theme in the Jewish secular world. Most secular Jews who did not value their Jewish identity did not bother with any religious alternative. There were enough political, cultural, and academic communities around to rescue them from isolation. And if they wanted to fight anti-Semitism, they could always send money to the Anti-Defamation League — or subscribe to some revolutionary ideology that promised to get rid of it.

For Enthusiasts who valued their Jewish identity, the new passion was Jewish nationalism. It seemed the reasonable alternative to Jewish religion, rabbinic or otherwise. It could be both intensely Jewish and intensely secular.

Secular nationalism has been the rage throughout the nineteenth and twentieth centuries. It has replaced religion and family as the focus of fanatical love. In a secular urban industrial world, it satisfies the need for transcendent goals and tribal connection.

The two requirements for an up and coming nation are language and territory. Without its own language, the nation will have no uniqueness. And without its own territory, the nation will have no self-determination. Nations with well-developed languages and territories, like the English and the French, have been role models for the rest.

Jewish secular nationalism faced many problems from its beginning. Before the Secular Revolution, Jews had defined themselves as a nation in exile. And their view of themselves was reenforced by segregation and social ostracism. But secular emancipation provided them with the opportunity to become citizens of other nations in Western Europe and North America. How could one be a loyal member of two nations at the same time? Being nationalistically German and religiously Jewish seemed feasible. But being nationalistically German and nationalistically Jewish seemed to be an impossibility. The Reformers had gone to great pains to redefine the Jews as a religious denomination. And the Western Jews, themselves, had abandoned their Yiddish linguistic uniqueness to become experts in English, French, and German.

In Eastern Europe, where Jewish emancipation was retarded, Jews retained their Yiddish specialty. They were a linguistic nation. But they were dispersed among the Poles, Ukranians, and Russians. They had no territory of their own. And none of the rival nationalities was willing to give them any.

The Secular Revolution opened up secular studies to the Jews. And secular studies made them more universalistic and cosmopolitan. But secular anti-Semitism, the new racial anti-Semitism of Drumont and Chamberlain, made them aware of their Jewish identity.[2] The urge to merge was met by rejection. And the Jews were thrown back on their "racial" identity. However, in the interim, they had lost all the ethnic skills that would make them comfortable with their newfound Jewish nationalism. They had become universalists by training and ethnics by bigotry.

The Jewish cosmopolitans faced a new problem with the new anti-Semite. They had to be Jewish whether they wanted to be or wanted not to be. Either they could bemoan their Jewish fate and devote their lives to regret, or they could choose to value their Jewish identity in a positive way and search for a respectable noble reason to make it worthy of choice. But in their new intellectual posture, they had difficulty finding universal reasons for remaining particular.

Despite its many problems, Jewish nationalism took center stage in the secular Jewish world. There simply was no other vital alternative. Only the nation and the socialist revolution could arouse the same passions that God used to arouse. And the revolution was not that easy to arrange.

From the very beginning, Jewish nationalists had difficulty staying together. While they all agreed that Jewish identity was a national identity (not a religious one), they did not agree on the recipe for nationhood. Some wanted Yiddish as the national language and Eastern Europe as the territorial homeland; others wanted Hebrew as the national language and Palestine as the place to live. Some wanted capitalism and free enterprise; others wanted socialism and collective settlements. Some desired to be different forever; others desired to be Jewish only until the final revolution.

Secular Jewish nationalists often had very little time to fight the old-time religion because they spent so much time fighting each other. Bourgeois Yiddishists hated Bundists.[3] Bundists hated Zionists. And Zionists had no use for minority culture-niks.[4] The nationalist disputes rivaled the arguments of the old fanatical religious sects. The vocabulary changed. But the self-righteousness remained.

The Yiddishists seemed to have the edge at the start. Although they excluded the Sephardic and Oriental Jewish world from their nation, although they were not compactly settled on a given piece of territory, although they were divided between capitalists and socialists, secularists and traditionalists; they represented a real living nation of six million Yiddish-speaking people. When Hebrew as a national language was a fantasy in the minds of a few idealists, Yiddish was the mother tongue of the European Jewish masses.

As a folk language that had been repudiated by the scholar class, its power for centuries was never really visible. Everybody spoke it. But nobody wanted to recognize it. Although most Jews could no longer speak Hebrew and were not encouraged to speak it, Hebrew was still regarded as the official Jewish language by the rabbinic rulers. Some day the Messiah would return the Jews to Palestine and give them back their ancient tongue.

By the time of the Secular Revolution, Yiddish was a thousand years old. Born in the Jewish communities of the Rhineland, it spread eastward to Poland and West Russia. While it was a sister language to German and had little connection with Hebrew, it gave an ethnic uniqueness to most European Jews. From Metz to Minsk, it gave a linguistic unity to the Ashkenazic Jewish world. Much more than Messianic fantasies, it gave national self-awareness. Obscured by religious ritual and religious segregation, it was revealed in its full glory when religion became less important.

Many secular Jews despised it. Since German was regarded by the people of Central Europe as the language of science and high culture, Yiddish, as the language of the oppressed, rubbed people the wrong way. To social-climbers, it suggested centuries of degradation. If a Jewish language was to be chosen for the secular age, it should be viewed as "noble" by its Gentile neighbors. Since Hebrew had the classic reputation of Greek and Latin, it seemed much more suitable.

But the socialist devotees of the common man loved Yiddish — precisely because it was the language of the common man. They used it for books and newspapers. They refined it for prose and poetry. They even tried to make it a language of science.

Like most folk speech that is just beginning to gain respectability, Yiddish blossomed with popular fiction and poetry — the kind of literature with which the masses could identify. Writers, like Peretz and Sholem Aleichem, rescued Yiddish from anonymous folk tales and gave it the prestige of literary heroes.

In Eastern Europe, Yiddish had a good chance of surviving as a secular Jewish language and of providing cultural stimulus to the dispersed Ashkenazic Jews around the world. There were enough Jews in the cities and towns to give depth to the linguistic community. If the right to separate schools and separate cultural institutions could be granted by law, then the Jews of Poland, Russia, and Romania would be as culturally secure as the Chicanos of southern Texas. Minority guarantees would become a substitute for territory.

The Yiddish diasporas in North America and Argentina took advantage of this secular alternative. They became creative outposts of the motherland. Minority nationhood thrived in the streets of New York and Buenos Aires.

But Yiddish was doomed by destiny. Western secular states did not countenance enduring ethnic minorities. There was no political and economic future in America or Argentina for people who wanted to keep Yiddish as their first language. The Bolshevik Revolution undermined the stability of Jewish communities in Russia. While the official policy of the Communist regime was to promote Yiddish ethnicity and Yiddish culture, the unofficial policy was to Russify the Jews and to break their connection with world Jewry. Linguistic assimilation was inevitable. Yiddish is not a viable long-run language for people who wish to flee the isolation of village life and to participate in the intellectual and cultural endeavors of the major urban centers of the world. Yiddish can compete with Albanian and Ukranian. It cannot compete with English, Spanish, and Russian.

But the major reason for the fall of Yiddish was Adolf Hitler. The Holocaust wiped out the "motherland." The dense Jewish community of Poland and West Russia was destroyed. The home base of secular Yiddish nationalism, with its schools, its theaters, and its political parties, ceased to exist. With that devastation, no nostalgia could revive it. The countless numbers of little secular Jewish institutes devoted to the teaching of Yiddish disappeared. There was no vital population of Yiddish speakers. Ironically, Yiddish survives most intensely, in both America and Israel, among the Orthodox enemies of the Secular Revolution who cultivate it as an expression of their hostility to secular Hebrew and Zionism.

ZIONISM

Secular Hebrew is the success story of Jewish nationalism. When the revival of Hebrew as the popular language began, Yiddish was, by far, the front-runner. Although some members of the new secular scholar class praised it and used it, there existed no community of Hebrew speakers and no special territory where they lived. There were no intimate memories of parents and grandparents speaking it — and no nostalgic Hebrew vocabulary of love and humor. As the language of prayer and religious study, it had no secular roots that anybody could remember.

From the start, the Hebrew revival was an attempt to separate Jews from their Diaspora past. Its very novelty as a secular Jewish language was its appeal. The odor of degradation and humiliation did not penetrate it. If anything, it smelled of Biblical victories and ancient independence. Moreover, its prestige in the Christian world increased its stature. And the fact that Sephardic Jews loved it too made it seem more universal than Yiddish.

Modern Hebrew is an extraordinary achievement. It is no slowly evolving folk language that was elevated by scholars. It is a national speech that was invented by scholars and given to the masses. Most successful languages, like English, French, German, and Ukranian, worked their way up. But Hebrew started at the top and worked its way down. French began with the people and was polished by the elite. Hebrew began with the elite and was transformed by the Israeli masses. No other language experiment in modern times can make that statement.

The Hebrew revival is part of the most successful expression of secular Jewish nationalism. The Zionist movement is the stellar Jewish development of the twentieth century. Zionism did what Yiddishism did not do. It provided an independent national territory and a viable national language. Today, three million Jews speak Hebrew in a Jewish state.

Zionism was an expression of the Secular Revolution. The Rejectionists rejected it. And the Ambivalents were uncomfortable with it. Only the Reconstructionists embraced it wholeheartedly.

The founders of Zionism were estranged from rabbinic Judaism, and they found little meaning in its liberal variations. Whether it was Herzl, Nordau, Ben Gurion, or Jabotinsky, they viewed their work as part of a Jewish "revolution." Jews must repudiate the religious notion that their fate is in the hands of God and that they must wait for salvation. The new Jews, the revolutionary Jews, must take their fate into their own hands and do what destiny has failed to do. The Jew of humility and humiliation must be replaced by the Jew of action and dignity.[5]

The modern movement to establish an independent
Jewish homeland has been the most successful Jewish
enterprise in the twentieth century. No other project has
claimed the support of so many Jews. The state of Israel has
become the single most important institution in Jewish life,
uniting divided communities and giving passion to Jewish
identity.

The organizers of political Zionism were secular Jews who
believed that the homeless condition of the Jewish masses
could only be alleviated by the establishment of a secular
culture in a secular state. They found in Zionism an alternative to religion. Some of the early Zionists were traditional.
But the overwhelming majority were searching for a secular
way to save Jews and Jewish identity.

Secular Zionists came in three varieties. Bourgeois Zionists, like Herzl and Weizmann, wanted a Jewish state that
resembled a European capitalist democracy. Nationalist
Zionists, like Jabotinsky, preferred a more militant state that
would be defended by proud and fearless warriors.[6] Socialist
Zionists dreamed of a model egalitarian state where clerical,
bourgeois, and military domination would cease to exist.[7] As
time went on, the bourgeois and nationalist Zionists discovered that opposition to religion subverted their political ambitions. Only the socialist Zionists remained fiercely secular.

The kibbutz commune became a dramatic example of a
secular socialism. Most kibbutzim rejected religious behavior
and religious authority. They sought to secularize Jewish
holidays and life cycle ceremonies. Because they were self-
contained communities united by a strong ideology, they
succeeded in fashioning a secular ceremonial alternative to
traditional ritual. They stood in sharp contrast to urban
humanists who were never really able to go beyond the
negative rejection of religion to a positive secular identity.

From its inception, Zionism, as a secular movement, ran
into trouble. Many Ambivalents found much of it attractive.

Anti-Semitism and the nostalgia for Palestine made them overlook the non-religious thrust of its founders. Modern Orthodox and Conservative Jews, in particular, liked its ethnic affirmation and began to join it. After Hitler, even the Reform Jews repented their old hostility and swelled the ranks.[8] The result was a shift to ambivalence. God — without the Messiah — now became the engineer of Zionist redemption.

After the state of Israel was established, Sephardic immigrants arrived in large numbers. Oriental Jews, who had never really been exposed to the assault of the Secular Revolution, now poured into the country and changed its cultural complexion. Their orthodoxy was much milder than that of the militant rejectionists from Eastern Europe since they had faced no challenger in their home environment. But they were traditional. The idea of Jewish identity without God — or any identity without God — was simply inconceivable. While they were too pious to have initiated Zionism, they were religious enough to change it. The government of a Jewish state could not be separated from rabbinic Judaism.

Ultimately, even the Rejectionists had to come to terms with the Jewish state. Although they despised a secular Jewish government, they willingly accepted its financial and political gifts. The secular dream of a separation of religion from government faded away. Rejectionist rabbis and their institutions received state aid. Marriage, divorce, and Jewish identity were put into the hands of clergymen who, fifty years before, would have been anti-Zionist.

As the Zionist state became less secular, the internal problems of a secular Jewish nationalism also began to surface. If Jewish identity is tied to language and territory, what is the status of secular Jews who do not speak Hebrew and who do not live in Israel? Radical Zionists, like Ben Gurion, maintained that Jewish existence was impossible in the Diaspora. The logic of Jewish nationalism (once the Yiddish variety perished) demanded that its adherents immigrate to Israel. Any other environment would inhibit the development of a Hebrew-speaking culture. Is it possible to do Jewish nationalism in English or Russian? Does Zionism have any real meaning for secular Jews who choose to remain in Beverly Hills or Leningrad? Are Hebrew tidbits enough to sustain a significant Jewish identity in Boston? Ethnicity without language or territory becomes an illusion.

Diaspora nationalism had initially been sustained by Yiddish solidarity in the Ashkenazic world. In Israel, Yiddish was replaced by Hebrew. But in North America, Yiddish was replaced by English. Culturally and linguistically, North American Jews became part of the Anglo-Saxon world. Americanized Jews and Poles found it easier to communicate with each other than to talk with their ethnic compatriots in Israel and Poland. Ethnic power in the United States — other than Hispanic — is often just play acting. Jewish culture in English is about as real as Polish culture in English.

Another internal problem for secular Jews was the historical identification of Jewish secular commitment with socialism. Of course, there is no necessary connection between secularism and socialism. Non-theistic philosophies of life range from the arch-capitalism of Ayn Rand to the radical anarchism of Emma Goldman. Elitists like Thomas Hobbes[9] and Vladimir Jabotinsky were mockers of religion. In fact, atheism was the child of the Secular Revolution. And the Secular Revolution was the child of the bourgeoisie. The workers were far more devout than the intellectual children of the middle class. The mistake of Marxism was its secularism.

For many Jews, secularism was an aspect of their socialist commitment. While some romantic socialists, like A.D. Gordon, were mystical and religious, hoping to turn the Jews into a nature loving peasantry,[10] the so-called scientific socialists followed Marx and found in atheism a personal liberation.

These Jewish socialists could not separate secularism from egalitarian politics. Dismissing God went hand in hand with elevating the proletariat. Atheistic fervor was tied to revolutionary passion.

Jewish socialists were never united. They were divided by many controversies. The Russian Revolution and the policies of the Soviet government sparked an endless debate. The rise of Zionism posed the question of where the socialist paradise should be created. And chronic anti-Semitism undermined the ritual hope that proletarian self-awareness would replace Jewish identity. Jewish socialist atheism became a carnival of internal arguments.

The strongest socialist group was the Bund. Founded in 1897 in the Russian Empire (one year before the establishment of the Russian Social Democratic Party), it was committed to Marxism and Yiddish nationalism. Standing in opposition to socialist Zionists and the assimilationist Communists, the Bund mobilized thousands of Jewish radicals. After the Bolshevik Revolution made Russia a hostile territory, it flourished in Poland. As a political and cultural force between the wars, it spoke for a large part of the Jewish community. Immigrants brought the Bund to North America. Embraced by the Workmen's Circle, it created its own system of schools and cultural institutions. But America was not an environment conducive to the survival of either Yiddish or socialism. While the Holocaust destroyed the Bund in Poland, the power of Anglo-Saxon capitalism undermined it in the New World. The bourgeois Jewish descendants of the Bundists were in no mood for the revolution.

Zionist socialism is the only surviving Jewish socialism with any constituency. But secularism and humanism have become less important themes for many of its adherents. The

left socialists of Hashomer Hatzair are still holding the line.
But the right socialists of the United Kibbutz Movement and
their urban counterparts are waffling. Hostility to religion is
less meaningful in an environment where religion is no longer
hostile to either Zionism or socialism.

However, the identification remains. Many secular Jews
shy away from secular connections because they see the
bogeyman of Marxism behind them. In North America, hosts
of humanistic Jews are tied to conventional institutions of
religion that are meaningless to them because they associate
religion with capitalist respectability. And in the Soviet
Union, thousands of Jews, assaulted by anti-Semitism and
disgusted with socialism, play at religion to express their
hostility to a vile regime. Ironically, the Secular Revolution,
which was a bourgeois creation, has lost its economic
neutrality.

Still another internal problem for secular nationalists and
secular Zionists is the Bible revival. Biblical literature was
edited by the leaders of rabbinic Judaism and became the
most dramatic part of its sacred scriptures. Although the
Bible is an anthology of many documents from many eras
"cut-up" and "pasted" together, its authors and editors view
Jewish history as part of a divine supernatural drama.
Yahveh and the Bible go together.

However, the Bible is the only surviving collection of
Hebrew literature that comes out of the period of Jewish
history when the Jews were an independent Hebrew-speaking nation in their own land. For many of the early Zionists,
even the most secular, the Bible was irresistible. It gave them
roots. It provided epic heroes. It was a document shared with
the Christian West that offered the Jews title to the land of
Israel. The Bible, despite its ideology, became an essential
Zionist document.

Radical Zionists tried to teach the Bible as literature, in the same way as Greeks might approach the Iliad and the Odyssey. But the approach was naive. There is no sizable Greek population that still believes in the Greek Gods. And Greek ideologues do not quote Zeus to justify the Greek claim to Greece. But Yahveh is still real for many Jews — and for many Christians. And the "pronouncements" of Yahveh are still politically convenient in a country where the Jewish claim is contested by the Arabs.

Using the Bible as a teaching document of the Secular Revolution is not easy. No one can use the Bible better than the people who really believe in its truth. Ambivalents, like the Reformers, have been struggling with this dilemma for a long time. Turning Leviticus into a humanist manifesto requires no mean intellectual skill. It may also be a waste of energy.

The most important internal problem secular Zionists face is the limitation of any nationalism. Once the language and the state are firmly established, they run by themselves. English people do not build a philosophy of life around English identity. French people, despite the Messianism of Napoleon and DeGaulle, do not normally search for the value of French identity. They derive their "spiritual" kicks from either self-absorption or goals more universal than national survival. For the Zionist pioneers, Jewish nationalism was a "religion." But for their children, it is a normal part of the local propaganda. Israeli humanists can be humanists in the same way as English humanists are humanists. If they do it in Hebrew, they do not have to worry about being Jewish. They can just focus on being human.

Some Zionists sought to give the Jewish state an ethical mission that transcended mere national survival. Instead of being monotheistic missionaries proclaiming the one God (a la the Reformers), the citizens of the Jewish state would be moral role models, teaching the rest of the world the basics of egalitarian behavior. Herzl envisioned the future state as a social utopia.[11] Asher Ginsberg (Ahad Haam), the Russian Jewish intellectual who was opposed to political Zionism, spoke of ethical values that a Jewish cultural homeland would express.[12] The notion of the "Chosen People" seemed to be revived in secular clothing.

The problem with national missions is the number of competitors. The British, the French, the Russians, and the Americans have all dabbled, for a time, in special historic "assignments." The "white man's burden," "manifest destiny," and the "revolutionary homeland" were, and still are, popular slogans in the repertory of modern nationalism. But why limit the job of role modeling? Is it not the task of every nation to be ethically respectable? Elevating one nation demotes all the others. It is an embarrassing parochialism — all in the name of universalism.

The second problem is behavior. It is easy to sign up for a mission. It is harder to carry it out. While some Israelis (like some English and some French) are worthy of imitation, others are quite ordinary. What intrigues the world about the Jewish state is not its ethical behavior. The military power of so small a nation fascinates the public.

Inventing missions offers the danger of appearing ridiculous. It may be the last desperate attempt to avoid confronting the logical consequence of Jewish nationalism. An established nation does not need to value its national identity. It is simply there, unavoidably present. The question is not: Why preserve it? The question is: How do we use it?

The Jewish Enthusiasts of the Secular Revolution who live in the Diaspora and who feel a need to work at their Jewish identity end up with the same frustration as the Ambivalents. Choosing to remain Jewish and choosing to become Jewish requires an approach to Jewishness that goes beyond a pale imitation of rabbinic Judaism and fantasies about Israel.

If there are no special gifts from Yahveh, what is the value of Jewish identity?

The following chapters will attempt to explain the view of Humanistic Judaism.

CHAPTER IX

Jewish Identity

Before we explore the value of Jewish identity in a secular age, we need to clarify what Jewish identity is.

We need to evaluate certain words that people use to describe Jews. *Religious, racial, cultural, national* are common designations. They have been used frequently by both friends and enemies.

What friends and enemies think is not irrelevant. Useful labels are public creations. They belong to a world of shared meaning. Groups have boundaries. What those boundaries are for Jews is determined not only by Jews but also by those who stand on the other side of the boundary. We are not only what *we* say we are. We are also what *others* say we are.

Sometimes what we think about ourselves and what others think about us is not part of our awareness. It is unconscious and can only be detected through behavior. Our actions are always more interesting than our words. They reveal what we really believe about ourselves. If we want to understand the nature of Jewish identity, we have to watch how Jews behave, not just how they choose to present themselves to others.

Are the Jews a *religious* group?

Certainly, in the countries of the Western world, that designation is the most convenient. It avoids the accusation of dual nationality and identifies Jews with a community activity that is viewed as positive. In Eastern Europe, it is less convenient. Religion is given a pariah status and religious ideas are classified as superstitious. In Israel, a definition of the Jews as a religious denomination would subvert the reason for a Jewish state. Theological fraternities do not need countries of their own.

The truth of the matter is that while many Jews *do* religion, many do not. No common set of theological beliefs unites all Jews. Many have no theological beliefs. Many openly denounce religion. Many espouse atheism. But their Jewish identity remains intact. Jews are proud to claim both Sigmund Freud and Albert Einstein as members of the tribe.

The Reformers' attempt to define the Jews as a religious denomination — and nothing more — failed. It excluded too many people who were obviously Jews. A definition that cannot accommodate Theodore Herzl and Golda Meir is less than convincing. Even the Rejectionists, who defend rabbinic Judaism, live by the criterion that the children of a Jewish mother are Jewish and remain Jewish, no matter what they believe or do.

When the Israeli Supreme Court denied Jewish status to Brother Daniel, a born-Jew who had become a Catholic monk, they did not behave appropriately.[1] They had no difficulty giving Jewish Marxists what they had denied to him. Was the fact that Brother Daniel suffered as a Jew in wartime Poland, despite his religious beliefs, irrelevant?

In fact, anti-Semites always ignore Jewish religious behavior. Conversion to Catholicism meant nothing to the persecutors of the Marranos. And the Nazi bullies never believed in "former" Jews. In their eyes, creedal statements could neither make nor unmake a Jew.

It is quite clear that the Jewish status of a Mr. Cohen is usually determined long before anybody bothers to ask him what his religion is. In the secular age, as a Jew, he has many options — both religious and secular.

Are the Jews a *racial* group?

Ever since Hitler, Jews have avoided this designation. It reeks of persecution and concentration camps. Jews go to great length to prove the diversity of physical form that exists among Jews. The differences between Western and Oriental Jews, so apparent in Israel, are obvious examples.

But it is quite clear that the Jews, at the very beginning of their history, enjoyed some form of racial conformity. They were a collection of Semitic tribes. They were part of the gene pools of Western Asia. They viewed themselves as the descendants of a single ancestor called Abraham.

In the nineteenth century, the word *race* was loosely used to describe a group of people who shared a common origin and who behaved as a nation. But in the twentieth century, the word has been given a more precise scientific meaning. Physical characteristics, more than pedigree, are the criteria.

After twenty centuries of breeding with slaves, converts, and outsiders, the original Semitic mix has been diluted. And the new rage for intermarriage in Europe and North America will make any racial classification more difficult.

Oddly enough — or not so oddly — Rejectionists, like the Lubavitchers, retain the racial outlook of the Biblical editors who view outbreeding as religiously dangerous. They maintain that Jews have an inherited disposition to spirituality. Even if well-intentioned Gentiles want to become Jewish, their desire is a hopeless one. They lack the genetic equipment to become what they want to be.[2] Racial theories are not confined to Nazis.

Are the Jews a *national* group?

The Zionists think so. The authors of the Bible think so. And the rabbinic fathers concur.

A nation, in ancient times, was a confederation of tribes who shared a common language and a common territory. Outside Judea, rabbinic Jews believed that they were in exile, that they were not part of the nations among whom they lived, and that they would return someday to their territorial homeland. Their hostile hosts agreed with them and gave them the status of aliens.

But very early, the dispersion of the Jews created sub-nations. Hebrew and Jewish Aramaic faded away. New territorial enclaves with unique Jewish languages emerged. Northern Europe produced Yiddish. Spain invented Ladino. Jewish Arabic united the Jews of the Near East. And Jewish Persian became the mother tongue of Jewish Central Asia.

Were the speakers of Yiddish and Jewish Arabic one nation because the Bible said so and because they shared Hebrew as their devotional language? Or were they separate nations, distinct from their neighbors and distinct from each other? The coming together of Western and Oriental Jews in modern Israel is similar to the experience of Anglo-Saxon and Italian ethnics on the streets of Boston. If there is an Israeli nation today, it is being molded by secular Hebrew, Arab hostility, and "intermarriage."

The Jews were a single nation. They divided up into several smaller nations. And now some of them are creating a new Hebrew-speaking nation. But the majority of the Jews of the world have abandoned unique Jewish speech to adopt the language of their local environment. In America, Jews are pragmatically identified with the *white* sub-nation, those Americans who share American English and who are visibly neither black nor Chicano.

For most of their history, Jews were part of unique Jewish nations because they spoke unique Jewish languages, even though they did not possess territory of their own. Today, linguistic assimilation has undermined Jewish nationality in most parts of the world. If many Israelis did not speak English, American Jewish tourists would feel less sentimental about Israel.

Nations without territory are possible. (Look at the Yiddish nation.) But nations without either language or territory are illusions. Communities of Hebrew-speaking Jews form the only viable Jewish nation today. Israel is a Jewish nation. But not all Jews are part of that nation.

Israel is a unique phenomenon. Its roots lie in the Diaspora. It is the creation of the Diaspora. Other diasporas are the creation of their homeland. They have their roots there. They have their linguistic memories there. Israelis have to deal with their past in the same way that most Americans do. They have to think about Europe, Asia, and Africa. They have to deal with the fact that their families are recent arrivals. They have to confront the fact that their grandparents speak Hebrew less fluently than they do.

Italian-Americans look back to their homeland. Israeli Jews look back to their Diaspora. The importance of the Bible in Israel is related to this strange reversal. By emphasizing the Bible, the early Zionists wanted to negate the two thousand years of the dispersion. They wanted to create the illusion that the roots of modern Israel are in the ancient kingdom of David and Solomon. But the connection is tenuous. The real connection is with that disturbing Diaspora that refuses to disappear or to come home. Jewish identity in Israel can never be "normal" in the same way that English identity is taken for granted in England because the creation of Israel was abnormal. No invading illiterate barbarian tribes invented it. Israel was the planned project of urban sophisticates with long written memories. Some Jews today are part of a Jewish nation. But it is highly unlikely that most of them will ever be.

Are the Jews a *cultural* group?

Many secular Jews like to refer to themselves as *cultural* Jews. By that description, they mean to suggest that while they no longer have any attachment to rabbinic theology, they do have a sentimental connection with Jewish holidays, Jewish music, Jewish food, and Jewish symbols. They may even enjoy Jewish literature and dance Jewish dances. They may even dabble in Jewish languages.

Cultural attachments are what survive when linguistic and religious behavior disappear. They survive on pick and choose. They can often be done in translation.

But cultural attachments are different from living cultures. Vital cultures are the merging of language with life style and daily activity. They require their own unique space and exclude others. Hasidic Jews and Shiite Persians understand that reality. American Jews who eat matsa and dance the hora have Jewish cultural attachments. But they do not live in Jewish culture.

The culture of most Jews today is Western European secular culture, which has been refined by North America and which is spreading all over the world. Modern technology and modern architecture have no real nationality. They are international in the same way that science is. World languages like English, French, and Spanish unite the educated elites of all participating nations. Even the insular Japanese patronize symphony orchestras and collect Renoirs.

Modern Israel is nationally distinct. But it is not really culturally distinct from North America. A world of shared artifacts and shared education does not breed separate cultures. Tourists today are getting less for their money. They are finding it harder to visit quaint nations and to view charming local customs. Even the natives find it demeaning to be quaint, and they are cynical enough to turn local customs into tourist traps. Jewish visitors to Israel prefer Jerusalem to Tel Aviv. But Tel Aviv is where the action is.

Some Jews, Rejectionist Jews who live behind the walls of segregation, have their own culture. But most Jews, including Israeli Jews, have become part of a culture that is not uniquely Jewish. Western culture, as a consumer culture with many options, allows for cultural attachments. American Jews can choose Passover and Hebrew classes. But they can also choose Chinese food, karate, and French lessons.

Some people may deplore the disappearance of grand old cultures and the emergence of an international style with cultural options. But the old cultures will survive only as segregated islands. The wonders of the new culture are too attractive.

As for many Jews, they do not choose to indulge any of the Jewish cultural options that are available. But they still are Jews. And some of them value their Jewish identity.

KINSHIP

It is quite obvious that Jewish identity includes religious, racial, national, and cultural behavior. But it cannot be adequately defined by any one of them. A broader and more inclusive concept is required.

What realities should this concept embrace? What are the parameters that surround *all* Jews, whether they choose to engage in uniquely Jewish activity or do not choose to do so, whether they value their Jewish identity or do not value it?

Jewish identity, first of all, means a sense of shared ancestry. The Jews began as a nation, an ethnic federation of tribes. Their epic literature, which has become part of the sacred scriptures of the Christian world, speaks of their common ancestors. Whether Abraham, Isaac, or Jacob were real personalities or personifications of tribal invasions is irrelevant to the issue. The Jews saw themselves (and their neighbors saw them) as a *true* nation, a people united by "blood" ties and family loyalty. Even in Talmudic times, joining the Jews was never a mere religious conversion. It was an "adoption." New Jews severed all connections with their old families and adopted the ancestry of Abraham and Sarah.[3]

The Jewish people was dispersed from its homeland and became a family of new nations. But Jews never lost their sense of kinship. No matter where they lived, no matter what language they spoke, no matter what culture they adopted, no matter what racial elements they incorporated — they believed (and their neighbors believed) that they were united by the bond of "blood." Nineteenth century writers would not have hesitated to use the word *race* to describe this awareness — even the most pro-Semitic. But the dangers of that word in the twentieth century forbid its use. The more benign word *kinship* may be more discreet. Or the phrase *family sense.*

All Jews — even those who hate being Jewish — have this awareness of other Jews being their "relatives." New Jews, those who choose to become Jewish, also sense that they are joining a family fraternity where enthusiasm may confer fewer privileges than birth. Outsiders too, both the pros and the antis, have this view of the Jewish tribal connection. The phrase *member of the tribe*, although offensive to some, captures the awareness of a condition that is less than national but more than ideological.

The second parameter of Jewish identity is shared memories. Kinship means family roots and family history. The story of the Jews, whether positive or negative, fills the popular culture in the Western world. Christians give the Jews center stage in their drama. Muslims assign them a more peripheral role. But both traditions force Jews — even Jews who want to run away from their history or who are indifferent to or ignorant of it — to confront their past. The

Jews have a secure place in the popular memory. Announcing that you are a Jew is different from announcing that you are a Swedenborgian. Receivers of the news can fit you into their cultural memory. Even the peasant folk who have "never met a Jew before" know that Jews are not novelties. Even Jews who claim that they "know nothing about Judaism" know that they have a secure place in the history of any Western culture.

The third parameter of Jewish identity is shared danger. Jews are a vulnerable family. For whatever historical reasons, we are surrounded by hostility. The potential of anti-Semitism is part of the self-awareness of all Jews. It is also part of the awareness of Gentiles who deal with Jews. The events of the twentieth century have reenforced this apprehension. The Holocaust has tied Jewish identity to such fundamental emotions as fear, anger, loyalty, and pride. Frequently, Jews and Jewish leaders complain about the overemphasis on the negative side of Jewish existence. But Jewish anxiety and Jewish behavior do not pay any attention to this warning. Most parents who seek a Jewish education for their children want their sons and daughters to feel "proud" of their Jewish connection. They are obviously afraid that someone will make them feel less than proud. Being defensive is part of the Jewish condition.

Vulnerable kinship is an imperfect classification of Jewish identity. But it is more accurate than the words *religion, race, nation,* or *culture.* The word *people* is a convenient designation. Yet its usefulness is its vagueness. You can make it mean whatever you want it to mean. The word is part of public relations, not clarification. If a *people* can be a vulnerable international family — then fine.

Jewish identity is not an enigma. It is not a mystery. Vulnerable kinships exist elsewhere. Gypsies are an example. They are lower in the social scale than we would prefer as a parallel. But they are less than a nation and more than an economic function. And they know that when they announce themselves, they are in danger.

Apprehensive international families can provide many positive benefits. Danger — if it is not physical — can be an exciting condition. It keeps you on the alert and forces you to be very aware of your environment. It trains you in the survival skills of flight, appeasement, and confrontation. It persuades you to try cooperation and group solidarity. It makes you always envision alternatives to what you are doing presently. If anti-Semitism is not overt, Jews have one of the best training programs for survival in the modern urban world.

Of course, the value of Jewish identity cannot derive only from the positive side effects of being nervous. There must be an alternative to such a training program that does not involve the risk of holocaust. Otherwise, we shall be in the absurd position of the charming Chinese people in the Charles Lamb essay who accidentally discover the delights of roast pork when a house with a pig in it burns down — and then deliberately burn houses to achieve the same result.

VALUE

So what is valuable about Jewish identity? What is valuable about cultivating membership in an endangered tribe and encouraging others to share the same fate?

Judaism is a doctrine — not only from Jews — but also *about* Jews. It is specifically a doctrine about the value of Jewish identity.

Rabbinic Judaism is the traditional justification of Jewish identity by the rabbinic scholar class. It promises rewards for being Jewish — not only in this life — but especially in the next one. Yahveh, the one God of the whole world, has chosen the Jews to be his own special people and has offered them divine protection, ultimate victory, and a unique share in the world to come — benefits that he has granted to no other people. The Jews, in return for these colossal rewards, separate themselves from all other people and their false gods, assume a priestly regimen as the chosen servants of Yahveh, and allow him to use them as a way of advertising his power and glory.[4]

Jewish vulnerability and suffering is neatly integrated into this doctrine. The Jews were allowed to suffer for four hundred years as slaves in Egypt so that Yahveh could demonstrate his might to the Egyptians.[5] They were routed — the long way — through the wilderness of Sinai on their trek to Canaan so that Yahveh could demonstrate to them their total dependence on his supernatural grace and to other nations his extraordinary power to keep a nation of thousands alive in a killing desert.

The "advertising" doctrine had variations. If Jews needed to be punished for their violation of their priestly vows — as in the days of Jeremiah when they were offering sacrifices to Astarte — Yahveh could use the punishment of his own people as an advertisement of his power. Yahveh's punishments were extraordinary events. He could arrange for the Chaldeans to come to chastise the Jews.[6] He could arrange for the Persians to come to take care of the Chaldeans.[7] He could motivate the Assyrians to come to make the Hebrew Samaritans feel his anger.[8] The world will know: If you sign a contract with Yahveh, you better keep it. There is no place in this universe that he cannot enforce his will.

If the vulnerable Jews needed more justification for suffering, there was a backup team of reasons. Yahveh is testing your faith in his power by letting you suffer for a while. And true believers will not allow their agonies to interfere with their beliefs.[9] Yahveh is letting you suffer now so that you will be all the more worthy of the rewards of the world to come.[10] And true believers are grateful to take their medicine early. Yahveh's plan for salvation is too complex to be explained to dumb mortals. And true believers know that what appears to be bad is really good.

Yahveh's investment in his covenant with the Jews was the hope that the Jews would be a living reminder of the purpose of God on earth — a dramatic testimony to his power and justice.

Rabbinic Judaism gave Yahveh a vested interest in the Jews. They were his earthly advertising. They were the living testimony to his power and his might. They were the witnesses to his justice and compassion. Just as the rescue of the Jews from the slavery of Egypt let the Egyptians know who Yahveh was and what he could do, so did Jewish history, as a whole, announce his undisputed rule over the earth.

But the faith of the believers has been tested — not only by the skepticism of the Secular Revolution but also by the events of Jewish history.

It seems irrational that Yahveh would choose to advertise himself through the experience of a bunch of "losers." Promises about the afterlife might console the Jews. But wouldn't his constant failure to protect them from disaster be bad publicity for him? Even Moses warns him of this danger in the Torah.[11]

The Jews were the least likely candidates for the promotion of any ambitious deity. Large doses of guilt, administered by both priests and rabbis, allowed them to interpret "losing" as "winning." They were simply being punished for their own sins; if they would shape up, victory would follow. When this excuse ran its course of usefulness, they were encouraged to believe that vindication had only been postponed to test their faith. The imminent final judgment would show the world.[12] But the Messiah never seemed to arrive. Believing was an effort.

Very early in Jewish history, Jewish experience became separated from Jewish establishment ideology. The official party line presented Jews as the agents and chosen symbol of the all-powerful God of the world. But their experience of reality was quite different. Defeat, suffering, and humiliation — or at least a continuous subjection to intruders — was the gift of fate. Their propaganda spoke of their glory. But their neighbors saw only their degradation. In order to cling to the ancestral faith, they had to practice a lot of denial. They had to hide their anger and disappointment.

The worst insult of all was that their enemies explained their suffering very well. For the Christians and the Muslims, God had rejected the Jews because they had rejected his true prophet.[13] The suffering of the Jews was a well-deserved punishment for their stubborn infidelity. If they suffered more than anybody else, their agony was appropriate. They, above all, as the chosen of God, should have embraced his true emissaries. If God allowed them to live, it was only to demonstrate that they were no longer chosen — a living testimony of what happens to the unfaithful. For the Christians, in particular, the Jews, as the assassins of God, were getting exactly what they deserved.

Jewish experience and Jewish theology did not fit each other. Dreams of future vindication in a world to come could not hide the painful reality. Jewish history had very little to do with any reasonable concept of chosenness. It had no decent connection with a God who was kind and compassionate. The rabbis said one thing. The reality said another. The prayers announced the presence of God. Experience announced the absence of God.

The survival of the Jews was no great benefit. If the Jewish people had vanished, like many of the nations of the ancient world, their descendants still would have survived under different labels. The Romans were not killed. They just turned into Italians. In fact, more descendants of the Jews would be present now if Jews had abandoned the Jewish label. What value was there in embracing a religious posture that offended everybody and provoked anti-Semitism through its arrogant denial of other people's gods — if the only reward was intense suffering? A surviving remnant is not testimony to a just God. It is a tribute either to masochism or to prideful persistence.

In order to deal with this reality, the Jews developed two personalities and two traditions. One personality and tradition — the official one — was pious and religious. It praised God, justified his behavior, and responded to every disaster with more prayer and more attention to ritual observance. The other personality and tradition — the unofficial one — was skeptical and angry. It shrugged its shoulders a lot, distrusted all authority, and learned to laugh at the absurdity of things. Piety and laughter are two contrary emotions. They arise from two different human responses to danger: appeasement and confrontation.

The first tradition is the establishment posture of the rabbinic fathers. In an age of censorship and scarcity of written materials, it monopolized the published literature. It produced the wealth of prayers and Bible and Talmudic commentaries that most Jews think of as "the Jewish tradition." Its hero is the Torah-loving scholar who sometimes questions the justice of God but who always finds some rabbinic reason to maintain it. Innocent joy, like Haisidic dancing, is permissible. But mocking, skeptical laughter is alien to its nature. It is the very stuff out of which reverence is made.

The second tradition is the "underground" behavior of the Jewish people. Since it was opposed to the rabbinic mood it never saw the light of publication. It lingered in popular customs and folk humor. But it helped to mold the Jewish personality that so many of us are familiar with and like. Its heroes are the angry mockers of authority who conform reluctantly because they have to — and who are more comfortable laughing than praying. Yiddish humor is the best legacy of this tradition. If it had a motto, it would go something like this, "With God as your friend, you do not need enemies," or maybe, "Why should I complain? I'm still alive."

People often ask where the Jewish intellectual of modern times comes from. How does one derive a critical, skeptical, agnostic surveyor of the human condition from a pious devotee of Torah tradition? Literacy and education are not enough. The scholar class of the Christian and Muslim theological academies never produced such a troublemaker. Talmudic reasoning sharpens your logical skills. But it does not encourage you to mock the fates and to challenge authority. Without anger and skepticism, you simply get a brilliant fundamentalist.

The driving force of the contemporary Jewish intellectual spirit — whether it is used to justify capitalism, Marxism, psychoanalysis, or Zionism — is a deep rage.[14] It is an angry refusal to accept what is unacceptable, to praise what is unworthy of praise, to label injustice, justice. It is a strong conviction that traditional religion and humiliation go together. The world that persecutes us does not deserve our passive acceptance. It needs our defiance.

When Erich Fromm defined the Jewish spirit as the refusal of all idols, he certainly could not justifiably derive it from rabbinic Judaism.[15] Reverence is reverence, whether it is directed to a Torah scroll or to a statue. And invisible gods are idols so long as they are treated as gods. The true refusal of idols is the unwillingness to worship anything, the *hutspa* to investigate everything. That refusal is not part of the official tradition. It is the gift of the "underground."

The Jewish intellectual has Jewish roots. But they are not pious roots. They are twenty-five centuries of emotional resistance to an official ideology that demeaned Jewish suffering. Not only were the Jews persecuted by their enemies. They were persecuted by their own excuses.[16]

The nineteenth and twentieth centuries have replaced the rabbis with a new Jewish scholar. Some of them are boring academicians. But some of them have transformed the thinking of the modern world. Freud, Marx, and Einstein helped to undermine the view of nature which supported rabbinic Judaism and all other traditional religions. Ironically, their assault has its emotional origins in the historic experience of the Jewish people.

For the "underground" tradition, the Secular Revolution was one of the first good things to happen in centuries. It freed their unofficial adherents from rabbinic censorship and government oppression. They could now state freely and easily what they really believed. They were not confined to gestures, jokes, and private conversations. Skepticism and agnosticism were in the spirit of the age. Reason and dignity insisted on them.

If the Middle Ages was the era of the official tradition, the nineteenth and twentieth centuries are the heyday of the "underground." Neither one is older than the other. They are simply different.

There are *two* Jewish emotional and philosophic traditions. They have lived side by side. They have competed with each other. They have appealed to different temperaments and personalities. Some Jews tried to embrace both and suffered from ambivalence. Other Jews acted out the one while really believing the other. But all had to conform in some way so long as the rabbis were in charge.

The "underground" tradition is strong. But it is less
visible than the rabbinic one. There is no body of easily
available literature that clearly defines it and establishes its
presence. There is no famous collection of books, like the
Bible, that dramatizes it. Only the nature of the modern
Jewish personality is a witness to its power.

The Jewish personality is less the consequence of rabbinic
ideology than of Jewish experience. Skepticism, mocking
humor, and nervous ambition do not come from Torah study.
They do not come from a faithful awareness of a well-ordered
universe. They come from a sense of chaos, an experience of
absurdity. Jewish history is not the tale of a triumphant people and their triumphant God. At best, it is the story of a *shle-
mazzel* god who is too weak and incompetent to defend the
people he promised to defend. At worst (and the most reasonable alternative), it is the story of a self-deceived people who
fight the reality of an indifferent universe and *unjust* fates.

The personality of the Diaspora Jew lacks the serene
peasant faith of Biblical theology. It is much more nervous. It
expresses the tension between reality and ideology. The Jews
were compelled to deny their anger and their fury — not
toward their enemies, but toward the God they said they
loved. Or they were tempted to think the unthinkable — that
there was no God either to love or to hate.

For a while, the Secular Revolution turned the thoughts of
many Jews away from the behavior of an "irrational"
destiny. Political emancipation in Western Europe improved
the conditions of the Jews and opened to them new opportunities for freedom and power. While secular reason continued to undermine rabbinic theology, the dramatic easing of
Jewish suffering made Jews less aware of their uniqueness.
A new euphoria of universalist and cosmopolitan hopes seized
the imagination of secular Jewish intellectuals. In a world of
scientific humanism, both God and Jewish identity would

become irrelevant. They would simply fade away. For the liberated rational citizens of the future, remaining Jewish would be as reactionary as remaining religious.

But the arrival of secular anti-Semitism changed all expectations. For the secular anti-Semite — even one who hated religion and despised Christianity — Jewishness was still important. In fact, it became the key to the understanding of human history. The Jew — and the secular Jew, in particular — was the devilish embodiment of all that was wrong in modern society. As the "inventor" of both capitalism and communism, the Jews undermined the moral foundations of civilization. They made money more important than honor and freedom more important than family. The competitive and collectivist nature of the Jewish conspiracy divided the Gentile masses and forced them to fight each other and not the true enemy who manipulated them. For many people, the Jews became more monstrous in the age of "reason" than they had ever been in the age of faith.[17]

In the face of the new anti-Semitism, the secular Jews retreated from universalism. Dignity and survival revived their interest in Jewish identity. But it did not revive their interest in God. If human beings now appeared less rational than they used to, the universe, in turn, appeared less orderly and more chaotic. The bourgeois attempt to rescue the word *God* and religious affiliation by turning God into a vague benign order of things became even less tenable. If it was undignified to deny your Jewishness to your enemies, it was equally undignified to offer thanks to God.[18]

Recent history provided the ultimate outrage. The Holocaust remains the supreme manifestation in Jewish history of the absence of God. Even those who seek to rescue God's reputation by chastising the modern Jew for the sinful abandonment of traditional religion cannot explain why the Nazi fury was directed to the homeland of the pious.[19] The victims who loved God the most, suffered the most. No future resurrection can compensate for the injustice of this genocide. Did the Yahveh who used the Persians to punish his people in ancient times also use the Nazis to do so in the twentieth century? The theology of the prophets is an insult to the memory of the innocent dead.

No interpretation of Jewish history and Jewish identity can escape the Holocaust. Even though it is recent, even though it is difficult to develop an historical perspective, the deliberate extermination of six million Jews in a short period of time, as a state policy and in a European setting where reason and dignity found strong adherents, is a monumental event that will not be easily forgotten (and should not be forgotten). If people appear *less* trustworthy, does God appear *more* trustworthy?

The Holocaust is dramatic testimony to the sublime indifference of the universe to undeserved human suffering — and to undeserved human pleasure, for that matter. In the twentieth century, the Jew learned that the reward for faith and humility is despair and humiliation. If they did not resist reality, they were confronted by an ironic truth. The Jewish people, whose official establishment proclaimed for over two thousand years that Jewish history is a testimony to the presence of God, is, indeed, the strongest testimony to the absence of God.

In the secular age, the Jews, above all people, discovered that the old theology was a harmful illusion. It encouraged Jews to be passive and grateful when they should be active and angry. If ever a people had been mislabeled, the Jews were. The people who supposedly discovered "God" were the painful witnesses to the fact that divine justice did not exist. In the history of no other nation were experience and ideology so far apart.

In the twentieth century, the true meaning of Jewish identity has been dramatized. It is no pious call to faith and humility. It is no saccharine invitation to prayer and worship.

It is a summons to all that a modern humanism stands for. If a people will not assume responsibility for its "fate" and its "destiny," no one else will. If human beings will not take charge of their own happiness, the indifferent forces of the universe may arrange for human suffering. Reason and dignity are not built into the structure of the world. They are difficult human achievements.

Jewish history and Jewish experience — especially in the twentieth century — are vivid witnesses to the absurdity of the universe, to the absence of any moral order in the "running" of the world. They are expert testifiers to the futility of expecting inorganic energy to conform to the ethical standards of an ambitious species on a hostile planet.

They are also sobering reminders to a secular world. If "God" is uncaring or non-existent, people too can be uncaring and "inhumane." Education and naive wishing will not guarantee the triumph of human dignity. Only painful discipline and realistic expectations will enable us to manage our disappointment and to use it constructively. Secular visions often suffer from religious enthusiasm. Like traditional religion, they often offer more than they can deliver.

In the century of Hitler and Stalin, in the age of the Holocaust, returning to God is a denial of dignity. It is an insult to the victims of war and undeserved "punishment." But returning to a naive view of human "goodness" is equally a denial of dignity. It is an insult to the countless number of "nice" people who discipline their passions and train their generosity with great effort and with a strong awareness of the "dark" side of their nature.

Jewish identity has humanistic value because Jewish experience testifies to the need for reason and dignity. To be Jewish is to feel the indifference of the universe and the terror of self-reliance. But given the gifts of destiny, there is no alternative to self-reliance.

Jewish identity is attached to Jewish memory. And Jewish memory is an encyclopedia of reasons for agnosticism, skepticism, and human striving. The theistic tradition of the Jewish establishment, so in conflict with the Jewish experience, makes the humanistic message all the more vivid. Being Jewish — with an authentic and realistic attachment to Jewish history — is a way of reenforcing a humanistic approach to life, a way of strengthening our awareness of the importance of reason and dignity.

Judaism (as we pointed out at the beginning of this book) is a doctrine about the value of Jewish identity. The old Judaism finds theological value in Jewish identity. The new Judaism finds *humanistic* value in Jewish identity.

A humanistic Judaism demands a *new* view of Jewish history. It demands a radical departure from the traditional way of describing what Jews feel and believe. It requires the ability to make a distinction between experience and propaganda, between reality and official ideology. It needs to focus less on theological ideas and worship practices and more on the actual skills that Jews developed for their own survival.

What are the details of this *new* view?

CHAPTER X

Jewish History

Jewish history is the saga of a vulnerable international family. It is the tale of its struggle to survive. What is worst in Jewish history is the surrender to faith and humility. What is best in Jewish experience is the discovery of reason and dignity.

The Jewish personality is far more than the official piety. It is a collection of useful skills that do not derive from theology but come from human ingenuity, from the response of a desperate people to the cruelty of fate. Alertness, ambition, intellectuality, skepticism, and absurdist humor — although not present in all Jews — manifest themselves in enough Jews to make them group characteristics.

So many historians of the Jewish people have devoted their attention to what Jews theoretically believe that they have been unable to focus on what they actually do. Monotheism can produce placid peasants just as easily as it can produce nervous intellectuals. Torah study can create rote memorizers just as easily as it can produce analytic thinkers. What is most interesting about the Jews is not a devotion to an invisible deity, who has his rivals in other traditions, and to moral platitudes, which are present in all cultures (even the heathen Chinese believed in love and family), but a personality style that deeply distrusts destiny and finds itself more comfortable with change than with eternity.

A proper understanding of Jewish history is the key to a humanistic Jewish identity. Without a distinction between establishment ideology and real experience, the Jewish story is a tale of religious piety that is quite ordinary and that cannot explain why Jews are the way they are. Only when we discard the conventional approach to the Jewish past, can we understand the humanistic dimension of the Jewish experience. Human ingenuity and the absence of God are not the themes of Talmudic commentaries.

A *new* approach to Jewish history is necessary. But it is also difficult. Most popular presentations of the Jewish experience insist on the primacy of religious ideas. God and Torah (even when they are viewed as human creations) are regarded as the basic Jewish glue and the motivating powers of Jewish behavior. The implication is quite clear. If God and Torah are illusions, they are positive illusions. If they fade away, so will the Jewish personality — and the Jewish identity.

This religious emphasis distorts the way we approach the past. Since the most important religious figures lived a long time ago, the distant past becomes primary. The age of the prophets, priests, and rabbinic fathers outshines any other time. Moses becomes more significant than Einstein. Amos becomes more definitive than Nathan Rothschild. The epic period of rabbinic Judaism stands out as the crucial time of Jewish achievement.

The consequences of this approach are harmful. They prevent us from seeing what we ought to see. Literature replaces events. We become more interested in the description of events than in the events themselves. If the author of the Torah tells us that Abraham was a real person and that he was very important, we tend to accept the statement — not because we have any reason to believe it, but because we are persuaded that trusting the Torah is essential to the preservation of Jewish identity. If the editors of the Torah inform us that Moses transmitted the Ten Commandments and was the supreme prophet of all times, we see no reason to question that assertion, especially when we have no alternative Jewish document to challenge it. Since the book is real — and preserving the book is tied up with preserving the Jews — we find many reasons to praise the book and fewer reasons to look at the events behind the book. Despite all the evidence that much of what the Torah says happened is different from what really happened, no one has boldly written a popular alternative to this priestly epic. The real history stays hidden in scholarly journals. No matter what deficiencies critical research discovers in the narrative of the Torah, the Torah never loses its status. The study of the Bible becomes a substitute for the study of Jewish history.

Since the rabbinic elite had a monopoly on published literature, personalities and events that did not fit into the rabbinic scheme were never mentioned. If you were a rabbi and you had an opinion about whether chickens should be eaten with milk, you got a handsome citation in the Talmud. If you were a poet and you sang the praises of Yahveh, the prayerbook acknowledged your contribution. But if you were the first Jewish banker or the best Jewish humorist, history has forgotten your name. The rabbis, like most religious elites, were not interested in preserving your memory. Only in the last two centuries would you have a chance for recognition.

Even in modern times, after the emergence of history as a secular discipline, Jewish history for the Jewish masses does not fit scientific guidelines. Since many Jewish historians use Jewish history to save Jewish theology, they are reluctant to shift their emphasis from mystics to merchants. A secular history of the Jews would undermine the sacredness of historic documents and make God-talk less important. While it is

now fashionable to downplay miracles and supernatural intrusion, it has become all the more urgent to emphasize the
significance of religious leaders. You may dismiss the
prophet's embarrassing ecstacy. But you may never dismiss
the prophet.

Since many of the names of priests, prophets, and rabbis
are already known, they are better objects for hero worship
than unknown middle class achievers. Nevertheless, getting
Einstein from Jeremiah and Akiva is about as plausible as
getting Bertrand Russell from Thomas a Beckett.

For the humanistic Jew, a proper understanding of
Jewish history is the key to a positive Jewish identity. Both
the events of that history and the responses to those events
need to be uncovered.

A *humanistic* approach to Jewish history needs certain
guidelines.

NATURALISTIC PERSPECTIVE

A humanistic approach to Jewish history needs a naturalistic perspective. The supernaturalist approach of the priestly
and rabbinic theologians who edited the Bible and the Talmud
is unacceptable. And the semi-supernaturalist approach of
contemporary historians who describe Jewish survival as a
unique "mystery" is equally unacceptable. The causes of
Jewish behavior and Jewish endurance are open to public
investigation. If they are presently unknown, they are not
permanently unknowable. "Mystery" and "enigma" are contemporary coverups for supernatural direction. They suggest
that the causes are beyond rational inquiry.

The laws of the Bible and the Talmud, the stories of sacred
scriptures, the petitions of the prayerbook are of human

creation. They are the products of human insight, human desire, and human vested interests. They are reflections of particular times and particular places. They are passionate propaganda in religious and political arguments. The stories of King Saul were written by the priestly employees of his enemy King David. The tale of Jezebel was composed by her prophetic opponents. The sacrificial ritual of Leviticus was designed by the priests who would benefit from it.[1]

Human need — not divine aloofness — is responsible for what Jews did and said. It is also responsible for distorting what Jews did and said. The motivation for recording events and happenings was no dispassionate desire to keep a diary. It was the obvious need to use history to push political programs and religious ideologies. Is the story of the covenant between Abraham and Yahveh a journalistic observation of an actual event? Or is it a justification for the Jewish claim to all of ancient Canaan?

Holidays are not the children of supernatural decrees. They have their beginnings in the human response to natural events. Passover is not the spontaneous invention of a heavenly king. It is an evolving festival that served the nationalist fervor of patriotic rulers. Nor is Yom Kippur the creation of a judgmental god. It is a priestly device to increase the dread of Yahveh. The supernatural did not use the natural to promote its agenda. The human used the supernatural to advance its vested interests.[2]

Seeing God behind all events is not necessary to explain what happens; human desire and natural laws do quite well. It is also potentially embarrassing. If Yahveh arranged for the Exodus, he also arranged for the Holocaust. The theological mileage that one can get from Jewish history is definitely limited. Theology is always more interesting when it is relegated to its appropriate niche in the department of anthropology, a study of human fear and human imagination.

BEYOND LITERATURE

A humanistic approach to Jewish history needs a determination to look beyond literature to *real* events. The Jewish experience is not the same as the description of that experience. The Bible is not the same as ancient Jewish history. It may be a key to what happened. But it is not a mirror of what happened. The Bible says that Abraham was a person. But he, most likely, was a whole Semitic invasion. The Bible says that Joshua followed Moses. But Moses, most probably, followed Joshua by three hundred years. The Bible says that the Ten Commandements were delivered by Moses to the Hebrews at Mount Sinai. But the evidence suggests that they were prepared by the priests of Jerusalem during the reign of the Davidic kings.[3]

Nor are pious legends the same as Jewish history. A Talmudic story may make Hanukka an eight day festival because the one day supply of holy oil burned for eight days. But the winter holiday was an eight day festival long before it was ever called "Hanukka." The Mishnah may trace rabbinic law all the way back to Moses. But the Oral Law was the creation of the rabbis themselves.[4] A tradition may ascribe Davidic ancestry to Hillel. But there is very little evidence to indicate that either Hillel or Jesus was descended from King David. Their respective protagonists simply wished to give them divine authority.

The history of a people is distinct from the value of its literature. The Torah may have a literary and religious importance above and beyond any narrative truth it may convey. But that religious importance is irrelevant to its accuracy when that accuracy counts. There is a difference between the Torah as an event in Jewish history and as a description of events. That people believed that Moses wrote the Torah is one issue. That Moses actually wrote it is another.

The Jews may have lived for four hundred years with the House of David without any formal Torah and with little awareness of the personality of Móses. With the downfall of the Davidic dynasty, the priestly relatives of Moses may have revived his memory in their bid for power. The Torah may be their justification to rule the Jews in the place of secular monarchs. If that observation is true, the love of David preceded the love of Moses in Jewish experience. Monarchists preceded theocrats, even though the Torah claimed that the theocrats came first. It may not be true that the Torah molded early Jewish experience. A part of early Jewish experience may have molded the Torah.[5]

Jews are the products of their *real* experience — not the products of what the rabbis said their experience was. The struggle for power between kings and priests, priests and rabbis was an important political dimension in Jewish development. The Bible and the Talmud were the result of these political controversies. And the editors of these documents do not deal kindly with their opponents — who were equally as Jewish. The enemies of Jeremiah were just as Jewish and just as patriotic as Jeremiah when they refused to surrender Jerusalem to the Chaldeans.[6] And the Sadducee enemies of the rabbis were just as committed to Jewish survival as their competitors when they refused to accept the authority of the Oral Law (Talmud).[7]

It is dangerous to pick your heroes and villains when you are able to read only one side of a religious controversy. The rabbis made sure that their view of Jewish history would prevail when they suppressed or destroyed all opposing points of view.[8] As the victims of religious censorship, we should be aware of our victimization. The enemies of the rabbis might have given us a more balanced view of early

Jewish history if their writings had survived. If we fail to give them their due, we shall end up with a history of the Jews that is as credible as a Herbert Hoover biography of Franklin Delano Roosevelt.

POPULAR RELIGION

A humanistic approach to Jewish history needs to make a distinction between official religion and popular religion. The obsession with God is part of the official documents of the religious establishment. But it may not have been an obsession of the masses of the people. In fact, we know from all the denunciations in the Bible that polytheism was common in ancient Israel and that female deities (whom the prophets abhorred) were very popular.

Monotheism is no more "logical" than polytheism. In fact, if you are a devotee of supernatural explanations, polytheism explains evil better than one-God theories. A devil is easier to blame for cancer than a just God. The source of monotheistic ideas is no great spiritual ingenuity. It is a political structure called imperialism. World gods are the reflection of world government. Just as tribal government features tribal gods and national government features national gods, so do empires sponsor the birth of supergods. Monotheism was no Jewish invention. The Egyptians, the Persians, and the Greeks all had their fling at it. Aton, Mazda, and Zeus became divine superstars just like Yahveh — and with more reason. Yahveh, the world ruler, coincides with the advent of Assyrian, Chaldean, and Persian empires. He is a political explanation, not a spiritual revolution.[9]

From the very beginning, monotheism was an ill-fitting shoe. It could never adequately explain the defeats and humiliations that pious Jews experienced. Only the addition of future rewards and punishment made it fit better. Popular religion still kept its demons and evil spirits, reflections of the disorder and disharmony of things. The masses experienced the terror of the world. No serene orderly deity was enough to handle the difficulties of daily living. In the end, the groom broke the glass at the end of the wedding ceremony to frighten away the evil spirits (whom Yahveh was obviously incapable of disciplining). Folk religion and the official religion very often did not coincide.

A humanistic approach to Jewish history needs to give a special place to Jewish secular achievement. So often the popular versions of the Jewish experience make it seem that religious behavior and religious aspirations were the chief concern of the Jewish past. They fail to describe the secular skills which made the Diaspora and group survival possible.

The most significant event in the early development of the Jews was not the change from polytheism to monotheism. It was the transformation of the Jews from an agricultural and pastoral people into a dispersed urban nation. Jews became a city people and remained a city people. Today, Jews are the most urbanized ethnic and religious group in the world.[10]

One of the reasons why the Bible is more appealing to rural Southerners than to Westchester County Jews is the fact that the authors of the documents were writing for farmers and shepherds. When the Torah was finalized the Jews were a conventional Near Eastern mini-nation, settled on its own land and pursuing the basic procedures of a near subsistence economy. With a few fortress cities and little surplus for export, they were far more parochial than the God they had promoted. As a nation of shepherds and peasant

farmers, they were very different from the Jews of the last
two thousand years.

The urbanization of the Jew had many causes.

Like their Canaanite and Phoenician racial cousins, the
Jews found their land too rocky and too dry to sustain a
growing population. The Phoenicians dispersed. And so did
the Jews. They left Judea for the same reason that New Eng-
landers came to Michigan and that Greeks went to Italy. The
homeland could not provide well for its own children. Later
on, political and religious persecution added to the outflow.

The Jewish refugees settled in the cities of the host
nations. In the Greek period, they were welcomed into the
new growing urban centers of the Hellenistic world. Joining
the native peasantry on the land was difficult because the
land was occupied and the village social structures could not
accommodate intruders. In later centuries, Jews were forbidden to own farm estates by their Christian rulers.

But the chief reason for the urban conversion was simply
that city life was more stimulating, more interesting, and
more profitable than farm life. The crafts and trading were
more attractive to the Jews in the same way that they were
more appealing to their "Syrian" compatriots (Phoenicians
and Arameans). Once you leave the village for the city (as we
know from modern times), you have very little incentive to
return. Jews, like many other people, were voluntary recruits
to urban existence.

Unfortunately, modern Jewish historians are very often
apologetic about this development. They are ashamed of the
urban skills that Jews have acquired. They are intimidated by
anti-Semitism. Modern anti-Semites denounce the Jews as
city-slickers, rootless cosmopolitans who undermine peasant
virtue and patriotism. For the Jew-hater, the city is the
setting for both greedy Jewish capitalism and subversive

Jewish communism. Both the family and religion decay in its corrupting environment.

In the face of this assault, many Jews protested their "innocence." They maintained that the Jews were only urban draftees, compelled by historical circumstance to do what they did not want to do. Given the chance, they would love to return to the land and resume farming. Some of the earliest Zionist propagandists, like A.D. Gordon, echoed this rationalization.[11] Jews could only create a true national culture if they went back to the soil. And being close to the land would make them more virtuous.

But if, indeed, this argument is valid, Jewish history is a long tale of corruption. Focusing on Biblical patriarchal shepherds and warrior kings (which embarrassed Jews love to do) will not hide the fact that, for most of Jewish history, the Jews were a mobile, urban people developing attitudes and skills that would make them ideal candidates for the capitalistic world. Money and trade, not manure and sheep, were motivating forces in their lives. Manufacture and distribution, not plowing and seeding, were the stuff out of which daily activity was made. To be ashamed of urban existence and a monetary culture, to fervently wish that more Jews were farmers and worked with their hands, is an act of self-hate, a refusal to come to terms with what the Jews were and are.

Some of the current emphasis on the Biblical period in Jewish history comes from religious conviction. (The time when Yahveh spoke is the most important time of all.) Some of it comes from the special place of the Bible in the eyes of Christian believers. Some of it arises from the Zionist need to identify with a period in Jewish history when the Jews were free and independent on their own land. But much of it comes from the enormous discomfort that many Jews feel with what they are. They have the same distaste for a mobile, individualistic urban milieu that most historic conservatives do. They want to identify with what Jews used to be a long time ago — even though, if this option were offered, they would reject it.

The Jewish experience moved away from Jewish ideology. While the establishment religion praised the life of shepherds and farmers, exalted the return of agricultural sacrifice, and elevated the land to a sacred status, the economic development of the Jews turned them into bookkeeping entrepreneurial wanderers. Nothing in traditional Jewish literature praised urban existence, even though Jewish life was tied up with town life. The Jews became what their leaders were not prepared to like.

Yet the Jewish personality, with all its verbal pushy edges, is not a product of peasant lovers of the Torah. It is an urban product, finely tuned to city life and city anxiety. If a high percentage of Jews have intellectual or "cultural" interests (or pretensions), it is not because they memorized Bible verses. If most Jews adapt easily to the demand and requirements of modern urban living (and are successful out of all proportion to their numbers), it is not because they were verbally skilled in Talmudic arguments. Quite the opposite. Polish *pilpul* (Talmudic verbal games) was the direct result of an urbanized culture that placed great emphasis on talking and verbal exhibitionism. City communities value verbal skills even more than physical prowess.

Coming to terms with the Jewish urban past and with Jewish urban skills is absolutely necessary for an authentic Jewish history. Jews do not need to apologize for being pioneers of our modern urban culture. Without that development, the Secular Revolution would never have taken place and the contemporary Western world of individual freedom and opportunity would never have emerged. Attachment to Manhattan or central Tel Aviv does not mean corruption. Jewish apologists should be wary of imitating anti-Semites.

EQUAL TIME

A humanistic approach to Jewish history gives equal time to both the immediate past and the distant past. It avoids the propaganda needs of rabbinic Judaism.

The official ideology (both in its traditional and liberal forms) does not see the last two thousand years of Jewish existence to be of equal value to the first two thousand years. In the eyes of the rabbinic establishment, Amos, Hosea, Isaiah, and Jeremiah have no modern duplicates. They were spiritual phenomena unique to olden times. The events of their time are more important because these "divine" messengers responded to them. And the people of their time are more important because the prophets used them as an audience. Later centuries are inferior because they simply did not produce the prophets or the rabbinic fathers.[12]

But such an approach is naive. Not only does it imagine that the most important determinants of Jewish identity were the pronouncements of prophets and scholars. It also ignores what happened to these statements. What the prophets said is less important than what later centuries did with what they said. (Just as what Madison and Hamilton intended is less significant than what the American Supreme Court did with the American Constitution.) The anti-urban economic egalitarianism of Amos never became part of the Jewish experience. It was rejected by the Jewish establishment and found no willing supporters among the Jewish masses (who had no desire to return to the *equal* poverty of the old shepherd existence). If his prophecies survived, they survived because some of what he said was misunderstood as a prediction for the coming of the Messiah.[13]

The anonymous urbanites of later years used Amos for *their* purpose. And their opinions were more powerful in the development of Jewish identity than the rejected advice of an executed prophet. You will not understand Christianity by studying the life of Jesus. And you will not understand the story of Jewish identity by focusing on the life of Amos.

It is certainly interesting to speculate on why Amos said what he said. But Amos is Jewishly important — not because what he said was morally unique in the annals of moral pronouncements, but because the rabbis chose to include him in the Bible, for *their* purposes, not for his. And he is interesting in modern times — not because he was in favor of "good" and opposed to "evil" (who isn't?), but because *both* bourgeois Reformers and Marxist ideologues ironically find in him a spiritual father of their own ethical programs.

What is historically important is not the Amos of the distant past — but the reformers and radicals who use him. Dead heroes are the most useful authorities. They cannot challenge what you make their words mean. Amos may have been the defender of a stern Bedouin morality that most progressives would find appalling. But today, he is dressed up to fit neatly into either liberal charity or radical redistribution. It is this phenomenon that is far more interesting than the self-proclaimed prophet of Tekoah. Most of what Amos "said" is really a reflection of what most modern Jews think and believe — and of those more recent events that produced such opinions.

Jewish radical intellectuals are not the children of the distant Amos. They are the children of verbal, alienated urbanites who have no reason to love a hostile establishment.

Understanding this alienation has far more to do with Jewish identity than quotations ripped out of their pastoral contexts.

Our need to use the distant past to "kosherize" the present has two harmful effects. It prevents us from really understanding the past. We are less interested in finding out what Moses and Amos and Akiba really did and said and more interested in making sure that they are on our side. It also minimizes the importance of the present and the immediate past by pretending that recent developments are really old ones. We focus on the quotation and not on the people who use it.

Most of the people whose decisions determined the character of Jewish identity are now unknown. They lived in a time when "sacred scriptures" were rampant, when nothing labeled original was deemed to have any value, and when new opinions were always disguised as interpretations of old ones. "Distant pastitis" is an old religious disease. It corrupts our judgment and prevents it from being fair to either the past or the present.

HUMAN MOTIVATION

A humanistic approach to Jewish history looks for human motivation. If the author of the opinions in the Bible, the Talmud, and the Siddur were God, then we would be searching for divine motivations (if God can have any) that have nothing at all to do with jealousy, hatred, and the struggle for power. But if the authors of these opinions are people, then it is appropriate for us to investigate the human desires that motivated them to write what they did — which, indeed, may have a lot to do with jealousy, hatred, and the struggle for power.

Personal fulfilment and fame — important modern motivations — were not the reasons why the special documents of the religious establishment were written. They were written as persuasive literature, what we call propaganda. They were intended to persuade Jews to defend certain ideas, to adopt certain practices, and to obey certain authorities. They were also intended to persuade Jews to reject certain ideas, to discard certain practices, and to ignore certain authorities.

Each author uses his document to make us see Jewish history the way he wants us to see Jewish history. If he is a royal scribe, his viewpoint will be different from that of a priestly writer. And the priestly writer will not see things the same way as the rabbinic scholar. Each author is defending a different master. Royal scribes want us to revere the royal members of the House of David. Priestly writers want us to give our allegience to the priestly members of the "House of Moses." And rabbinic scholars want us to obey the guardians of the rabbinic tradition.

The Book of Samuel is more than a collection of stories. It makes David and his descendants legitimate kings. The Book of Deuteronomy is more than a collection of laws. It makes Moses and his relatives legitimate priests and leaders. The Sayings of the Fathers is more than a collection of epigrams. It gives the rabbis a legitimate chain of command.

Jewish history is the tale of intense rivalries. Different groups vie for power. And their literature is their propaganda. The dead David and the dead Moses become the symbols of competing elites, who tell their stories to serve their interests.[14] What happened to the Jews is no different from what happened to other nations. New groups tried to overthrow old groups. And having succeeded and feeling vulnerable, they felt the need to justify their rule.

The Secular Revolution upset this game. Emancipation liberated Jews from the involuntary control of Jewish authorities. History might be used to push passionate points of view (like this book). But rival interpretations were no longer destroyed. And the emergence of the social sciences made judgments more open to public scrutiny and challenge.

There has been more diversity of opinion and belief in Jewish history than the rabbinic establishment ever wanted to reveal. There is no unbroken chain of tradition from Moses to the present. The propaganda of the early tribal *shofetim* was replaced by the propaganda of the Davidic kings. And the royal tradition was replaced by the priestly tradition. The rabbinic triumph was a radical break with the priestly authority that came before. Jewish elites were quite human in their ambitions. We make them less interesting when we turn them into noble parrots of supernatural perfection. Love, kindness, generosity, and dignity would not be commendable achievements if they did not arise out of a more sordid context. Saints are boring. And supernatural advice is always patronizing.

CHAPTER XI

Anti-Semitism

Anti-Semitism must take its proper place in a humanistic approach to Jewish history. Much of the Jewish personality that is humanistically interesting was produced by anti-Semitism.

The Jews of ancient Judea were pious peasants. They were more likely candidates for the Moral Majority than for the A.C.L.U. Attached to their families, clans, tribes, and ancestors, they revered them all. Like most village people, they believed in the rightness of their own ways and were hostile to aliens.

The Diaspora made the Jews less comfortable and more cosmopolitan. In the Greek and Roman Empires, the Jews became what they had despised in their own homeland — alien intruders. The urban Christian world that followed turned them into bourgeois pariahs who were tolerated because they were economically necessary. And once they were no longer useful, they became "devils," conspirators of evil who were worthy of death and destruction.[1]

After the Enlightenment secularized a good part of the Christian world, the Jewish "devil" became a secular "devil." Instead of the old accusations of ritual murder and the stabbing of wafer hosts, the image of the world conspirator emerged. No longer viewed as only a religious enemy, the Jews became the racial foe, the atheistic planners of both materialistic capitalism and immoral communism. Since they invented both sides of the quarrel, they kept the Gentile world in social turmoil.[2]

The danger of secular anti-Semitism was its exportability. A Christian setting was no longer necessary. Even Arabs (who were Semites) could enjoy it.

The Christian personality was not altered by anti-Semitism. Hostility to Jews flowed quite naturally from its dogma, its intensity, and its fanatic piety. Since the Christian world experienced power and success and kept Jews in a lowly position, fact and faith coincided. Experience and propaganda did not seem too far apart. The world had the semblance of order and justice.

But anti-Semitism had the opposite effect on the Jewish personality. It separated fact from faith, experience from propaganda. The suffering of the Jews hardly seemed consistent with divine justice and love, especially for the favorites of God.

Some Jews responded to the onslaught with guilt. They assumed that their suffering was due to their bad behavior and not to God's injustice. They became even more pious, even more faithful. Some Jews discovered that resignation and appeasement were comfortable postures. They felt safer as pitiable creatures than as powerful ones.

But many Jews responded with anger. Since the religious establishment would never allow such an unworthy feeling to be openly expressed to God, it was redirected. Hostility to Gentiles was a safe alternative, so long as it was verbalized within the group.

THE JEWISH PERSONALITY

Ultimately, the anger manifested itself in three behaviors and attitudes which became an important part of the Jewish personality in modern times, especially the European Ashkenazic one. These responses were attempts to preserve Jewish dignity, since anger as a positive emotion is an expression of defiance, a defense of one's own space against intruders.

The first behavior is *skepticism.* Jews developed an enormous distrust of the Gentile authorities who governed their lives and determined their fates. They felt alienated from the official world of power and suspicious of its right to rule. In a religious world of conformity, the skeptics had to bide their time. But in the secular world of the modern democratic state, this angry distrust made the Jews the most creative intellectuals of the nineteenth and twentieth centuries. Jewish alienation enabled pioneers like Marx, Freud, and Einstein to challenge established ways of thinking and to present alternatives. The verbal skills and literacy that derived from Torah education were not enough. Anger was the essential added ingredient, the fuel of challenge and creative defiance. And Jews had sufficient anger to launch a thousand assaults against the smug conclusions of a self-satisfied world.[3] In time, the anger and skepticism would be turned on the rabbis themselves and their ideology of divine justice.

The second expression of anger is *humor.* While some Jewish humor is self-deprecating, a clowning to humiliate oneself and to appease the anti-Semite, much of it is healthy mockery. Laughter and hostility are evolutionary twins. They both show teeth and are frequently "biting." Religion and humor have been historic enemies because one must never show anger to God, veiled or otherwise. Piety prefers resignation, appeasement, and worship.

While the official Jewish personality was pious and worshipful, the unofficial personality became mocking and humorful. Since what Jews experienced was very different from what they professed to believe, they developed an underground culture of jokes and laughter to drain the anger. Once the restraints of the religious establishment were removed, Jews became the comic champions of the secular world. No one felt the absurdity of the world more completely than the Jew, and no one derived greater pleasure from expressing it. Woody Allen is just as Jewish as the Lubavitcher *Rebbe.*

The third manifestation of anger is *self-reliance.* The drive to achieve and to become master of one's own life is not a natural response to divine love and protection. It is a ready state of alert in the face of cosmic danger. Jews ultimately know that they cannot rely on the goodwill of God. They know that only self-reliance will save them in the face of a hostile world. The pioneers of Zionism articulated this ideal when they spoke of the "revolution" in the Jewish spirit. Jews must take their own fate into their own hands.[4] That is the message of Jewish history.

Skepticism, humor, and self-reliance were never advocated by the Jewish religious establishment as strategies for personal and group salvation. And yet they are eminently Jewish. They arise out of Jewish experience. They are responses to anti-Semitism. They are part of Jewish history.

JEWISH SURVIVAL

A humanistic approach to Jewish history abandons the cliches about Jewish survival. While it certainly dismisses supernatural providence as a credible explanation (thirteen million Jews after four thousand years, in comparison to one billion Chinese, is a pretty sad record for any ambitious deity), it would also rethink the old argument that adherence to rabbinic faith and discipline (even though based on theological illusion) was responsible for Jewish continuity.

The argument for rabbinic Judaism has shifted. Before the Secular Revolution, the discipline and the theology went together. You practiced because you believed. Since the Secular Revolution, discipline and theology are conveniently separated. Even if you do not believe or cannot believe, you should commit yourself to traditional practice because it is good for Jewish survival. In fact, it is indispensable to Jewish survival.

Many secular Jews, who value Jewish identity in a strong and positive way, end up buying this argument. They believe that traditional religion is responsible for Jewish survival. If it disappears, so will the Jews. "Non-believers" often commit themselves to a traditional life style, not because of God, but because of the Jewish people. In the absence of any other alternative, even integrity must be sacrificed.

But the argument is invalid. While rabbinic Judaism has been *one* factor in the endurance of the Jews, it is not the *only* factor. In fact, its insistence on segregation and its refusal to mingle sociably with other nations provoked the anti-Semitism that ultimately destroyed most of the Jewish people and inhibited its growth. There is even no indication that the Jews as a Christian nation (assuming they had converted like all the others) would not have survived more comfortably and with less difficulty. The Copts of Egypt, the Chaldeans of Iraq, the Maronite Syrians, and the Armenians are still around to tell their story. As the people of Christ, the Jews might have achieved special honor. Christian theology would have found it less embarrassing to accommodate itself to Jewish acceptance than to Jewish rejection.

In the Christian world of the West, where religious conformity was religiously enforced, rabbinic Judaism meant non-conformity and invited assault, expulsion, and destruction. The only reason Jews were allowed to survive as Jews was the fact that they came to perform a unique economic role that no other group was willing or able to undertake. Selling money was their life saver. It made them indispensable for a while. When rival money lenders emerged in Western Europe, they lost their royal protection and were thrown to the mobs.[5] Had new nations like Poland not needed their services, Ashkenazic Jewry might have totally perished.

In modern times, anti-Semitism, the child of rabbinic Judaism and the hostility it engendered, is a major factor for Jewish survival. In its non-lethal forms, it restricts Jewish choice. Jews are either unable to give up their Jewish identity or they are unwilling to give up their Jewish identity in the face of an external assault. Guilt and pride involve thousands of non-observant Jews in Jewish celebration and in the support of the Jewish community.

Nationalism is also a major factor for survival. Although political Zionism was stimulated by anti-Semitism, it produced a national setting that has generated its own continuity. The revival of the Hebrew language as a secular language has enabled thousands of Jews in Israel to be Jewish without being religious and without being self-conscious about their Jewishness. They are distinct from their neighbors in the same way that most territorial nationalities are distinct. The state of Israel becomes an important new secular component of Jewish continuity.

While anti-Semitism and Jewish secular nationalism are newer than rabbinic Judaism, they now provide more powerful motivation for group survival. An accurate survey of Jewish history indicates that there have been many reasons for Jewish persistence and that they are always changing.

JEWISH EXPERIENCE

Jewish experience is different from what the leaders of the Jewish people wanted the Jews to experience. Jewish experience is the internal response of the Jewish people to the events of their history. The Jewish personality is the external response to those events.

Jewish experience is a continuous tension between what was promised and what was delivered. Piety alternated with anger and resentment. Sometimes, the piety was a coverup for the anger and resentment, in the same way that excessive politeness is a conventional way to mask rising hostility. Sometimes, it was simply the safest posture in the face of a hostile and punishing authority.

Jewish history has to explain the contemporary Jewish personality. It has to explain how piety produced so much skepticism. It has to explain how so much faith in divine providence produced so much nervous self-reliance. It has to explain how the People of the Book so quickly produced so many champions of the Secular Revolution.

Perhaps the emancipation which followed the Secular Revolution allowed the Jew to express freely what they had been secretly thinking. Perhaps the Jew found secular culture very congenial because they had been prepared for its agnostic approach through centuries of frustration and disappointment.

If we pay attention only to the official literature, we will never understand the Jewish experience. We will never be able to explain why Jews are the way they are. The theological frosting will hide the reality of our emotional cake.

Reconnecting the Jewish experience to Jewish history is an important task. Reconnecting the Jewish personality to the Jewish experience is equally important. We have no reason to be puzzled at what the Jews are. Their "family" style flows quite naturally from the events of the past.

Because they prefer the Jewish experience to establishment theology, humanistic Jews have a very different perspective of Jewish history than do traditional Jews. This perspective is the basis for their understanding of their Jewish identity and for the reasons they value it.

The humanistic Jew does not see the evolution of monotheism as the major event in Jewish history. That development did not arise from folk culture and folk experience. It arose out of the need of the Yahveh prophets and priests to rescue the reputation of their god from the embarrassment of defeat. The worship of one God did not come from Jewish experience. It was an attempt to deny it.

The major event in Jewish history was the advent of the Secular Revolution. The breakdown of traditional religious authority gave the Jews a freedom they had never before enjoyed. They were now free to express alternative viewpoints that the old conformity never allowed. The skepticism, anger, humor, and self-reliance that had arisen out of the Jewish experience and that the official literature sought to disguise could now be fully expressed. The Secular Revolution allowed the Jews to become more authentic. It brought their personality and their expressed opinions together. The uncomfortable theological mask no longer had to be worn.

The humanistic Jew, therefore, does not view Jewish history as a decline from the heights. The official tradition sees the beginning as the mountain top. The age of Abraham, Moses, Isaiah, and Ezekiel was the age of spiritual heroes that will never again be duplicated. Even the time of the rabbinic fathers is an inferior sequel. And what follows is a continuous decline. By the time we come to the Secular Revo-

lution, we have reached the spiritual "pits." The age of
science is the age of apostasy and unbelief, a tragic contrast
to the period in Jewish history when Yahveh spoke directly to
his people. Even Reform Judaism, by its continuous attempt
to derive its legitimacy from the Torah and the prophets,
gives secondary status to modern times.

In the humanistic perspective, Jews have been improving.
The secular skepticism of the nineteenth and twentieth
centuries is superior to the theistic piety of the first. The
developing skills of self-reliance are stronger in the present
than they were in the past. The openness and honesty of the
contemporary world, where the "underground" tradition of
good-humored naturalism can now be freely exposed, is
better than the theological narrowness of ancient times. In
fact, Jewish identity, by virtue of the nature of Jewish
history, is much more meaningful now than it was before the
period of trial and testing.

Humanistic Jews do not find most of their Jewish heroes
in famous Jewish personalities of the past. The official literature praises Moses and Malachi, Shammai and Akiba. Their
fame derives from the political and religious agendas of the
religious establishment. What they said, or presumably said,
reenforced the theological viewpoint the ruling elite sought to
impose. As a result of this program of indoctrination,
rabbinic Judaism is "loaded" with many old famous heroes.

The heroes of a humanistic perspective are chiefly anonymous. Until the Secular Revolution, they were neither
praised nor noticed by the "official" writers. Although they
are not known through their personal biographies, they are
known by their works. The bold wanderer, the daring
entrepreneur, the skilful banker, the busy organizer of
community charity, the comic inventor of absurdist jokes —
all of them in their collective anonymity are the unheralded
role models of the past. The famous secular spokespeople of

the last two centuries — a Berdichevsky, a Sholem Aleichem, and an Albert Einstein — are the visible continuity of an invisible tradition.

Humanistic Jews do not see the Jewish story as a testimonial to God and faith. They view it as an evolutionary development in human self-reliance. Jews are not interesting because of the firm attachment of their official teachings to rabbinic monotheism. They are interesting because they resisted "fate" and found ways to survive, despite official piety, through their own human ingenuity. And the contrast between the official and the real makes them all the more intriguing.

CHAPTER XII

Evolution of the Holidays

The value of Jewish identity emerges from Jewish history. The humanistic value of Jewish identity emerges from a humanistic view of Jewish history. The absence of God and the need for human self-reliance are "messages" from the Jewish experience. Jews are living testimony to the importance of reason and dignity.

Strengthening Jewish identity means strengthening an awareness of Jewish history. But how?

One way, quite obviously, is to study it. For many Jews, remembering and interpreting the events of the Jewish past is the best way to reenforce their Jewish self-awareness.

But for others, this historical study is too private and too academic. Something more is needed. Mastering Hebrew and Yiddish provides the extra bond of cultural identity. But in a Diaspora environment, where no substantial community of people speaks these languages, linguistic uniqueness is difficult. Something more practical is required.

Jewish holidays have become the lifeblood of Jewish identity. Although they are less informative than historical studies and less ethnic than Hebrew or Yiddish, they are regular events in the lives of most Jews. Because they involve small pieces of time and few special skills, they are available to large numbers of Jews. Because they are public and communal and feature ceremonial "pizzazz," they can involve all elements of the population.

Jewish holidays — like the holidays of most national and religious groups — are connected with historical and mythical events. Even if you never study Jewish history, you cannot escape it if you celebrate Jewish holidays. They will introduce you to the Exodus, the Maccabees, and the state of Israel. The Jewish calendar gives you more than uniquely Jewish things to do. It gives you a short and "repetitious" introduction to the Jewish past.

Yet for humanistic Jews, Jewish holidays — as they are generally presented — are less than satisfactory. While they were not invented by the leaders of rabbinic Judaism, they were appropriated by them and put to rabbinic use. Religious authority made them convenient vehicles for rabbinic propaganda and for the rabbinic view of Jewish history. In "orthodox" Judaism, the holidays became testimonies to divine power and supernatural intervention. You could not celebrate them without bumping into God.

The Passover Haggadah is a perfect example of the problem. It turns the Exodus from Egypt into a divine event. Without Yahveh, the Jews would never have escaped from slavery. Human effort and human self-reliance are irrelevant to the victory. Suffering and redemption are all part of some noble divine plan. Both Moses and Pharaoh become mere puppets of the Lord.

Hanukka suffers the same fate. A Talmudic legend about holy oil lasting for eight days becomes the focal event of the Maccabean triumph. Supernatural intrusion is the guarantee of Jewish survival and Jewish identity. Since the rabbis did not like the Maccabees, they consigned their winter celebration to oblivion for many centuries and gave them very little credit for their hard-won victories.

Sukkot is no better. A harvest and rainmaking festival is rendered absurd with Yahvistic tampering. The holiday is tied to the forty years wandering in the desert when the

Hebrews found their only food in droppings from heaven. The farmers' harvest hut, where workers rested in the field during the heat of the day, has been turned into a desert house for nomadic shepherds. The blood, sweat, and tears of Jewish farmers taming their own land is lost in a sea of false and silly connections.

Jewish holidays are marvelous opportunities for reliving Jewish history. But not in their present form. They need to be reclaimed for humanistic use. Since the rabbis did not invent them, they have no exclusive right to them. They are the property of the Jewish people. And they need a better showing.

HUMANISTIC CHANGE

Humanistic Jews insist that their holidays give them integrity. The prayers and stories that turn the Jewish experience into a testimony to supernatural reliability have no place in the holiday celebration. They distort the true meaning of the events and prevent Jews from understanding their own history. To say one thing and to believe another is not an act of poetry. It is an act of cowardice. Praising Yahveh on Passover demeans human effort and ingenuity. There must be a way to tell the story that will reenforce human reason and human dignity. No divine plan can make slavery acceptable. Matsa can be as much a symbol of self-reliance as it is of divine providence.

Of course, a humanistic approach to the Jewish calendar must be pragmatic. The rabbinic dates for established holidays are unavoidable. They are the familiar annual mile-stones when Jews become most aware of their Jewish identity. Without a sense of community with other Jews, the holidays fall flat. Doing them at the same time — yet differently — balances integrity with identity.

Radical proposals to celebrate Jewish holidays on dates that nobody recognizes as Jewish are counter-productive — especially the attempt to "restore" the connection between the Jewish calendar and nature.[1] Making Hanukka coincide with the winter solstice or Passover with the spring equinox may have a rational appearance. But, in an urban global culture, where the beginning of the school year is more important than the beginning of autumn, and where Hanukka inaugurates the summer in Argentina and Australia, tying holidays to the seasons is meaningless. It simply diverts our attention from Jewish awareness.

Now this restriction does not mean that we cannot be creative. On the contrary, humanistic Jews assume that they have the same right to invent new holidays as their ancestors did. The old holidays connect them to all who share Jewish identity. The new holidays reenforce their humanistic uniqueness. Einstein's birthday in March is a meaningful addition, even if rabbinic Jews do not want to celebrate it.

We may also decide to discard. Some old holidays may not be worth the effort of reinterpretation. The Fast of Esther, the 17th of Tammuz, the 9th of Av have little to commend them. They divert our energies from more important holidays. The destruction of the Jerusalem Temple was certainly part of a national disaster and a grisly testimony to the absurdity of the fates. But Holocaust Day covers that theme more vividly.

Ultimately, the humanistic decision to revive old holidays, to reinterpret existing ones, and to invent new ones is part of a very clear agenda. Holidays are the best way to teach Jewish history and the value of Jewish identity to a busy public.

Holiday selection and interpretation must be guided by a realistic understanding of the history of the Jewish calendar. Priestly and rabbinic Judaism were so busy trying to prove that Yahveh invented everything Jewish that they obscured the natural origins of Jewish celebrations. Before we can outline the humanistic Jewish calendar, we have to go beyond the rabbinic perspective to certain historical realities.

Jewish holidays come in three varieties. There are holidays that started out as nature festivals, as responses to the seasons and universal experiences. Rosh Hashana, Yom Kippur, and Tu Bi-Shevat have no specific connection to Jewish historical events. They are much more the expression of human experience in general, the "judgment" of destiny.

There are holidays that began as nature festivals and were later identified by the rabbis with so-called historical events. Sukkot started out as the autumn harvest festival and was later attached (quite irrationally) to the mythical forty years wandering of the Hebrews in the desert. Hanukka began as a winter festival of lights and was later identified with the Maccabean victory. Passover started out as a shepherd fertility celebration and was connected, in time, with the exodus of the Jews from Egypt. Shavuot was a summer harvest holiday that was later linked to the proclamation of the Ten Commandments at Mt. Sinai. Whether appropriate or not, the linkage conferred a Jewish historical meaning on these festivals.

The third variety is the holiday that has nothing to do with nature. It only points to an event in Jewish history. Holocaust Day and Israeli Independence Day are examples of this more modern approach. In an urban society, nature events become less important while human events become more important.

There are also *three* calendars into which the holidays fit. The Sabbath is a part of the *week* calendar that counts time in units of seven days, seven weeks, and seven years. Most of the holidays derive their dates from the *lunar* calendar that reckons time in units of twenty-nine or thirty days and follows the repetitive travel of the moon around the earth. All of the holidays are ultimately adjusted to the *solar* calendar that imitates the movement of the earth around the sun and marks the seasons. Astrological weeks, lunar months, and solar years do not always fit neatly into each other. Each of them is a reflection of a different period in Jewish history.

Jewish holidays evolved slowly. The old holidays started out as days of fear. In the minds of our ancestors, hostile spirits made all forms of human activity dangerous. Sabbath rest was hardly restful. It was a time of high anxiety when danger lurked around every inappropriate action. Compulsive rituals were the only way to maneuver safely through all the peril. Even today, many Jewish holidays arouse the fear of ritual disaster in traditional people. Sloppy or missing rituals become more than mistakes; they endanger the whole community.

In time, joy and festivity crept into the days of forbidden action. Ceremonial dancing, poetic prayers, colorful processions, group feasting, and large assemblies added a happy touch. Shepherd holidays turned into farmer holidays. And farmer holidays became urban events. Passover moved from the rapid outdoor eating of sacrificial lamb to the munching of agricultural matsa. And matsa ultimately became only one of many goodies at an elaborate home feast worthy of Roman city manners.

Jewish holidays have never stood still. They have accommodated themselves to many economic conditions and to many ideologies. They are the most flexible items in the Jewish cultural treasury. They are more universal than language and less pushy than theological ideas. They are able to embrace the widest number of Jews.

In their development, the festivals featured different orders of importance. In the royal period of David and

Solomon, Sukkot was the annual spectacular. By the time of the priestly Ezra, Passover moved into first place. The rabbinic period transformed Rosh Hashana and Yom Kippur into the *high* holidays. In modern Christian America, Hanukka is emerging as a shining highlight. Different ruling classes and different settings favored different holidays. Our selection is not the same as that of our Biblical ancestors.

Priestly Judaism and rabbinic Judaism covered the holidays with religious activity. Sacrifice, prayer, and scripture readings dominated the festival routine. And new stories emerged to give the holidays a connection to Yahveh and to divine revelation. The Mosaic priests pushed the royal exploits of the House of David out of the picture and attached Moses and the Exodus to almost every festival.[2] Everything major came to involve Moses. Even the rabbis were so intimidated that only minor festivals, like Hanukka and Purim, could remain non-Mosaic.

Under the direction of rabbinic Judaism, the familiar rabbinic calendar emerged. The weekly Sabbath dominated all. Five holidays became the major solemn days of restricted activity: Rosh Hashana, Yom Kippur, Sukkot (first and last days), Pesakh (first and last days), and Shavuot. Two festivals became minor celebrations with free activity: Hanukka and Purim. Two other holidays survived with little attention: Tu Bi-Shevat and Lag Ba Omer. A series of minor fast days was added to ward off perceived evils and to commemorate catastrophes.

The major festivals reflected an obsession with two rituals: the lighting of fire and the drinking of wine. Kindling flames is a universal religious practice. The significance of fire is no mystery. Its discovery and taming are the basis of human civilization. Before people learned how to manufacture it, fire was captured and preserved as a sacred supernatural treasure. Fire and life, fire and survival went together. Sacred fires are important themes in almost all ancient cultures. Altar fires and temple candelabras are both Jewish and universal. They point to our evolutionary roots. Unconsciously appreciated, they usually need no explanation.

As for wine, it is less universal and Jewishly more controversial. Like conservative Semites, like conservative Arabs, many of the ancient Hebrews objected to its use. Being nomads and shepherds by origin, they were suspicious of the grape and the farmers who cultivated it. But its ready availability and its power to transform consciousness made wine more attractive when the Jews shifted from shepherding to agriculture. As in many Mediterranean farm cultures, it became a suitable gift for the gods and an "obvious" way to share in their power and enthusiasm. The similarity in appearance of red wine to life-giving blood gave it a supernatural edge.

Fire and wine are the two most familiar repetitious aspects of traditional Jewish holidays. Even the minor festival of Hanukka features sacred flames. And life cycle ceremonies insist on wine.

Like fire and wine, the Jewish holidays have no intrinsic divine connection. They derive from the evolution of the human species and human culture. They are as comfortable with a natural explanation as they are with a supernatural one. For humanistic Jews, the holidays need to be rescued from rabbinic tyranny and given a secular language and a secular story. Timid adjustments will not do. They will only appear as uncomfortable variations on a rabbinic theme. Humanistic Jews have to be as bold as the priests and the rabbis who gave the holidays to Yahveh and Moses. We have to claim these festivals for the *other* view of Jewish history.

If we do exactly that, what kind of a calendar do we end up with?

CHAPTER XIII

The Jewish Calendar

The Sabbath and nine annual holidays define the basic schedule of a humanistic Judaism.

SHABBAT

The Shabbat is the most frequent Jewish holiday, occurring once a week. It is the one holiday that is totally independent of the moon-sun calendar. The seven day week and the thirty day month do not comfortably accommodate each other. Every year, the Shabbat chooses different days of the month.

The origin of the Shabbat is obscure. The Genesis myth maintains that it was the special creation of Yahveh. On the seventh day of the world, Yahveh rested, and so must we. Needless to say, such a rationalization leaves a great deal to be desired.

The more likely story involves an understanding of the word *shabbat*. It does not mean *rest*. It means *stopping activity*. As a designation, it originally described the full-moon holiday.[1]

A day of no activity is different from a day of rest. It is more than abstinence from work. It is a time of fear when all forms of motion are dangerous. It is a time of appeasement when angry gods and spirits are abroad and when it is safest to be inconspicuous. The first Shabbat was hardly a day of rest and relaxation. It was an awesome day when the least dangerous posture was to stay at home and to stop doing everything, including such "restful" and necessary activities as lighting fires and cooking foods. The traditional rabbinic Sabbath retains this negativeness, this fear of doing the wrong thing.

The Mosaic priests shifted the Shabbat to the seventh day of the seven-day week. Devotees of the sacred number *seven* and the calendar to which it was attached, they elevated the seventh day *Shabbat* to supreme importance as the special day of Yahveh.[2] With male circumcision, the Shabbat became one of the two major symbols of Jewish identity.[3] As a priestly celebration, it was a dour and severe time. The Torah restricted the people to their homes all day and to unrelieved darkness all night. (This restriction was one of the reasons why the early Reformers' "go back to the Bible" movement ultimately seemed so silly.)

The rabbinic establishment relieved the severity of the Shabbat. They added fire and wine, public assemblies, and Torah readings. They allowed people to leave their homes and to congregate in the synagogues. While they still prohibited most activity and movement, socializing and minor mobility relieved the severity of the day. There was less anxiety. But it was hardly a day of rest.

When Jewish emancipation came to the Christian West, the Shabbat was sorely tried. Secularized Jews found it difficult to stop working on a secular workday. The prohibition also seemed less than rational. The Reform Movement offered its usual ambivalence. The Shabbat was praised as a day of rest in the prayer service, but all the inhibitions were removed. The result was a bizarre distortion. A holy day that had never really been a day of rest was now designated a day of rest for people who rarely rested on that day.

Zionism finally saved the day. The Jewish state simply designated the Shabbat as the official day off. Secular Israelis could now treat the day in the same way as Americans treat a secular Sunday. Despite annoying religious intrusion, they could still choose the beach over the synagogue or have recreational fun with family and friends. But the Israeli solution offered no help to humanistic Jews in the Diaspora.

From a humanistic point of view, the Shabbat can be a very useful symbol. Once the charade of trying to turn any day in a modern urban world into a day of rest is dismissed (our individualized schedules now provide for chunks of time called vacations or long weekends), the holiday can be reconstructed.

As a day of fearful anxiety, the rabbinic Shabbat was the ultimate reminder of divine control and supernatural intervention, a vivid expression of the theology of rabbinic Judaism. As a humanistic symbol, the Shabbat becomes a testimony to the human bonds which alone make survival possible. Ironically, the traditional prohibitions made the few positive activities of the Shabbat stand out as items of human solidarity. Against the stark cruelty of the fates and destiny, the family, gathered around its Shabbat dinner, represented the chief power for personal survival.

On the theological level, the Shabbat was perceived as a day of God. On the experiential level, it was a time of heightened anxiety, relieved only by the image of family unity and love. If the world (or God) made you nervous, at least your family offered you support and caring.

The terror of the original Shabbat is a reflection of the terror of Jewish existence. To the indifference of nature and destiny, we reply with human care and human connection.

For humanistic Jews, the Shabbat is family day. It is a time when we celebrate the human support systems that give us life and that make Jewish and human survival possible. Our Shabbat dinner is a tribute to the family that sits around the table. Our Shabbat service is a tribute to the Jewish extended family that shares our history and social fate.

Ironically, the terror of the original Shabbat is not an expression of a just and well-ordered universe. It is a mirror image of the cruel indifference of nature itself. Against the intimidation of blind destiny, human solidarity is the human answer. The traditional rationalization must yield to experience. "Family day" is much more realistic than "stop all activity creation day."

ROSH HASHANA — YOM KIPPUR

Rosh Hashana and Yom Kippur go together. In rabbinic tradition, they are the *Yamim Noraim,* the Days of Fear: a ten day period of divine judgment. Next to the Sabbath, they became the most important holidays of the Hebrew calendar.

Their origins are obscure. Rosh Hashana (which means *new year*) began as a day of fearful appeasement of the rain god, a time of judgment for agriculture and group survival. Although it may have initially followed the autumn festival of Sukkot (just before the beginning of the rainy season), Rosh Hashana ended up on the first day of the Hebrew month of Tishri.[4] In the minds of the natives, it was a scary day with threats of drought hanging over everyone's head. Solemn suffering was appropriate behavior. A shepherd ram's horn, a primitive trumpet of warning, was blown to keep anxiety high.

In the Torah, Rosh Hashana is not the new year celebration. Tishri (September-October) is the seventh month, not the first month. Since the new moon of the seventh month was a day of dangerous supernatural intrusion, the priests designated the day a time of warning, a *Yom Truah*, with shofar blasts for admonition.

In early times, Yom Kippur most likely preceded both Sukkot and Rosh Hashana. It was a day of purification when sacred places and temples were cleared of supernatural defilements so that subsequent celebrations could proceed without peril.[5] In the Torah, it follows Rosh Hashana and is the one day of the year when the high priest confronts Yahveh face to face through a screen of incense smoke to plead for the forgiveness of communal sins and to ask for reconciliation.

In rabbinic Judaism, Rosh Hashana and Yom Kippur are elevated to supreme importance, replacing the old stars of Sukkot and Pesakh. They constitute the beginning and the end of the *Yamim Noraim*, the Days of Terror. The seventh month has become the first month. *Yom Truah* has become the New Year.

The theological rationale for the new structure is imposing. An omnipotent Yahveh, now promoted to world domination, undertakes an annual judgment of humanity, especially of his chosen servants, the Jews. Descending from heaven, he enthrones himself in Jerusalem and for ten days sits in judgment, rendering his initial verdict on Rosh Hashana and his final verdict on Yom Kippur. In the face of his terrifying presence and power, the safest human response is to appear as pitiable as possible. Temporary starvation, torn clothing, weeping, and obsequiousness are effective procedures for arousing pity and reducing divine anger. In a sense, the annual judgment is a preview of the final judgment of Resurrection Day when the living and the dead will confront their ultimate destination.

When the secular age arrived, much of the rabbinic theological setting became embarrassing. While the Rejectionists clung firmly to the old ideology, the Ambivalents searched for alternatives. The compromise was less than satisfactory. The prayer service would continue to talk about divine judgment, but the sermon would introduce the new humanistic themes of self-reflection and self-judgment. In the last two centuries, very few Conservative and Reform rabbis have preached divine terror. Under the influence of the new psychology, great emphasis has been placed on the human power to re-evaluate one's own life and to change it for the better. The prayers and the fasting went one way — and the sermon went the other.

Humanistic Jews find this compromise unacceptable and avoid its lack of integrity. They insist that meditation and message fit together. While they recognize the importance of relating destiny and the fates to individual existence and to Jewish history, they do not see them through the eyes of rabbinic theology. They conceive them more realistically.

The world we live in is filled with terror and painful surprise. It is also filled with "unjust" pain. The courageous response to all this undeserved suffering is not obsequious pleading. It is defiance.

For humanistic Jews, the High Holidays are a necessary time to reflect on the relationship of the universe to human need and human desire. Evolution has equipped us with a set of wants to which the rest of nature is generally indifferent. Only through the use of human will and human intelligence can we tame our environment, making it less terrifying and more conducive to human happiness. Exploding stars and galactic circuits may be beyond our control. But cancer and floods are natural enemies that we may some day conquer.

The face of "god" is not an invitation to fawning praise. It is a provocation to human awareness, an affirmation of how little trust can be placed in passive reliance on the goodness of nature. Our time should not be spent talking to "God," but talking to ourselves and to others. And the language of our resolution should be clear and unmistakably humanistic.

Rosh Hashana and Yom Kippur open our Jewish year with the most important message of Jewish history. Human dignity is not the gift of destiny. It is a human achievement, requiring courage and human self-reliance. If we seek to reconcile ourselves with anybody, we reconcile ourselves with the men and women who share our struggle and who offer us the only realistic support we can expect.

SUKKOT

The Jewish calendar features three seasonal holidays, which are grand celebrations stretching over a week or eight days. The autumn gives us Sukkot. The winter presents Hanukka. And the spring delivers Pesakh. Tied to the agricultural year, these are the splendid old festivals of our Hebrew roots.

Sukkot was the major celebration during the era of the royal House of David. Rosh Hashana was its climactic last day and Yom Kippur was a preceding day of preparation. Lying between the summer harvest and the rainy season, Sukkot featured both satisfaction with the past and anxiety over the future. The parade with the palm branches and citrons — with its passionate cry of *Hoshana* ("save us") — provided the pageantry and the magic. Hopefully, Yahveh (or whatever god was in fashion) would respond to this appeal with the gift of rain.

In the priestly period — when the Torah was completed — Sukkot was transformed. Yielding to Pesakh as the chief holiday, Sukkot also developed an Exodus theme. Although it

was essentially an agricultural festival, Sukkot was now tied
to the legendary forty years of Jewish wandering in the
desert. The decorative harvest booths (*sukkot*) — that gave
the holiday its name and that were initially used by
harvesters for rest during the midday sun — were now
bizarrely described as the housing of the Hebrew nomads
wending their way from Egypt to Canaan.[6]

This distortion fit into the demands of priestly theology.
The Exodus story in the Torah was the ultimate tribute to
Yahvistic power and divine providence. All holidays were
ripped from their original contexts by the priestly editors and
given an Exodus setting. If they did not commemorate any
events, at least their place of origin became Mt. Sinai.

In rabbinic Judaism, Sukkot suffered from two problems.
The first was the proximity of Rosh Hashana and Yom
Kippur, which overshadowed it. The second was the urbanization of the Jew, which diminished the importance of a rain
festival. While Sukkot remained a major holiday, it lacked its
former emotional clout. Ultimately, it was rescued by tying it
to the Torah. The last day of the festival was chosen for the
end and the beginning of the annual cycle of Torah readings.
Renamed Simhat Torah, the celebration provided attachments more relevant than agricultural memories.

With the coming of the secular age and the Industrial
Revolution, Sukkot fell on hard times. Metropolitan Jews
found an agricultural celebration to be slightly quaint. And
there was no grand idea or striking historical event to give it
dramatic shape. Rescuing Sukkot for some useful purpose
became the difficult task of the Ambivalent clergy.
Ultimately, only the Zionists in their new agricultural settlements in Israel were able to rescue it.

From a humanistic point of view, Sukkot has special significance. Agriculture was the beginning of human
civilization, a quantum jump in the human mastery of the

environment. The emergence of farming some ten thousand years ago revolutionized human existence. Territorial settlements, cities, population growth, surplus wealth, and written language followed quite naturally from this technological success. It lay the foundation for the human self-confidence that led to the secular age.

Farming is not, as many misguided urban nature lovers imagine, a manifestation of being close to nature and loving its generosity. It began as the painful struggle against the hostility of swampy river valleys and waterless plateaus. Human ingenuity transformed the inhospitable wilderness into the tailored countryside that we find so pleasing and that we so often call "nature." Parks and farmland and wilderness trails are human creations that shield us from the brutal reality of our evolutionary past.

But farming is only one of many steps in the cultural unfolding of human talent. The taming of wild animals and the breeding of "meat" is another. The invention of the crafts and the manufacture of technological assistants is still another. And the transformation of fortresses into cities of trade and production is yet another.

Theology may seek to turn Sukkot into a tribute to divine providence. But experience teaches us that if tributes are to be paid, they should be paid to the millions of unsung experimenters and inventors who struggled to make the earth yield a decent living.

Jewish history is a living testimony to human ingenuity in the face of overwhelming odds. The same intelligence that made agriculture possible made cities and urban living possible. City existence is not the "artificial" antithesis of "close to nature" farm life. Villages and farms are just as artificial. Neither context, fortunately, resembles the primeval muck that our hunting ancestors struggled to endure.

An imaginative and humanistic use of Sukkot would avoid making invidious comparisons between the pure and divine harvests of agricultural life and the sullied "harvests" of manufactured goods and services that modern urban existence provides. Both farming and industrial technology are expressions of the human will to change and to improve what is not satisfactory. The breeding of juicy oranges is no less scientific and intrusive than the invention of computers.

A humanistic Sukkot is a tribute to human culture, agricultural, pastoral, and urban. There are many "harvests," all human, all "artificial," all significant. The space ship is the natural brother of the plow.

The early entry of the Jew into urban life, as part of the Jewish survival saga, is not alien to the mood of Sukkot. It is an expression of the same human ingenuity that cultivates the *lulav* and the *etrog*.

HANUKKA

Hanukka started out with another name. Before the Maccabean triumph it was called *Nayrot* (Lights). It was the winter festival that celebrated the rebirth of light. At the winter solstice, darkness ceases to expand, and the day begins to grow longer. Since darkness is death and light is life, the reversal is a dramatic moment in the year.

As an eight day festival, *Nayrot* conformed to the two other seasonal holidays, Sukkot and Pesakh. Fires were lit on each of the eight days to imitate the change and to encourage nature, by suggestion, to continue its good work. Ultimately, the fires were confined in each household to a board of eight lights. The eight days and the lights were part of Jewish life long before the legend of the holy oil made its appearance.[7]

Like many folk festivals, *Nayrot* never made its way into the priestly Torah. The priests were wary of sanctioning any practice that could not easily be identified with Yahveh and the Exodus experience. *Nayrot* flunked its entry test, leaving Torah Judaism devoid of a decent winter festival.

With the conquest of Israel by the Greeks and the subsequent rebellion against Greek rule, the Maccabee family rose to power. Of priestly origin, the Maccabees became the military leaders of the rebel forces and pursued their own independent road to political power. Having defeated the Greeks and captured Jerusalem, Judah Maccabee decided to rededicate the temple shrine to Yahveh. He chose the folk festival of *Nayrot* as a perfect vehicle for the continuing commemoration of his victory. He renamed the holiday *Hanukka* (Dedication) and elevated it to official importance.[8]

But the Maccabees had a run-in with the rabbis because of their pretentious assumption of the royal title. When the rabbis came to rule under Roman guidance, they wrought their vengeance. Hanukka was demoted to minor status, since, as a popular folk festival, it could not be easily eliminated. The other Maccabean victory celebration, Nicanor's Day, was replaced by Purim.[9]

In later centuries, the rabbis sought to diminish the importance of the Maccabees by attributing the victory to the intervention of Yahveh. The Talmudic legend that focuses on holy oil lasting for eight days has a political purpose. It shifts the emphasis from the brilliant skill of the Maccabees (who are barely mentioned) to the magic tricks of Yahveh.

By the dawn of the secular age, Hanukka was one of several minor celebrations of the Jewish calendar. The possibility for a winter festival with grandeur had been stymied by political hostility.

However, secular emancipation in a Christian world provided a revival. The lure of Christmas, the Roman-Christian version of a winter solstice festival, was very strong. In its new secularized form, many Jews were finding it irresistible, especially since they had no decent dramatic winter holiday of their own.

In North America, in particular, the competition of Christmas rescued Hanukka. It was taken from its theological mothballs and elevated to a status that even the Maccabees never imagined. Suddenly, candles, dreidels, potato pancakes, and the story of a minor military victory were dressed up to compete with Christmas carols, Christmas trees, the birth of a god, and the excitement of a new year. The quick rise to fame was, to say the least, less than satisfactory.[10] Nevertheless, for many North American Jews, Hanukka has become *the* holiday — especially if there are children.

Even if we dispose of the Talmudic legend about holy oil, the Hanukka story remains uncomfortable for humanistic Jews. While the Maccabees did, indeed, arrange for national liberation from Greek tyranny, they were no more tolerant of dissent than their Greek enemies. The concept of personal freedom was as foreign to them as it was to any of their contemporary competitors. If Antiochus was unwilling to allow Torah Jews to practice their religion, the Maccabees were equally unwilling to allow the Hellenists the option of their preference. As we know from present events, national liberation, the removal of foreign rulers, does not guarantee personal freedom. It may simply replace a foreign dictatorship with a domestic one.[11]

However, humanistic Jews recognize that the roots of Hanukka precede the intolerant fanaticism of much of priestly and rabbinic Judaism. The old holiday of *Nayrot*, and its fascination with fire, has a strong connection to the story of human survival. It provides a better basis for a humanist celebration.

As the Feast of Lights, Hanukka is the preeminent holiday of fire. The kindling of fire is part of almost every festival. But, with Hanukka, it becomes the focus.

The taming of fire is the major human revolution that preceded agriculture. It enhanced human survival in dramatic ways. Wild animals could be held at bay. Cooked food made eating less time consuming and opened the daily routine to new activities. Heat made cold places accessible to our tropical bodies and allowed the human race to inhabit the earth. Without fire, we would have been confined to the safe environment of central Africa.

As the guarantor of survival, fire became the symbol of life. In all early cultures, the "sacred" fire took on a special importance, especially before our ancestors learned how to make fire. "Captured" fire seemed to possess a supernatural power beyond the ability of human beings to manufacture and control. Maintaining the fire and never allowing it to be extinguished became the passion of communal activity. The extinction of the flame meant death. Shades of Eternal Lights, Menorahs, and Hanukka legends!

Although much of religion has preserved this early anxiety, the fear has been inappropriate for over eighty thousand years. The fire revolution took a major turn for the better when our human ancestors discovered how to make fire. No longer dependent on thievery from available flames, they changed fire-finding into fire-making. The evolution of metalworking, technology, and human self-confidence flows from that event.

The story of fire is the story of the discovery of human power. Men and women discovered that they did not have to be passive infants waiting for parental nature to give them the things they needed and wanted. Making fires was the first step in the harnessing of the energies of the universe for the enhancement of human dignity.

In Jewish history, this growing maturity and self-reliance is part of the Jewish experience. Waiting for Messiahs to rescue the people from foreign adversaries may be the official line. But the Maccabean resistance did not wait. Nor did the Zionists of the twentieth century.

If Rosh Hashana and Yom Kippur are testimonies to the assumption of human responsibility for human life in the face of an absurd and indifferent universe, if Sukkot is the witness to the power of human ingenuity and creativity; then Hanukka is the celebration of human power, the increasing power of people to *use* the world to enhance the quality of human life.

We do not have to wait for fortune's gifts. Like the Maccabees, we can manufacture our own.

TU BI-SHEVAT

The Jewish National Fund made Tu Bi-Shevat. Before the advent of Zionism, before the massive land reclamation and tree planting in the land of Israel, this holiday was one of the least familiar to most Jews.

The 15th day of the Hebrew month of Shevat (corresponding roughly to February 1) is one of twelve full moons in a regular Hebrew year. Like all full moon days, it aroused the anxiety that supernatural forces arouse when they show up in large numbers in the neighborhood. But it also held the honor of being close to spring and the rebirth of nature (a prelude festival like the Chinese New Year or Valentine's Day).

Priestly Judaism and the Torah gave it no acknowledgment because it was initially associated with the worship of one of Yahveh's detested rivals. Asherah, the consort of Baal, started out as a sacred tree.[12] Like the Druids, the devotees of this goddess had a thing for trees. The Yahveh prophets, in their hostility to this powerful female competitor, kept urging the people to turn Asherah shrines into stumps and may have been partly responsible for the deforestation of Israel. Tu Bi-Shevat was adopted by the Asherah cult as a day for the planting of new trees. Since many Jews were devotees, it was indeed a Jewish holiday, even though the narrow-minded priests did not agree.

Rabbinic Judaism, which cultivated many of the folk practices of the Jewish masses neglected by the priests, rescued Tu Bi-Shevat for official practice. Detached from Asherah, it lingered as a minor festival with the additional title New Year of the Trees.[13]

Zionism gave the holiday a new lease on life. The contents of thousands of little blue boxes provided for the reforestation of Israel. The commitment of the new pioneers to the restoration of the land gave new meaning to the festival. In Palestine, it was a time for the planting of new trees. In the Diaspora, it was a time to reflect on the importance of the Jewish homeland.

The connection with Israel gives Tu Bi-Shevat humanistic value. Already secularized by Zionism, it stands out as the one celebration during the year when the Jews of the Diaspora join with the Jews of Israel in constructive deeds to rebuild the Jewish homeland.[14]

Israel is an important part of Jewish identity. It is the historic setting for the evolution of the Hebrew language and of Jewish culture. In modern times, it is the center of Jewish ethnic activity. For thousands of Jews, it has become the reason for their involvement in Jewish communal work. As an international people, the Jews now have developed a symbiotic relationship between the Jewish state and the Diaspora. Each part is vulnerable without the other.

Despite all its problems and shortcomings, the Zionist movement is the major expression of Jewish humanistic commitment in the present century. As a rebellion against the passive acceptance of whatever destiny dished out to the Jews, the Zionist passion sought to give the Jews greater control over their own lives and fate. National liberation became national self-esteem. People would have to do what prayer could not.

Tu Bi-Shevat has evolved into Israel Day, a time when we can celebrate the important connection between the Jewish homeland and the Diaspora. More comprehensive than Israel Independence Day, it allows us to include the attachment to the land during *all* periods of Jewish history. It is less narrowly political. And it gives us the life-affirming ritual of the trees.

In the middle of the winter (or summer, if you are in Buenos Aires), when the Hebrew calendar provides very little holiday excitement, an expanded Tu Bi-Shevat (no longer in the minor league for humanists) is a welcome addition.

PURIM

In rabbinic Judaism, Purim is less major than Sukkot and less minor than Tu Bi-Shevat. Like Hanukka, it enjoys a not too solemn middle status.

Purim has a built-in ambivalence. On the one hand, it features masks and plays and Mardi Gras type fun. On the other hand, it insists on reading a serious story about a Persian anti-Semite who plots to destroy all the Jews and is, in turn, destroyed with all his cohorts. Anti-Semitism and Carnival, on the surface at least, do not seem to mix very easily.

This odd combination is due to Purim's history.

The original Purim may have been celebrated on the full moon of Adar (somewhere around March 1). Like Tu Bi-Shevat, it was one of several "welcome to spring" fertility festivals that were available for public use. Yahveh was not in its original cast of characters. Rival deities who had their origins in Babylonia held center stage. Marduk (Mordecai) was the god of the heavens. Ishtar (Esther) was the goddess of the fertile earth. Haman was an underworld devil with pretensions. Zeus, Demeter, and Hades would be comparable stars in a Greek setting. Ishtar and Haman, the forces of life and death, vie with each other. Ishtar triumphs. And so, of course, does the spring.[15]

Like the Mardi Gras festival, the day was filled with dramatic reenactments of the story and sexual liaisons to promote fertility. Ishtar was served by impersonation, masks, and disguise. Fun was inevitable.

The name Purim is obscure. And the place of origin is also not clear. Was it a native Palestinian holiday dressed up in Babylonian clothing? Or was it a Babylonian import adopted by a growing community of Babylonian Jews? No one is sure.

What is sure is that the priests and rabbis cleaned the holiday up for official Jewish use. Marduk and Ishtar could not remain in the story as gods. They reemerged as two nice Persian Jews (the Persians had replaced the Chaldean Babylonians as the conquerors of the Jews) who were now being persecuted by a Persian devil called Haman. The Book of Esther is the result of these revisions.

If there is no reference to Yahveh in this entire story, it is only because Yahveh was not part of the original story. The authors simply turned the pagan gods into people.

However, the rabbis never really trusted Purim. It was not pure enough for their tastes.[16] Only political controversy rescued the holiday. Rabbinic hostility to the Maccabees gave Purim a chance to succeed. The major celebration of the Maccabean victories was not Hanukka but Nicanor's Day, which fell on the thirteenth of Adar. (Nicanor was a Greek general whom the Maccabees had defeated in a fierce battle.) Simply abolishing Nicanor's Day would not work. Substituting another holiday for it, on the very next day, would divert public attention with alternative activity. Purim was ready and available for this new role. The people fell in love with it.

Some humorless modernists have difficulty with Purim. They deplore the vengeful treatment of Haman. And they are wary of celebrating a holiday about people who never really existed.

But humanistic Jews are reluctant to discard a fun-filled holiday with as much potential as Purim, especially one that ironically gave up its theology for theological reasons. While the story of Mordecai and Esther is indeed mythical, it can be treated as a legend. A charming tale that demonstrates how human ingenuity and human courage prevail is much more humanistic than pious truths about pious rabbis.

Since dressing up as a Purim character is part of the traditional celebration, why not expand the idea to include all the heroes of Jewish history? We need a hero day to honor the humanistic role models of our past and present. In this way, the legendary story becomes the setting for broader honors to real people.

Heroes are important. They are the embodiments of our ideals. Even when we exaggerate their virtues, honoring them is preferable to not having them at all.

We need two kinds of ancestral roots. We need folk roots, the memories of persons and places that describe our beginnings and development. We also need ethical roots, role models of behavior from our family tree. After all, the gods of traditional religion started out as revered ancestors.

Traditional Jews already have their human pantheon. Most of it is ancient and, therefore, open to mystery and myth. Abraham, Moses, David, Ezra, Hillel, Akiba, Isaiah, and Jeremiah are the major stars. And there are dozens of minor ethical performers who people the pages of the Torah and the Talmud.

Humanistic Jews are still in the process of assembling their hero list. While most of the traditional heroes are appropriate memories for our folk roots, many of them are inappropriate as moral guides, as ethical role models. Some of them adored the supernatural and deplored any reliance on human effort. Others were militantly parochial, viewing any social connection with Gentiles as defiling and abhorrent.

We cannot simply borrow the traditional list and doctor it up a bit. We have to create our own list. It will include not only ancient luminaries, but also modern sages; not only those who stayed within the framework of organized religion, but also those who denounced it. Our list of heroes will include fewer people who can hide behind the myths of an unknown past and more people who are forced to face the scientific scrutiny of the present.

But how do we choose?

What are the criteria for a humanistic Jewish hero?

If we expand Purim to Hero Day — retaining all the fun and using Mordecai and Esther as legendary models — we will have a guide.

Humanistic Jewish heroes have to be *famous*. They have to distinguish themselves in some field of human endeavor so that their names are widely known. The heroes must be identifiable, not only to their friends, but also to their enemies. A model figure who nobody knows is hardly the stuff from which heroes are made.

They have to *enjoy their Jewishness*. Humanist heroes of Jewish origin who have no positive interest in their Jewish identity can hardly be models for those who choose this value.

They have to make decisions in a *rational* way. If they

were always talking about faith and sacred authority, they would be an embarrassment to recommend to humanistic youth. This criterion does not mean that they must be explicit devotees of empiricism and the scientific method. Our heroes simply may be commonsensical people open to changing their opinion on the basis of new evidence and able to live with uncertainty and the unknown.

They have to be *people of action*. In times of crisis, they must avoid passive waiting and use their human skills to solve their problems. The child posture that places responsibility for action on outside protective powers is not morally acceptable. Prayer is harmful when it is a substitute for real action. Waiting for the Messiah does not qualify you as a humanist hero.

They have to be *bold*. They must be willing to publicly challenge old ideas when they do not conform to the evidence of experience and to defy old institutions when they no longer serve human needs. They are not afraid to be innovators.

They have to be *caring persons*. They must be able to transcend themselves to serve the needs of others. They must be sensitive not only to the desires of those who are familiar but also to the desires of strangers. Rational people who use their reason against the welfare of the community may be smart, but they are hardly humanist heroes.

Who, in Jewish history, fits these criteria? Many come to mind — David, Elisha ben Abuya (the radical rabbi of the ancient world), Baruch Spinoza, Theodore Herzl, David Ben Gurion, Albert Einstein, Sigmund Freud, Erich Fromm, Woody Allen, Sholem Aleichem.

These people are humanistic Jewish philosophy translated into the flesh. They are easier to understand and to imitate than are abstract principles.

The Purim play needs more characters. We start with Mordecai and Esther. But we do not have to stop with them.

PESAKH

Pesakh is the great spring festival of the Jewish people. It celebrates the liberation of the world from the slavery of winter. It speaks the joy of renewal, revival, and resurrection. Even if the exodus of the Jews from Egypt had happened at some other time of year, we would be compelled to celebrate it at Passover time. The rebirth of the Jewish people should coincide with the rebirth of nature.

Pesakh began as two separate fertility holidays. The first was a farmer's festival called *Matsot* that celebrated the spring grain harvest. Flat bread was made from the unfermented new grain to dramatize the change.[17] The second was a shepherd's holiday called *Pesakh* that celebrated the birthing of new lambs and kids. A feast of baby sheep was consumed. Skipping dances were performed. And the blood of the lamb was used to ward off evil spirits who were abroad in large numbers in this season of fertility.[18]

King Josiah, a descendant of David, combined the two festivals and designated the merger *Pesakh*. He also attached the spring celebration to an historic event, the flight of the Jews from Egypt some six hundred years earlier. This exodus was glorified and was turned into a national epic to stimulate national pride and unity.[19]

The priests, who followed the kings and who edited the Torah, made Pesakh the holiday of the year. Their ancestor Moses was made the human star of the Exodus story, just as Yahveh was made the divine star. In their hands, Pesakh was molded into a tribute to divine providence, and the Exodus was exalted to the status of super miracle story of the world.[20]

The rabbis gave Pesakh its most popular celebration, the Seder feast. The hurried lamb sacrifice of priestly times was transformed into a leisurely dinner, Roman style, where the Haggadah, the story of the Exodus, was read and where the special foods of the feast were presented and explained. This marvelous addition turned Passover into a sentimental family occasion. Even the inconvenient abstinence from the products of fermented grain did not dim its luster.

With the coming of the secular age, the Seder feast retained its hold on Western Jews. But the Haggadah, with its improbable stories of miracles and divine intervention, began to lose credibility. The Torah story was challenged. It was now hard to believe that two million Hebrews were rescued from Egyptian slavery through the miraculous intervention of Yahveh. And it was equally hard to accept the morality of killing first-born sons and drowning innocent Egyptian soldiers.

Meanwhile, modern archeology and Biblical criticism produced many new versions of the Exodus story.[21] But even these truer stories, devoid of supernatural trappings, had the same limited moral message of the original myth. In all the versions, the Hebrews pass from one authoritarian situation into another. Moses is no less dictatorial than Pharaoh. Although his dictatorship is less offensive because he is Jewish, Moses issues laws in the name of a divine authority; this neither provides for individual liberty nor allows public challenge. Conformity, humility, and obedience are the virtues of the theocratic system. Freedom, in any meaningful sense, is absent from the scenario.

However, there have been many exoduses in Jewish history. One, in particular, was a *true* liberation.

When I was a child, I was struck by an obvious irony. The immigrant Russian Jews who sat around my table chanting the Haggadah myth had been part of an exodus experience far more dramatic and far more significant in the revolution of Jewish values than the flight from Egypt they were singing about. My parents and grandparents had been part of a massive emigration from Russia, which dwarfed all earlier emigrations in Jewish history.

The exodus of 3,000,000 Ashkenazic Jews from Eastern Europe was the greatest and most traumatic exodus in the history of the Jewish people. And, unlike the departure from ancient Egypt, it involved Jews who are still alive today.

Here lies the irony. Jews who have experienced the ultimate exodus sit around a table singing about a less dramatic emigration. Justice and good humor would suggest that singing about their own experience would be more appropriate.

The exodus from Russia, unlike the itsy-bitsy Levite departure from Egypt, altered the whole face of world Jewry from feudal pious Eastern Europe to urban capitalistic secular North America. A century ago, two thirds of the world Jewish community lived in Russia and surrounding lands. Today, half of world Jewry lives in the United States and Canada.

The exodus moved Ashkenazic Jews from an economic and social system of poverty and class rigidity to a bourgeois setting of affluence, technological luxury, and social mobility. Never have so many Jews been so rich, so well-educated, and so intellectually powerful as they are in contemporary America. Going from the opportunities of Egyptian slavery to Bedouin poverty hardly compares.

This exodus was so powerful in its social consequences that the Jewish life style of twenty centuries was replaced by a new one in a matter of months. What twenty centuries of feudal persecution could not alter, urban secular society changed in a flash of historic time.

This exodus was truly an exodus to freedom. Only in countries influenced by the political patterns of Western Europe have Jews experienced the opportunities of individual liberty and free inquiry. The humanistic value system of American

Jewry was made possible by this traumatic emigration. The move to North America did bring *personal* freedom to individual Jews, not just *collective* freedom. America liberated the Jews, not only by rescuing them from anti-Semitic outrage, but also by subverting the traditional communal institutions which held them prisoner.

The Ashkenazic exodus has its contemporary parallel in Sephardic history. Ever since 1948, the overwhelming majority of Oriental Jews have been transported from Muslim countries to the newly founded state of Israel. The story of Yemenite Jews airlifted from medieval poverty to the Western democracy of the Zionist state, the adventure and terror of Iraqi Jews rescued from the feudal prejudice of Arab Baghdad to the secular environment of modern Israel, equals the Ashkenazic transformation.

A truly relevant, honest, and humanistic Haggadah would include not only the story of shepherd Hebrews but also the bold tale of twentieth century revolutionary migration.

Pesakh started out and remains the season of renewal and rebirth. It celebrates, on the human level, the rediscovery of human dignity and of the personal freedom that alone makes dignity possible.

The Exodus story is only the beginning of that discovery, and an imperfect beginning. The twentieth century — and all the centuries in between — are a continuation of that search for dignity.

REMEMBRANCE DAY

No dramatization of Jewish history can escape the Holocaust. No tragedy in Jewish history exceeds its horror.

The newness of the event does not diminish its importance. A thousand years from now, it will retain its significance.

This memorial has no long history. But, from the humanistic point of view, it is the equal of all the other holidays. The Holocaust is the "final straw that broke the camel's back." It is the final unmasking of the bankruptcy of rabbinic theology. After the senseless systematic murder of six million Jews, it is difficult to talk about a just God and a well-run world. The odor of absurdity and chaos is too pervasive.

Remembrance Day (or Holocaust Memorial Day) falls on the spring anniversary of the ultimate defense of human dignity. In April, 1943, in the Warsaw Ghetto, several thousand Jewish freedom fighters rose up to fight their Nazi overlords. Under the leadership of Mordecai Anielewicz and his secular allies, they defied the Germans in desperate battle. They knew that they could not win. But they refused to consent to the cruel decree of destiny and to resign themselves passively to deportation and extermination. Believing that they could not survive, they made their death an act of defiance, an affirmation of their dignity against a universe that did not care.[22]

Oddly enough, this ultimate testimony to the absurdity of the world is not some ancient catastrophe exaggerated by legend. It is an event of the twentieth century, the reality of which is beyond exaggeration.

Like the thousands of misshapen stones that mark the field of Treblinka, the horrors point to no ultimate benign divine plan. They point to nothing.

In the face of such a stark reality, our dignity demands the courage to speak the truth. The victims died for no good purpose. Their fate was an unmitigated tragedy.

Our only respectable response is the refusal to accept the unacceptable. We will not praise the fates nor thank destiny for murder — nor mumble sweet excuses about divine mysteries. We will garner our energies and our anger and strive to do the justice that nature refuses.

If we celebrate anything on this day of tragic memories, we celebrate the human dignity that gives human meaning to an uncaring world.

SHAVUOT

Shavuot comes fifty days after Passover and closes the holiday season.

The word *Shavuot* means "Weeks." It indicates the fact that the holiday appears seven weeks and one day after Passover. The festival is the survivor of an old calendar that preceded the existing Hebrew one. In this old calendar, the number *seven* was the sacred number. The seasonal year was divided into seven units, each of fifty days. Each unit of fifty days was, in turn, divided into seven weeks; each week, into seven days. Shavuot was the *atseret,* the closing day of the spring unit that Passover began. Only the Sabbath and Shavuot are surviving holidays from this old calendar.

Since the spring barley and wheat harvest lasted about fifty days and started with Passover, Shavuot evolved as the celebration of the end of the harvest. In the beginning, Shavuot was a farmer's festival, attached to Passover and identified with the fertility of the land. When Jews ceased to be farmers, Shavuot gradually lost its connection with Passover and developed its own uniqueness.

In the rabbinic period, the holiday was identified as the anniversary of the giving of the Torah on Mt. Sinai. This association was as arbitrary as the event was legendary. But the prestige of this connection maintained Shavuot as a major holiday. In traditional synagogues, it became the time for the public reading of the Ten Commandments.

When the Reform Movement rejected Bar Mitzvah and substituted the more egalitarian group Confirmation, Shavuot proved a convenient time for the new ceremony. Coming at the end of the school year and identified with commitment to the Torah, it seemed an ideal occasion for young people to pledge their allegiance to Judaism.

For humanistic Jews, the connection of Shavuot with the Torah is an insufficient reason for a celebration. But if we see the holiday as a tribute to the Jewish experience that the Torah authors sought to describe, then it becomes an important holiday.

Training to understand the nature of that experience is what Jewish education ought to be. Whatever literature gives an accurate insight into the character of that history is worthy of honor. Ahad Haam and Simon Dubnow were Russian Jewish intellectuals who were less famous than the Torah. But what they have to say about Jewish identity and Jewish self-awareness is the equal of the Torah, if not superior to it.

Shavuot — through a humanistic perspective — honors the tradition, both written and unwritten, that affirms the human dimension in Jewish history. That tradition may be as old as Moses or as new as Max Nordau.

Ten Jewish holidays — the weekly Sabbath and nine annuals — make up the basic humanistic Jewish calendar. Celebrating them humanistically is the easiest way to make the message of Jewish history come alive.

CHAPTER XIV

Passages

All kinship groups, including the Jews, provide ceremonies for dealing with birth, puberty, marriage, and death. Unlike the Jewish holidays, which may point to historical events that are uniquely Jewish, these "passages" are universal, events of the human condition. But they can use Jewish identity to enrich their message. In fact, they are the times in personal development when kinship connection becomes most important.

As a kinship identity, Jewish identity has historically been tied to family and to family loyalty. Rabbinic Judaism and the informal folk culture defined unique roles for men and women, husbands and wives, fathers and mothers, sons and daughters. These rigid guidelines became the heart of an ethical system that remained fairly unchanged until modern times.

But the Secular Revolution, with its affirmation of the ideal of personal dignity, has undermined the structures of the past. Life styles are changing all over the world, especially in North America where half the world Jewish population lives. The authoritarian family, with its authoritarian father, is disappearing. Jewish behavior no longer conforms to the traditional standards that the rabbis love to praise. And the new Jewish family, like most modern families, bears little relationship to the old propaganda.

More and more people are discovering that their work identity is as important as their family identity. More and more parents are spending their old age separated from their children. More and more women are choosing to have fewer babies than their mothers. More and more children are challenging the authority of their parents and teachers. More and more young people are arranging to find sex and love outside of marriage.

Humanistic Jews do not resist these changes. Nor do they approve of them unconditionally. They test both the old and the new with the measuring stick of dignity.

They also realize that a humanistic celebration of Jewish "passages" must be able to embrace what is good in these changes.

BIRTH

For families, tribes, and historic nations, new babies mean group survival. Birth is more than a personal event. It is a community happening of moral importance. Birth control and abortion become ethically offensive when too few babies are born and when too many infants die.

If the patriarchal family prevails, boy babies become more valuable than girl babies. Birth ceremonies focus more on male vulnerability than on female security. In a world where people believe in angry gods and nasty spirits, male infants need special protection.

Male circumcision most likely started out as a protective procedure against bloodthirsty, jealous divinities who would as soon kill the child as love it. Part of the child, the foreskin, was offered in the place of the whole, in the hope that the oedipal ancestral spirits would be appeased with this disposable tissue. Initially performed in childhood (as with the Arabs), the ceremony was often moved up to birth to provide early protection (in the same manner in which Christian baptism was moved to infancy).[1]

Male circumcision was widespread among the Semitic and Hamitic peoples of Western Asia and North Africa. It was not unique to the Jews. But priestly Judaism elevated it to supreme importance, interpreting it as a sign of the fertility that Yahveh had promised to Abraham and his descendants. Dire consequences would prevail, both for the child and the Jewish people, if any Jewish father should neglect the ritual circumcision of his sons on the eighth day (the sacred number seven plus one) after the birth. Even today, that anxiety lingers among traditional and most secularized Jews.[2]

While male circumcision ultimately turned into a Jewish birth ritual with a detailed prescribed procedure, virtually nothing was done to "protect" girls. Blessings and amulets were all that were provided. And they were not the stuff of which formal celebrations could easily be made.

In modern times, most Jews who openly denounce the morality of the patriarchal family still indulge this invidious distinction with little thought to its social message.

A humanistic morality that defends female equality would have a hard time justifying a birth ritual that excludes women. Adding clitoral circumcision to phallic trimming does not seem a reasonable alternative to good-humored Jews. And ignoring the issue in the name of venerable folk custom is an immoral evasion. The *Brit* (the covenant ceremony) is, by its very nature, inconsistent with a humanistic Jewish value system. While circumcision as a private surgery may be an appropriate modern hygienic measure, it is unacceptable as a public surgery and as part of a public celebration.

What is the humanistic Jewish alternative?

The alternative is a celebration (either family or community) that provides equal status to both boys and girls. This ceremony would dramatize the connection of the child with the future of the family, the Jewish people, and humanity. The announcement of a Hebrew name would be a fitting symbol of the Jewish attachment.

If we are sincere about our humanistic ethics, we do not trim the morality to fit the ceremony. We refashion the ritual to fit the morality.

PUBERTY

Leaving childhood and entering adulthood is an important time in the lives of all young people and in the life of the community in which they grow up. Entering adults, like entering babies, are guarantees of the future.

Most cultures provide a growing up ritual to dramatize the passage from dependence to community usefulness. Tests of hunting and farming skills, as well as exposure to pain and deprivation, were often part of the official procedure in tribal times. Urban civilization introduced the mastery of community laws and the reading of sacred texts.

The world of the Secular Revolution has undermined the significance of old rituals by postponing adulthood. The modern process of education is so complex and so long that most people do not achieve social maturity and usefulness until the age of twenty. And many who pursue higher education do not attain these goals until they are thirty. We now live in a world of physically mature people who continue to wait for their certificates of adulthood. In the centuries before formal education for the masses, thirteen seemed an appropriate age for celebrating growing up. It now barely represents the emergence from elementary education.

The Bar Mitzvah ceremony is the traditional rabbinic way of celebrating the Jewish boy's coming of age. But in its present form, it is an uncomfortable ceremony for humanistic Jews since it violates three essential humanistic commitments.

Humanistic Jews obviously reject, on the basis of present childhood development, the age of thirteen as the time when boys become men. They also reject any celebration that derives from male chauvinism and that denies girls equal honor to that of boys. While humanistic Jews accept the Torah as important Jewish literature, they do not deal with it as sacred scripture, and they deny its status as the fundamental symbol of Jewish identity and community loyalty.

Even classical Reform, which subscribed to only two of these three objections, dispensed with the Bar Mitzvah ceremony and replaced it with a class confirmation.

The Bar Mitzvah ceremony is an old ceremony. Throughout the centuries, it has undergone many changes. The first Jewish puberty ritual had nothing at all to do with reading from the Torah (since the Torah did not even exist at that time). It most likely was a circumcision rite that offered the foreskin as an appeasement to the gods, tested the boy's ability to endure pain, and prepared him for sexual activity as an adult male.[3] The practice of calling Bar Mitzvah boys to do the final reading of the Sabbath Torah portion is relatively recent. It goes back to the beginning of the fourteenth century and started only as a local custom.[4]

The essence of the historic Bar Mitzvah ceremony is not allegiance to the Torah. It is the celebration of the arrival of puberty. When the circumcision ceremony was moved to birth, a long period without dramatic puberty rites intervened before alternatives emerged.

Despite the postponement of adulthood in modern times, thirteen remains an important age for both boys and girls in our culture. It no longer marks the advent of adulthood. But it does indicate the arrival of adolescence, a recent development. In a modern industrial society, children are not able to enter the work force at thirteen. They require more training for the jobs they will choose. Adolescence is that difficult teenage period between childhood and maturity when the preparation for adult life continues. Entering the teenage years is an important turning point in a child's life. The body changes. The school changes. Personal desires change. Reassurance from the community that the child is competent and recognition from the family that the child is important are necessary psychic boosts. Thirteen is a perfect time for a public ceremony — not to celebrate the approach of adulthood, but to mark the reality of adolescence.

The puberty ceremony does not have to be male chauvinist. Both the Reconstructionists and the Reformers have been doing Bat Mitzvah for many years. It is just a matter of having girls do what boys do. While it is difficult to turn the ceremony of phallic circumcision into a girl's ceremony, it is easy to adjust a verbal experience to accommodate female needs. In fact, there is no good reason to designate the celebration Bar Mitzvah (Bat Mitzvah) where women always end up inside the parenthesis. You can simply name it the Mitzvah ceremony. If you want to "bar" it, you can "bar" it. If you want to "bat" it, you can "bat" it. After all, in popular Hebrew and Yiddish, the word *mitzvah* means more than "commandment." It also means "good deed." And the ceremony is indeed a good deed for the child and for the community.

Since the historic mitzvah ceremony has been changing throughout Jewish history, another radical change is not inappropriate. Obviously, a *required* reading from the Torah and from other parts of the Bible is inconsistent with a humanistic approach to Judaism. First of all, the Bible is essentially a theistic document. And secondly, given the range of Jewish experience and literature, the requirement is too narrow in its focus.

Of course, there is no dearth of effective alternatives. Selecting a hero or role model from the Jewish past, researching the hero's life, and sharing that research with the community is one alternative.[5] Presenting an answer to an important ethical or historic question of Jewish interest is another. Whatever project is chosen should celebrate the emerging talents and skills of the young adolescent. And it will provide families and humanistic Jewish groups with bonding experiences that are more than sentimental recollections of the past.

There is no reason why a developing child should have only one developmental ceremony. While the Mitzvah celebration marks the entry into adolescence, another celebration should be available to mark the beginning of adulthood. In many respects, the Confirmation ceremony developed by the Reform movement is a precedent for such an event. During the past fifty years, the age of Confirmation has varied (fourteen, fifteen, and sixteen). The drawback of the arrangement has been the exclusive use of class graduations and the avoidance of individual celebrations. As a result, Confirmation has never been able to equal the power of the Bar Mitzvah. A group ceremony cannot provide the ego satisfaction that an individual celebration confers.

As an experiment, the original Confirmation was a creative alternative. But it needs considerable reshaping. It needs to be an individual ceremony. It needs to be identified with a personal birthday. It needs to be linked directly with adulthood. Given our present culture and legal system, the eighteenth birthday seems an appropriate time. However, it is tied up with departure from high school and entry into college. There are too many distractions to allow the student to prepare properly for a significant celebration. Sixteen is less "adultish." But it is an age that North American culture has associated with growing up parties and the right to drive. It is also the beginning of the child's emergence from adolescence. Since the word *confirmation* (borrowed from the Lutherans) may not be the best word we can use, calling the second ceremony the Second Mitzvah may be more appropriate.

Certainly, since the process of growing up may continue for a long time, there is no reason why a Third Mitzvah should not follow the completion of professional education when social and financial independence become possible. After the traumas of university training and graduate school, many graduates might enjoy their day in the sun and the approval of their kinship community. And what they would have to say would provide a learning experience for their family and friends.

Whatever the format, a humanistic maturity ceremony (whether first, second, or third) must reflect the ethical commitments of humanistic Jews. It must provide *equality* for both boys and girls, men and women. It must provide *integrity*. The symbols and words should honestly express what the celebrant believes and what the community stands for. It must provide a sense of *competence,* a feeling of achievement. Presenting a lecture to an adult audience is only one of many options. It must reenforce a sense of *roots.* Jewish roots are not limited to religious roots. Music, dance, humor, science, and business are as much a part of Jewish culture as worship. It must allow the *community* to experience its own ideals and its own commitments. The celebration is not only for the celebrant. It also serves people in the audience who need periodic opportunities to affirm their own beliefs.

MARRIAGE

Marriage is at the heart of traditional family culture. As an institution, it provided the basis for orderly reproduction, childrearing, and continuity. As a ceremony, it was a public license from the community to have children. All historic societies regulate reproduction. Permission to marry was the major strategy for enforcing this regulation.

In a patriarchal society, like rabbinic Jewish society, the procedures of marriage were unrelated to love and romance. If these sentimental virtues emerged, they appeared by accident, not by intention. Husbands and wives were the agents of their families, chosen by venerable custom to arrange for appropriate children. Falling out of love was no disaster. But infertility was. No beauty or charm could rescue a childless woman from humiliation or rejection.

Grooms purchased brides. Fathers sold their daughters. Documents of sale were signed with public witnesses. Evidence of virginity was displayed so that no doubt could be cast on the paternity of children. Seclusion and mothering became the appropriate and universal task of women. In time, this total dependency made women as childlike as their offspring.

The wedding ceremony reflected these conditions. While initially the betrothal (purchase) was separate from the marriage (consummation), they were brought together for the sake of expediency. Outside the ritual praise of God, the guarantor of fertility, two important ceremonial events took place. The *k'tubah* ("purchase document") was signed and publicly read, and a ring was placed on the finger of the bride as the groom recited a ritual formula that declared his formal acquisition of his new wife. Although the woman ultimately acquired the right to reject the ring if she so chose, few women defied their families to take advantage of this freedom.[6]

The main activities were embellished by a canopy for shelter out of doors, two cups of ritual wine for conviviality, and the sound of breaking glass to drive away unwanted evil spirits. But the embellishments could not hide the male chauvinist heart of the ceremony.

Divorce was impossible for women. Only men were allowed this privilege. Since the reasons for permissible divorce were numerous and often trivial, the rabbis exercised some control over the harshness of masculine power by making the written bills of divorce so complex that husbands were incapable of writing them, themselves. Yet the plight of women who were bound to brutal marriage partners was not much alleviated by rabbinic intrusion. Happiness was secondary to reproduction.

When the Secular Revolution came, with its breakdown of family power and its elevation of the status of women, this ceremony became an anachronism, unrelated to the lives of the people who were mindlessly consenting to this ritual.

Humanistic Jews reject the idea that the purpose of marriage is the licensing of reproduction. Men and women may legitimately choose marriage, even though they have no intention of having children. And they may rightfully choose to bear children, even though they are not married.

In the eyes of a humanistic morality, marriage is more than living together. It is a public promise by two people to offer each other mutual support and exclusive sexual intimacy. Love and romantic loyalty are its initiators and its emotional glue. Friendship and equality are its style. Bonding becomes an end in itself, not a means to a reproductive end. Children may be chosen. But they complement the relationship, not define it.

Bonding will continue to be the choice of most people. But some may prefer to remain single, finding their support system for an individualistic society in their circle of friends and co-workers. Unlike birth, growing up, and death, marriage is no longer a natural and social inevitability.

A humanistic Jewish wedding must reflect this radical change in perspective. Canopies, winecups, and broken glass can be given new humanistic meanings. But purchase documents and marriage formulas that affirm the rabbinic view of family loyalty are verbally specific and unacceptable.

The humanistic Jewish wedding ceremony does not start out in the theater of a business deal. It begins with the conception of a bride and groom publicly declaring their commitment of support and loyalty to each other. The heart of this ritual is the articulation of this pledge by both partners in the presence of family and friends. What they say to each other should be no ritual formula. It should be a statement that they have either created or chosen.

This statement can be accompanied by an exchange of rings or other gifts as visible signs of their commitment. Songs and poetry (Hebrew or otherwise) about love and loyalty, a marriage contract designed to the character of their personal relationship, and philosophic statements about the humanistic meaning of marriage — together with a canopy, a winecup, and a glass waiting to be broken — may all be added, if desired.

Jewish identity enters the ceremony in two ways. As a kinship connection, it defines the extended family to which they belong. As history, it serves as a paradigm for the marriage relationship, itself. Just as Jewish experience teaches us that people must ultimately rely on their own talents and skills for their survival, so do the successful bride and groom acknowledge that the quality of their marriage will ultimately be determined by their own effort — and not by reliance on the kindness of the unpredictable fates. The special humanistic message of Jewish identity complements the humanism of their own commitments.

DEATH

For the living, the presence of death is terrifying. No matter how often it occurs, it never becomes familiar. It remains an unnatural intrusion.

Religion most likely began with the worship of the dead. The ancestral spirits are the fathers of the gods. In the beginning, religion granted immortality to the few. In the end, it conceded it to the masses.

The denial of death is the heart of traditional religion. Physical death becomes an illusion. The spirit of each person lives on and is indestructible. Rabbinic Judaism affirmed the resurrection of the dead and eternal reward and punishment. The promise of immortality provided the motivation that made the burdensome ritual regulations tolerable.

Traditional rabbinic mourning customs all derive from this denial of death. At the heart of the rabbinic response is the insistence on burial and the refusal of cremation. The preservation of the body, even in its skeletal form, was an act of faith in the forthcoming resurrection. Burning the body was an act of defiance. And tampering with the body to preserve it — such as embalming — was a denial of Yahveh's power to put flesh on bones. Even sealing the body in heavy coffins and vaults was forbidden. The ideal corpse lay in its shrouds, with the earth as its covering, ready to roll underground to the Mount of Olives on Judgment Day. Burial of the dead was to be on the same day as the death, if possible. The rabbis feared that the old custom of worshiping the dead would be revived and offend Yahveh, risking punishment and the loss of future rewards.[7]

The mourning customs that followed burial reflected more ambivalence. The bereaved feared that the wrath of God would strike again. Despite the promise of immortality, they were still afraid to die (the pre-rabbinic afterlife had been more like the Greek Hades, a somber place to spend eternity). To appease Yahveh's anger, it was necessary to avoid all displays of prosperous self-control. It was safer to appear pitiable. Wailing, fasting, and the rending of clothing would effectively convey the message of despair. Yahveh would be reluctant to punish again such dismal mourners. The seclusion and deprivation of *shiv'a* ("week") and *sh'loshim* ("month") reflect this strategy.[8]

As you can well imagine, humanistic Jews find most of these procedures offensive. Since the secular vision begins with the recognition that death is real, rituals that seek to deny death would compromise human dignity. And the willingness to confront unpleasant truth is part of that dignity.

The humanistic Jew starts with mortality as an unavoidable and final event. Life is valuable because it does not go on forever. Happiness is an urgent matter because it will not be available after we die. If there is "immortality," it is purely figurative. Only memory survives in the minds of others.

To accept this truth is to live courageously and generously in the face of every individual's personal tragedy. To surrender to fear and despair is to give the fates more than they deserve. Life can be long enough to be satisfying and to fulfill

important dreams if we accept time as a special gift and do
not waste it.

If we accept the reality of death, then both burial and cremation become Jewish options. Autopsies and the donation of
bodies for medical research become desirable. The disposal of
the dead does not have to be hasty and can be adjusted to the
needs of family and friends. Gifts of money and art should be
devoted to the living, not to the dead who cannot appreciate
them.

If we reject the personal intrusion of the supernatural,
then mourners do not need to appear despairing and pitiable.
They can behave like people who are in charge of their lives,
accepting what they cannot change and turning to the needs
of the living. Wailing, fasting, and the tearing of clothing
only make them more childlike and less able to cope with the
problems at hand. Uncontrolled grief, like uncontrolled
anger, can be harmful, since both destroy what they seek to
rescue.

A humanistic Jewish memorial service is an opportunity
to teach a humanistic philosophy of life. Both the meditations
and the eulogies must serve to remind people that the value
of personal life lies in its quality, not in its quantity. And, in
the age of the Holocaust, it would be an insult to victims and
martyrs to find in death the evidence of a well-ordered universe or the wages of sin. Jewish experience reveals the
absurdity of a world in which we can conceive of many biological alternatives "superior" to aging and death. A clever
God could have chosen to be kinder.

A humanistic culture does not devote its time and
resources to serving the needs of the non-existent dead. It
seeks to mobilize the living for the living. Constructive memory is a tribute to the past. It gives people identity and a place
in humanity. It does not wallow in useless nostalgia.

Death, marriage, puberty, and birth become times of testing for humanistic commitment and integrity. With a little creativity, humanism and Jewish identity become quite compatible.

CHAPTER XV

The Bible and Humanistic Judaism

An effective Judaism needs its own literature. Literature is more than an art form. It is the basic means of propaganda. It teaches. It reenforces conviction. It gives substance and integrity to public celebration.

Rabbinic Judaism has a famous literature. The Torah, the Bible, the Midrash, the Talmud, and the Siddur are a formidable array of prestigious words. A quotation from any one of them is all that some Jews require to kosherize whatever they think and do. As the old established sacred literature, they have earned the power to permit and to forbid. The Bible especially has extraordinary power since the Christian world pays it so much homage.

But Humanistic Judaism lacks this literary support system. A non-theistic, non-supernatural view of Jewish history and Jewish identity is comparatively new as an open Jewish alternative. For most of Jewish history, proto-humanists were not allowed to publish their beliefs. Heresy could be fatal. An underground system of humor, skepticism, and ambition became the only safe alternative. It produced much of the Jewish personality. But it was unable to provide a lasting commentary.

Many humanistic Jews handle their frustration by trying to "steal" the literature of their opponents. They desperately want the Torah and the Talmud to be seen as humanistic documents. Imitating Ambivalents like the Reforms and the Reconstructionists, they want the sacred texts of traditional Judaism to yield their humanistic point of view.

Turning rabbinic literature into its opposite is no easy task. It is something like proving that the Iliad and the Odyssey are really the same thing as Aristotle. Documents that were written and edited by Yahvist devotees and confirmed believers in supernatural authority are not generally the stuff of which humanism is made.

TORAH

The Torah, because of its centrality to priestly and rabbinic Judaism, is the prime target for liberal appropriation. For most Jews, the Torah is more than a book, more than a scroll. It is a sacred symbol of the Jewish religion. They can no more imagine a Judaism without the Torah than they can imagine a Judaism without God.

While most Jews do not study the Torah, they believe that they ought to. Even if they do not understand it, they believe that it contains eternal wisdom. And even if they are not interested in eternal wisdom, they believe that everything valuable in Jewish identity can be traced back to it.

No form of liberal Judaism has dared to dispense with it. Reform Jews praise it and provide the biggest arks for it. Reconstructionist Jews declare it to be one of the three fundamentals of their faith. Ambivalent Jews arrange to do Bar Mitzvahs with it. Even many secular Jews regard it as the source of their history.

In the face of all this attachment, how should humanistic Jews deal with the Torah?

Should they imitate rabbinic Judaism and make it the dominant symbol of Jewish commitment? Should they rescue it as a Jewish constitution and seek to give it a humanistic interpretation? Should they take it out of the ark and consign it to the library together with other books from Jewish history? Should they deal with it as a collection of charming outdated myths and not so charming outdated laws?

The Torah is certainly a problem for humanistic Jews.

The Torah is a theological document. Its authors and priestly editors firmly believed in a supernatural realm of supernatural beings. Yahveh is the central figure of the book. He — and not people — determines the course of human history. He — and not the Jews — determines the course of Jewish history. Without his consent, nothing happens. And without his intervention, salvation is impossible. Even Pharaoh does not "harden his heart" without Yahveh arranging for it. Even Jewish suffering in Egypt is no more than part of his plan to advertise his power through a dramatic rescue.[1]

The Torah is an authoritarian document. Laws do not derive their moral validity from their consequences, from their satisfaction of human needs. They derive their ethical clout from God's command. If Yahveh permits, the behavior is right. If Yahveh forbids, the behavior is wrong. Supernatural rewards and punishments are not intended to give authority to the laws. They simply motivate people to do what is obviously the right thing to do. "I am Yahveh your God," is the endless refrain of the Torah. It is a dramatic version of parental intimidation. "I am your father — and I deserve your obedience." With that kind of moral approach, reason and dignity go out the window.

The Torah is a confusing document. Scientific criticism has revealed that it was not written by Moses (as the rabbinic tradition maintained), but that it is a composite of at least four separate documents. Many of its stories contradict each other (Genesis 1 & 2). Many of its laws are incompatible (individual and collective guilt). Many of the events it describes either never happened or never happened in the way they are described. And most of the stories were written centuries after the so-called events occurred.[2]

The Torah is a reactionary document. It promotes a life style that is morally offensive to most contemporary Jews and is rejected by them on a behavioral level. While it is fashionable to lift individual commandments out of their social and supernatural contexts (*e.g.* you shall love your neighbor as yourself), the choice distorts the reality. The traditional Torah life style was a world of family tyranny, female inequality, tribal exclusiveness, theocratic government, and sacrificial ritual. It takes legal ingenuity and dishonesty to turn the Torah into a constitution for a liberal democracy. Even the Ten Commandments place Sabbath observance on the same level as not stealing.[3]

The Torah is a chauvinistic document. It views the Jewish people as a "chosen" people. The descendants of Abraham are selected out for special protection and special privilege, not because of their own intrinsic merits, but because they are the children of Yahveh's favorite. Very little attention is devoted to the role of non-Jews and to what Yahveh expects of them and will do for them. The world God behaves like a tribal God.

The Torah is a "sacred" document. It has become a book to be worshipped and defended — not a book to be enjoyed and studied critically. It is an "idol," set aside for public reverence and held up to public adoration. The contents of the book have become less important than the ceremonial marching and kissing and raising and praising. Sacred scriptures are dangerous because, so long as they are regarded as sacred, they cannot be treated as literature, as the creation of fallible human beings. Many Jews feel a compulsive need to rescue the Torah. They are afraid that, if they give it up, they will have no other "idol" to replace it. The result is an obsessive attempt to save it for contemporary use and a fixation with an ancient period in Jewish history that may be insignificant to the formation of the modern Jewish personality.

Given these difficulties, what is the place of the Torah in the educational and ceremonial life of the humanistic Jew?

Whatever answer we give to this question, it must be consistent with the basic affirmations of a humanistic approach to Judaism: the irrelevance of God, a rational ethic which derives its authority from human need, a life style consistent with reason and personal dignity, a naturalistic view of Jewish history, the rejection of all idols. It is not our job to fit these beliefs into the Torah. It is our job to fit the Torah into these commitments.

First, let us describe how *not* to deal with the Torah.

We do not need to rescue the Torah. We do not need to make the Torah do more for us then it can. The Torah is the supreme document of priestly Judaism. It is a skilful expression of a theocratic view of the world and society. Some ancient Sadducee enthusiast of priestly rule would be able to use it effortlessly. But for us, it is a desert of patriarchal regulations and sacrificial rules. Even the myths of Genesis carry moral messages about female subordination and tribal hostility that are less than noble.[4] No matter what interpretive genius we bring to the text, the Torah cannot be turned into a humanistic constitution — not even a shabby version of one. A document, two thirds of the contents of which are humanistically embarrassing, cannot — without dishonesty — be made to serve as the foundation code of a secular approach to Jewish identity.

We must not mock the Torah. It deserves it own dignity. It rightfully belongs to the traditional Jews who live by its prescriptions. Texts deserve their own integrity. They mean what their authors intended them to mean. They do not mean what desperate liberals want to make them mean. The writer of Genesis 1 believed in a flat earth and a flat heaven. He did not believe in galaxies and evolution. If he had endorsed these convictions, he would have said so. The writer of Exodus 19 believed in supernatural intrusion and divine voices. He did not believe in Moses the philosopher engaging in philosophic introspection on top of a mountain. The author of Leviticus 19 believed in divine dictatorship and priestly government. He did not embrace personal freedom and egalitarian democracy. There is a right of original intent, a moral claim to let texts mean what they say and what their authors meant them to say. The rabbis chose to distort some of the priestly intent. The Reformers chose to distort most of it. Humanists would have to use every ounce of their guile to turn the texts of the Torah into a plea for an agnostic egalitarian morality.

We must not avoid the Torah. It is so easy to use the Torah as a symbol without ever paying attention to its content that we tend to talk about what the Torah stands for and not what it says. Reform rabbis love to point out that the Torah is only a sign of God's continuous revelation (divine wisdom is present in the best thinking of every Jewish age).[5] But they never give equal honor to the books that followed. In the end, the Torah becomes a symbol of itself. The weekly readings become perfunctory. The alternatives never get read. An empty parchment scroll with a pretty gown could do just as well.

We must not misrepresent ourselves. We must not use false advertising. We must not imitate Reform Judaism and pretend that Zadokite priests were the precursors of the Enlightenment. The Torah is an appropriate emblem for rabbinic Jews. It fits their aspirations and the life style they are promoting. But for humanistic Jews, it is a lie. It points to the wrong tradition. Humanistic Judaism is not the child of the official documents of priestly and rabbinic Judaism. It is the child of Jewish experience, twenty-five centuries of human ingenuity in the face of cruel and unkind fates. Jewish history was different from the way priests and rabbis saw it. The Jewish personality is the product of Jewish history, not the product of the Torah.

If this is the reality of our roots, how then *should* we use the Torah?

A humanistic Judaism should use the Torah as an important historical document, a resource book for the study of the ancient history of the Jewish people. Although it seems to focus on the lives of Abraham, Isaac, Jacob, Joseph, and Moses, it actually describes the power struggles and ambitions of priests and Jews who lived many centuries after the death of Moses. The Torah is less a description of the life of the Hebrews in the nomadic period and more a revelation of the beliefs and anxieties of the Jews before and after the Chaldean conquest. The editors of the Torah put their sixth century laws and convictions into the mouths of the patriarchs and Moses.

The Torah is a book of clues. If it is studied scientifically (not piously), it will lead us to the real events that lie behind the mythology. Abraham, Isaac, and Jacob may turn out to be symbols of three Amorite invasions of Palestine. Joseph may be transformed into a Semitic occupation of Egypt. And Joshua may end up living three hundred years before Moses. The authors of the Torah saw the past through their own political and theological convictions. Jewish history is not necessarily what the priestly writers say it was. It is a collection of events that lie behind the descriptions. And the Torah is a collection of clues that lead us to the events.

The Torah is also a book about past and present beliefs. Even if all the historical statements of the Torah were false, even if all the laws of the Torah were ethically invalid; they are still assertions in which many of our ancestors fervently believed and which guided their behavior. It may be true that the earth is not flat. But it *is* true that believing in a flat earth determines your travel arrangements and the way you see your place in the universe. It may be true that Yahveh did not write the Torah. But it is true that believing Yahveh wrote the Torah would influence the way you approached new ideas and justified new laws. The rabbis of the Midrash and the Talmud found it necessary to connect their own beliefs with the affirmations in the Torah, even though they appeared to be different.

Much of establishment Jewish behavior comes from ideas that are to be found in the Torah and its commentaries. The study of these ideas is part of the study of Jewish history, just as the study of the conditions that undermined these ideas is part of the study of Jewish history.

The Torah is a book of shared conclusions. The priestly writers often reached ethical conclusions that humanistic Jews have also reached. The priests came to these moral precepts with the reasoning of an authoritarian God. Humanistic Jews come to these rules with a commonsensical testing of their consequences. Rabbinic Jews come to these commandments with the knowledge that the Torah gives them validity. Humanistic Jews approach them with the awareness that human experience makes them worthwhile (even if the Torah never existed). Millions of people in dozens of cultures have discovered that honoring parents and telling the truth are morally important, even though they have never seen a Torah. Ethics do not come from a book. They come from human needs and human experience.

Jewish morality did not come from the Ten Commandments. It came from Jewish experience. Even if the Decalogue had been dictated by Yahveh to Moses on the top of a fiery mountain, it would be no more valid than if it had been discovered by a school child in the process of studying human relations. No historic religious code, including the Ten Commandments, completely passes the test of a humanistic appeal to human dignity. Insisting that Jews remember their dependence on supernatural intervention is hardly an invitation to self-reliance and self-esteem. Prohibiting the sculpture of the human form does not elevate the independence and creativity of the artist. Arbitrarily choosing one day for everybody to abstain from all pleasurable activity has more to do with terror than with rest and recreation.

Most sensitive Jewish young people, using their commonsense, could draft a list of ten ethical guidelines that would equal the value of this old list. While they should know about the Ten Commandments, they should not be intimidated by their antiquity or by their authoritarian history. Rational guidelines are never inscribed in stone. They need to be continually adjusted and amended.

All literature is of human creation, designed to appeal to human audiences and filled with human imperfection. Books are never holy. They may be useful and inspirational. But they are never *all* true and *all* perfect. And they bear no guarantee of eternal validity.

The Torah belongs in the library. As a scroll, it deserves a place of special honor in the museum of famous Jewish books. Let students study it and evaluate it. Let teachers talk about it and explain its historic power. But let no humanist worship it or imagine that Jewish identity and ethical living depend on it.

PROPHETS

The same caution applies to the other books of the Bible, especially the books of the Yahveh prophets. For many Ambivalents, Amos, Isaiah, Jeremiah, and Micah were the most appealing figures in the Bible because of their compassion for the poor and the needy. The liberals sought to rescue the ethical relevance of the Bible by letting these prophets be their Biblical roots instead of the Torah. "Prophetic Judaism" became an important phrase for many modernists.

However, the prophets present several serious problems for humanists. They were self-righteous and authoritarian and gave no credence to the opinions of their enemies. They were always proclaiming, never discussing. As the voice of Yahveh, they had the non-humanist quality of infallibility. Some of their ethical pronouncements were humanitarian. But they were not humanists. They firmly believed in supernatural authority and in supernatural rewards and punishments.[6]

Most Ambivalents choose only to notice the thirty or forty verses that denounce the exploitation of the poor and conveniently fail to notice the hundreds of verses that predict the cruel and inhuman destruction of opponents and enemies. To really read the Prophets (the four books of Isaiah, Jeremiah, Ezekiel and The Twelve) is to wade through pages of blood, gore, and supernatural visions before finding the few nuggets of humanitarian sentiment. The punishments do not even seem to fit the "crimes." Any attention to deities other than Yahveh seems to warrant death and oblivion. Even Jeremiah suggests that the Jews surrender to the Chaldeans so that they can begin the sentence of suffering that they deserve.[7]

One way out is to attribute all the "nice" statements to the prophets and all the "mean" statements to later editors. But that approach is so blatantly partisan that it will not hold up under critical scrutiny. The truth of the matter is that the Yahveh prophets who were selected for the sacred scriptures display an annoying moral unevenness. Their words were not preserved for humanitarian reasons. They were preserved to satisfy the great need of the Jews for reassurance about their future — and especially to explain why the present was indeed so bleak. The ritual poetry of the prophetic books was read at public assemblies to bring visions of hope and vengeance to a humiliated people.[8]

Like the Torah, the prophetic books are more useful as clues to Jewish history than as moral directives. Obviously, most Yahveh prophets were never included in the Bible. They were simply denounced by the few that were chosen. As Jews, their ideas are just as Jewish as the beliefs of their opponents. Even though we only know about their viewpoint from the denunciations of their enemies, they were part of a public controversy of political and theological ideas that was not quite the "good guys-bad guys" argument the prophetic editors tried to present. It is quite obvious that the opponents of Amos did not go around saying "love evil, avoid the good." They disagreed with Amos about what the "good" really was.[9]

Part of our problem with the "kosher" prophets is that we are so grateful for their humanitarian pronouncements that we tend to revere them and to assume that their opponents had nothing worthwhile to offer. Pragmatic social justice is far more than loving the good and avoiding the evil. It is finding a social system that will motivate the talented to work for the less talented. The poor need more than compassion. They need intelligent alternatives.

The Bible is our most valuable resource book for the study of early Jewish history. It most effectively articulates the viewpoint of its final editors about what really happened and about how the Jewish people should behave. But it also reveals other Jewish options through its contradictions and denunciations. If used skilfully, it will reveal to us a wide array of Jewish opinions. As humanistic Jews, we are not obliged to accept the editors' choice.

Ultimately, no one can use Rejectionist literature better

than Rejectionists. Humanists will enjoy it for historical
reasons. But it cannot have the sustained ideological and inspirational quality that it has for rabbinical traditionalists.
The ethical nuggets are too few and far between. And the
rescue is too tedious. Too many statements have to be ripped
out of their historic contexts. Too many rules have to be given
false motivations ("The dietary laws, after all, were only
primitive rules of hygiene").[10] Too many apologies have to be
made for never accepting what the author of the text seems
to be saying ("On the surface it appears. . . but what he really
meant to say. . . "). The shoe does not fit. Priestly and
rabbinic literature was edited for priestly and rabbinic Jews
and for priestly and rabbinic purposes. A clever clergyman or
lawyer can twist the American Declaration of Independence
to justify the regime of Ayatollah Khomeini. But so what?

Humanistic Jews must not repeat the errors of the Ambivalents. Reform and Reconstructionist Jews lost their ideological integrity and their propagandistic clout when they
decided to dress up in their enemies' clothing. They must
always apologize. They must always explain why what does
not obviously fit them really does. The Ambivalents become
more desperate than the Kabbalistic mystics (who, at least,
were connected to the literature by their piety). They are
always looking for hidden humanistic messages that the
authors never intended. Truth, reason, and scientific integrity go out the window — all in the vain attempt to be kosherized by a history that never was.

CHAPTER XVI

The Alternative Literature

Humanistic Jews need a literature that clearly and boldly states what they think and believe — in the same way that Rejectionist literature clearly and boldly presents what Rejectionists think and believe.

This literature should defend reason and dignity in a clear and open way. It should talk about human power and human freedom with the same directness that rabbinic literature talks about divine power and divine freedom. The ordinary reader, who is not familiar with clerical and legal rescue strategies, should be able to hear the message without confusion.

This literature should present Jewish history and the Jewish experience in a scientific humanistic manner. Instead of explaining how the old establishment literature failed to tell the story in the right way, *it* should tell the story in the right way. Instead of pretending that the roots of the modern Jewish personality lie in the belief system of the priests and the rabbis, it should describe the *real* roots.

This literature should be straightforward and should not have to be defended against misinterpretation. Humanism is not served well by writing that seems to say the opposite. The texts should make it easy for us to teach, not necessary for us to apologize.

If we apply these three criteria to existing literature, what passes the test?

The classics of humanism pass the test. Epicurus, Democritus, August Comte, John Stuart Mill, Bertrand Russell, John Dewey, Jean Paul Sartre, and George Santayana speak their minds clearly and without reservation. They are not Jews. But they are articulate humanists. The literature of humanism is part of a humanistic Judaism, even more than the pious writing of pious Jews who did not defend either reason or human autonomy.

These writers did not deal with Jewish history or the Jewish experience specifically. But in their treatment of the human condition, they enable us to understand the values and ideas that make a secular Jewish identity possible. If Humanistic Judaism is a philosophy of life, it must be able to place the value of Jewish identity in a philosophic context. That context is universal and includes all humanists.

The writings of famous Jews who were humanists and who wrote about humanism pass the test. Albert Einstein, Sigmund Freud, Erich Fromm, Walter Lippmann, and Walter Kaufman came to their humanism out of the background of their Jewish experience. Although they were not aware of their Jewish significance, they were voices of the Jewish experience — an experience which had molded the Jewish personality but which had never been able, in the face of rabbinic suppression, to establish its own literature. The words are new. But the affirmation of the human spirit is an old Jewish response.

The literature of secular historians, sociologists, and archeologists, both Jewish and non-Jewish, who have uncovered the *real* history of the Jews, passes the test. Spinoza, Julius Wellhausen, Emile Durkheim, Max Weber, Simon Dubnow, Salo Baron, and Theodore Gaster went beyond the official story of rabbinic Judaism to reveal the events that were distorted or never noticed and the natural causes that made these events possible. It is the Jewish experience, not the classic description of that experience, that is important.

The writings of Jewish nationalists, whether Yiddishist or Zionist, whether socialist or capitalist, who rejected supernatural authority and who sought to persuade the Jews to take their own destiny into their own hands, pass the test. I.L. Peretz, Sholem Aleichem, Chaim Zhitlowsky, Ahad Haam, Micah Berdichevsky, Theodore Herzl, Max Nordau, A.D. Gordon, Ber Borochov, Shaul Tchernikhovsky, Vladimir Jabotinsky, David Ben Gurion, and Nahum Goldmann mocked the pious passivity of the old regime and sought to restore Jewish confidence in human planning and human effort. Their passion produced some of the best humanistic Jewish propaganda. Even exaggerated sentimental poetry like Tchernikhovsky's "Ani Maamin" still hits the mark: *"Laugh, laugh at all my dreams. But this I the dreamer proclaim. I still believe in man. I still believe in you."*

The celebration materials of secular Jewish communities qualify for admission. For seventy years, the secular kibbutzim in the land of Israel invented new humanistic ways to celebrate old holidays. Their efforts are collected in kibbutz archives, untranslated and presently unavailable to world Jewry.

The reflections of Jewish essayists and novelists who are ardent humanists and who value their Jewish identity are an important part of a humanistic Jewish literature. Saul Bellow, Albert Memmi, and George Steiner see the significance of Jewish identity in the history of Jewish alienation. The human context of Jewish self-awareness is what counts.

A humanistic Jewish literature differs in many ways from the rabbinic variety.

It is new and contemporary. It lacks the advantages of antiquity and wide popular recognition. It is not embedded in the folk cultures of Western civilization. It does not conjure up the image of books that grandparents revered.

It tends to be scholarly and intellectual. Folksy legends and naive stories that appeal to children are few and far between. Not that these rabbinic styles are not possible on humanistic terms. They just have not been indulged.

Its authors tend to be far more diverse. They are less involved in professional Jewishness than the historic prophets, priests, and rabbis. They lack the professional solidarity and intensity that these old fraternities engendered.

But, most important of all, it is incomplete. Rabbinic Judaism has had over two thousand years to say what it needed to say. Its view of Jewish history, its roster of heroes, its celebration formats, its sentimental symbols, its sacred scriptures, its folksy messages for the masses, are established. What remains is only repetition and reverence.

Humanistic Judaism has only begun. Most of the literature it *needs*, it still has to create. Two thousand years of censorship and official intimidation have put us far behind in the race. The Jewish experience is old. But having the opportunity to describe it in a humanistic way is new.

We still need a clear, popular, poetic, non-scholarly presentation of Jewish history. We still need folksy sentimental biographies of humanistic Jewish heroes. We still need vivid celebration formats that make the humanistic meaning of the holidays come alive. We still need naive didactic stories for children and inspirational anthologies for adults. We still need time for our symbols to touch the heart.

The test of a successful Humanistic Judaism will be its courage and persistent integrity. If the task of creating this new literature frightens the Jews of the Secular Revolution and freezes their talents, they will drift back to the compromises of the lackluster Ambivalents. They will strive to rescue the "scriptures" of rabbinic Judaism for their very own and fail. In the end, they will be neither here nor there — suffering the cynicism of lost integrity and deception.

But if the task inspires them with a sense of urgency and excitement, there is no doubt that the talent exists to tell the Jewish story the way it should be told.

CHAPTER XVII

Israel

No discussion about the value of Jewish identity is possible without dealing with the overwhelming significance of the Jewish state. No reality in the Jewish world arouses the widespread emotional fervor that Israel does.

For many Diaspora Jews, Israel is their Jewish passion. Thinking about her, worrying about her, and working for her are the chief ways that they express their Jewish identity. No prayer service or cultural endeavor can arouse the enthusiasm and interest that Israel does. Even the youth education programs of most synagogues build their curriculum around the life of Jews in the Jewish state.

Classical Zionism maintained that Israel was the solution to the problems of the Diaspora. Its creation would normalize the Jews as a territorial nation, revive the Hebrew language as a unique and secular instrument of Jewish identity, eliminate anti-Semitism by removing Jews from Gentile environments, and combat assimilation by concentrating Jews in one area. The Diaspora would fade away. Jewish identity and Israeli identity would merge. And the Jewish revolution would be complete.

But the Diaspora did not disappear, and Jewish identity and Israeli identity have not merged. Only a quarter of the Jews of the world live in Israel. This number may rise to forty percent by the year 2000 because of low Diaspora birth rates.

But over half of world Jewry will continue to live outside the boundaries of the Jewish state, most of them in North America.

If defining their relationship to Israel is a major issue for Diaspora Jews, clarifying their connection to the Diaspora is equally important for Israelis.

For Diaspora Jews, the relationship is confusing.

It is confusing because Israel prevents Diaspora Jews from functioning as a religious denomination. From the Zionist point of view, the Jews are a nation, bound together by ethnic and cultural solidarity. Like other national diasporas, Jews are tied to their ethnic homelands by national sentiments. But Diaspora Jews are not content being merely ethnic. Their major community organizations present themselves as religious institutions. As the major alternative to Christianity in the Western world, Jews are reluctant to forego their religious status to become one of many minority nationalities.

The relationship is confusing because Diaspora Jews are not members of the Israeli nation, even though they have strong attachments to it. It is hard for many Jews and Gentiles to distinguish between loyalty to the Jewish people and allegiance to the state of Israel. Anti-Zionists make a lot of noise about dual loyalty, which Zionists tend to dismiss with accusations of self-hate. The confusion persists because most Jews do not really want to deal with the issue.[1]

The relationship is confusing because Diaspora Jews view Israelis as more completely Jewish than they are. A Hebrew-speaking culture seems more Jewish, for obvious reasons, than an English-speaking society. However, non-Jews in Israel speak Hebrew fluently, far better than the eager Jewish tourists from abroad. While in most nations speaking the national language makes you part of the nation, Israel is different. The Hebrew-speaking Arab fails to become Jewish

even though the French-speaking Arab in France becomes French. Yet the rancher named Cohen, speaking English with a Montana accent and living far away in North America, remains Jewish.

The relationship is confusing because Israel is the creation of the Diaspora. Jewish nationalism was a European movement responding to the problems of European Jews and to the declining fortunes of the Yiddish-speaking world. Zionism, as a national liberation movement, did not start out with an oppressed native population resident on their own land. Before the Zionist pioneers could free their nation, they had to manufacture it. For many years, the Diaspora was the protector of the fledgling homeland and the source of its population. It still is. But there is no conventional national model that fits that pattern.

The relationship is confusing because Israel seems unique. Virtually all national diasporas — Irish, Italian, Polish, American — have their roots in their homeland. Their nostalgia, their memories, and their language leftovers have their source in the place where the nation first formed. But Diaspora Jews — since the Diaspora is so old — have their roots in the Diaspora. Russia and Yiddish are the nostalgia of most North American Jews. Israel and Hebrew were Biblical fantasies, subjects of study, not experienced realities. Italian grandmothers came from Italy. Jewish grandmothers came from Pinsk.

The relationship is confusing because Zionists and Israelis place a negative value on Diaspora Jewish life. Classical Zionists saw no future for Jewish identity in the Diaspora. Either anti-Semitism or secular assimilation would undermine Jewish community life and make it disappear. Only immigration to Israel could save Jews and Jewish identity.[2] The obligation of every Diaspora Jew was to make *aliya*, to move to Israel. Zionists who remain in the Diaspora lead lives of apology, always explaining why they stay where they stay. Feelings of guilt and inferiority underlie the dialogue between Israeli and Diaspora Jews. Ambivalence reigns.

The relationship is confusing because Israel is often described as the "center" of the Jewish world. But it is a center with very little input from the Jewish outside. Financial and political support are welcome. But Israelis do not feel that there are any Jewish things to be learned from the Diaspora. Israelis regard Jewish culture as an export, never an import. While the general culture of the West is lovingly embraced, the Jewish experience in the West is viewed as a cultural misfortune.

For Israelis, too, the connection with the Diaspora presents ideological and emotional problems.

There is the problem of roots. The early Zionists tried to pretend that the roots of the modern Jewish state existed in the ancient Jewish commonwealth, the kingdoms of David and of the Maccabees. The Bible took on a special political importance, even for secular Jews, because it emphasized the historic Jewish connection to the land of Israel. As for the Diaspora, it was conveniently ignored.[3]

But reality intrudes. Just as the real roots of the modern Diaspora lie in the Diaspora, so are the *real* roots of modern Israel in the same Diaspora. Israelis are always aware that their parents, grandparents, or greatgrandparents came from other places. They are not "natives" in the same sense that Italian peasants are natives or Danish burghers are natives. The dim memories of tribal invasions form no part of the Jewish self-awareness of the new Jewish state. The very division of the Jewish population into Ashkenazim and Sephardim, with all its tensions and conflicts, is vivid evidence of the imprint of Diaspora existence.

Since, in the Zionist perspective, the Diaspora has negative value, Israelis have never been able to deal honestly and realistically with it. They have never been able to see the Diaspora as their historic homeland from which their culture and their personality have largely derived. While it is true that the Jewish dispersion came out of Judea, it is equally true that the personality which conceived the Zionist enterprise was molded in the Diaspora. The Jewish people invented Israel. And the Jewish people, not the Judean nation, came into existence in the dispersion.

One futile enterprise was the attempt of certain secular Israelis to sever the connection between Israel and the Diaspora. Calling themselves "Canaanites" to emphasize their connection with the pre-Israelite inhabitants of the land, they demanded a Hebrew-speaking state in which "Hebrew" identity would be primary, the connection with the Diaspora would be severed, and the word "Jewish" would cease to have any public significance.[4] Needless to say, the absurdity of this proposal guaranteed it little success. But the very fact that seemingly rational people subscribed to this program indicates how uncomfortable many Israelis are with this persistent and indissoluble Diaspora.

No matter how hard certain Israelis try to be Israeli without being Jewish, they fail in their attempt. In the eyes of the world, Israel is a Jewish state with a fundamental connection to Jews all over the world. Just as American Gentiles identify Jewish Americans with the behavior of the state of Israel, so does public opinion identify Israel with Jews wherever they are. The connection cannot be undone. Israel is the Hebrew-speaking center of a larger social entity called the Jewish people — which, under present international conventions, enjoys no official political status.

The problem with the Arabs highlights this connection. Israel is a binational state.[5] Yet Israeli Jews feel a greater bond with the Jews of the Diaspora than they do with the many Arabs who are Israeli citizens. Even if there were a secular way to turn Arabs into Jews, it would be useless. Arabs wish to remain Arabs. Without substantial Jewish immigration from the Diaspora, they may become the majority culture of the state. The link with the Galut becomes a strategy for Israeli survival.

Even the experiences of the Diaspora are now being experienced by Israelis. Israel lives in a sea of anti-Jewish feeling on the margin of the Arab world. The military virtues of the Israeli army are a function of the very anti-Semitism and marginality for which Zionism was the supposed cure. The Diaspora personality adapts very readily to all the danger and alienation of the Israeli scene.

HUMANISTIC JEWISH RESPONSE

How does Humanistic Judaism respond to these problems and confusions?

A few simple insights guide the response.

It is important to remember that there is an old and well-established international kinship group called the Jewish people that is older than the state of Israel and that created it. Without its connection with the Jewish people, the state of Israel would not be strong enough or interesting enough to survive.

The Jewish people is a Diaspora phenomenon. Its history as an international family is much longer than its experience as a territorial nation. Its style and personality were formed in the outside world even though its official literature preferred to focus on the distant parochial past.

Most territorial nations in the world started out with territorial natives. But the decision to establish a nation in

Palestine preceded the arrival of the organizing population. Zionism did not start with Jewish natives. It began with the Jewish people. As a nation, Israel has a unique origin and a unique connection.

Jewish identity for Israeli Jews is not merely a territorial distinction. If it were, the word *Israeli* would be sufficient in the same way that the word *French* is sufficient.

For most Israelis, especially secular Israelis, Jewish identity is important for the very reasons that offend many classical Zionists. It points to the obvious connection of the Israeli "Hebrews" with the world Jewish people and its history in the Diaspora. Valuing Israeli identity and the Hebrew language is not the same as valuing Jewish identity. To value Jewishness in a humanistic way is to understand how Jewish history, especially Diaspora history, speaks a humanistic message. The absence of God and the necessity of human responsibility flow from its events.

Humanistic Judaism in Israel is more than humanism. It is more than humanistic philosophy in Hebrew. It is a doctrine about the secular importance of Jewish identity, an identity that is broader than membership in the Jewish state. It is a reversal of the historic Zionist reluctance to find its roots in the Diaspora and in the Diaspora experience. Despite the wish of many Zionist pioneers, the Jewish state can never be fully "normal" because Jewish Diaspora history has been less than normal.

The failure of secularism in Israel lies in the assumption that Jewishness will become as natural as Frenchness and will require no special effort. But the overwhelming presence of the Diaspora forces secular Israelis to deal with the fact that Jewish identity and Israeli identity do not coincide. Secular Israelis are only now beginning to realize the importance of the Diaspora connection, beyond the obvious need to recruit new immigrants. Just as Diaspora Jews have appropriately learned to make Israel the center of the Jewish world, so must Israelis learn how to affirm the Diaspora as their national roots.

For Diaspora Jews, the advent of the state of Israel is a turning point in Jewish history. Jews now have the option of either minority status or majority power. They have the option of going beyond being part of a kinship people to participating in the life of a territorial nation with a Jewish language. Both choices are equally Jewish. But the Jewish state is bound to be the center of the Jewish people by virtue of its Jewish intensity.

Although Israel is the center of the Jewish people, Diaspora Jews do not have to assume a passive role of acceptance and resignation. They have a right, by virtue of their Jewish connection, to influence its behavior. If they are humanistic Jews, they have a right to actively work to make Israeli behavior more humanistic. The separation of religion from government and the guarantee of equal rights for Arab citizens are urgent matters.

To live in a century when the Jewish state became real is a special privilege. As a successful attempt by Zionist pioneers to encourage Jews to take their own fate into their hands, the Zionist movement was initially filled with a humanistic spirit. Keeping that spirit alive is one of the tasks of Humanistic Judaism.

CHAPTER XVIII

Intermarriage and Conversion

Goyim have never been easy for Jews to deal with. Jewish feelings are too ambivalent. On the one hand, there are the bonds of shared humanity, shared work, shared culture, and personal friendship. On the other hand, there are the memories of assault, persecution, and the struggle for minority survival. Attachment and withdrawal are the theater of modern Jewish responses.

But no effective Judaism can avoid dealing with this issue. In the world of the Secular Revolution, whether in the Diaspora or in the "binational" Jewish state, the openness, freedom, and individualism of contemporary urban living means that we can no longer exclude Gentiles as forbidden strangers.

Historic rabbinic Judaism was hardly ambivalent. Segregation and separation were the established norms. Ritual purity and dietary laws prevented any meaningful fraternization. And the prohibition against intermarriage made social contacts potentially dangerous. Not only was the ghetto a Gentile imposition, it was also a Jewish desire. The reason was clear. As aliens seeking to avoid contamination while waiting to return to their homeland, Jews had no need for intimacy. Openness would corrupt Jewish integrity and invite divine punishment.

As Christian and Muslim hostility killed the missionary spirit of rabbinic Judaism, few Gentile converts joined the Jewish people. Those that attempted to were reminded of the hardships that Jewish identity brought. The Jews withdrew more and more into themselves, both fearing and hating the Gentile world, even when it was necessary to do business with it.

The secular emancipation created havoc in the Jewish community. Secular education, secular professions, and secular government forced Jews and Gentiles to work together on a regular basis. Freed from rabbinic authority, the Jews followed their own individual inclinations. Many of them chose to spend much more time with Gentiles than with Jews. Partnerships were established. Friendships blossomed. And love and marriage followed inevitably.

While the Rejectionists responded with denunciations of this new behavior, the Ambivalents were appropriately ambivalent. The Modern Orthodox and the Conservatives encouraged social intercourse but continued to ban intermarriage, thus promoting the cause and prohibiting the effect. The Reformers deplored mixed marriage but allowed their rabbis to officiate at mixed marriage ceremonies.[1]

The leaders of the Ambivalents were as ambivalent as their followers. They praised brotherhood and shared values at interfaith banquets but denounced effective fraternization when preaching in their own synagogues. They lacked the guts and the consistency of the Rejectionists.

For humanistic Jews, the question of fraternization and intermarriage becomes even more difficult because humanism as a philosophy of life is shared with many Gentiles. Humanistic Jews belong to two communities. One is the community of Jews who value their Jewish identity — a community that includes the whole spectrum of Jewish opinion. The other is the community of humanists, who may or may not be Jewish — a community that is not specifically concerned with the preservation of Jewish identity.

A humanistic Judaism must be able to respond clearly and consistently not only to the issues of intermarriage and conversion but also to the question of how to relate to other humanists.

INTERMARRIAGE

Should Jews marry only Jews?

Most Jews think that they should. Even the most sophisticated prefer the perils of atheism to the trauma of mixed weddings. The prospect that their children will be doing their reproducing with Gentiles arouses the deepest dread that their unconscious can conjure up.

Outspoken liberals, who are big on brotherhood, open pot, and female liberation, often turn hysterical when they learn that their Jewish son intends to cohabit in a legal way with a non-Jewish woman. Infamous Jewish anti-Semites, who are turned off by all forms of organized religion and who find Jewish culture depressing, are known to become violent when their daughter announces her intention to marry a Gentile man.

Why this overreaction to what appears to be decent love?

The answer is important because no issue in Jewish life is as explosive as the question of intermarriage. Even the Reform rabbinate, the so-called paragons of religious liberalism, are deeply divided on the issue. We are witnessing the ironic spectacle of radical egalitarians and libertarians turned into fanatic inquisitors eager to expel erring rabbis from the rabbinic fold for the unspeakable sin of officiating at mixed marriages.[2]

The reason for this behavior is no mystery. Tribal loyalty is an old and respectable human emotion. Although it is not uniquely Jewish, it has been strengthened among Jews by centuries of exile and homelessness. Jews have had to make a special effort to survive as a group. Without the dramatic differences in their rituals, food, language, and dress, they would have had great difficulty resisting the religious onslaught of their hostile neighbors.

Throughout the centuries, Jews worked very hard to maintain these differences. As a result, their descendants feel very guilty when they give them up. Even when they no longer believe in the viability of traditional customs, even when the tyranny of outmoded practices violates their individual integrity; they often consent to do them. The guilt of repudiating what so many of their ancestors died to preserve is too much for them to bear.

The most effective technique for group survival in an alien environment was social segregation and compulsory inbreeding. The ban on intermarriage followed logically from their overwhelming desire to preserve Jewish identity. People who reproduce together, stay together. As a technique for the maintenance of dispersed minorities, this prohibition is both universal and familiar. The Aryan conquerors of India used it well when they devised the caste system. And the English colonials found it useful in the preservation of Anglo-Saxon identity in the colonial environments.

The Jewish ban on intermarriage dates from the sixth century B.C. When the Jewish aristocracy was taken by the Chaldeans to a Babylonian exile, they found themselves a small minority in a sea of Semitic strangers. Too snobbish to assimilate and too affluent to forego the new luxuries of Babylon for the rural poverty of Judea, they turned to rigid inbreeding as a way of enjoying the best of two worlds.

Under the leadership of fanatic priests, they elevated their new custom into divine law. The Zadokite priests inserted this prohibition into the text of the Torah, which they were writing, giving it a divine aura.[3]

When some of the Babylonian Jews returned to Jerusalem in the fifth century, they brought with them both the Torah and the ban. Their charismatic leader Ezra forced the native Jews to accept the authority of the Torah and to divorce their non-Jewish wives.[4]

In the contemporary world, the prohibition against outmarriage is of crucial importance to Jewish survivalists. With the rapid disappearance of many unique Jewish forms of behavior and with the quick assimilation of Jews to the cultures of Western nations, the only barrier that seems to stand between group identity and the ethnic melting pot is segregated reproduction.

Since group survival for the sake of group survival is no longer publicly respectable, Jewish professionals are driven to find "noble" reasons for this parochialism. Jews and Gentiles are annually inundated by a variety of books which make the old claim that without Jewish exclusiveness, mankind would enjoy less brotherhood, justice, and intellectual greatness. A world without Jews, they claim, would almost be a world not worth having.

Threatened minorities do not survive unconsciously (like the Russians and the Chinese). They often survive only by becoming obsessed with the problem of their own survival. Everything in Jewish life today is seen from the perspective of group survival, from the perspective of group identity. For many Jewish professionals, synagogue social action, experimental services, and the updating of Jewish philosophy are not avenues for individual fulfillment. They are gimmicks for involving Jews in Jewish institutions. Their value is a function of their ability to promote Jewish identity.

Even most liberal rabbis who consent to officiate at mixed marriages are often apologetic about their own activity. Embarrassed by their natural empathy for two individuals who love each other, they feel impelled to justify their action. Maintaining that if they refuse to officiate, the couple will choose to get married in a purely secular or Christian setting; they opt for the lesser of two evils. Intermarriage is bad. But losing a Jew forever is worse.

So great is the fear of the vanishing Jew that the moral worth of individual happiness and personal love is lost in timid and defensive arguments about group survival. Irrational comparisons between the European Holocaust and assimilation crop up in the reasoning of self-proclaimed liberal theologians. How can we complete the work of Hitler, they cry, by allowing the Jew to disappear?[5] As though the physical extermination of individuals were equivalent to the opportunity of individuals to freely choose their marriage partners!

In the midst of all this anxiety and exaggeration, the factual and moral realities remain.

Since Jewish identity is not a belief identity, two Jews marrying each other may be further apart ideologically and morally than a Jew and a Gentile marrying. A truly Orthodox Jew may share his Jewish identity with his humanistic Jewish wife. But they will share little else. The negative critics of Jewish-Gentile intermarriage often complain about the loss of ideological and moral consistency for children, even though the "mixed" couple may share a secular approach to life and values, but they rarely discuss the "intermarriage" problems of two totally incompatible Jews. For traditionalists, a Jewish atheist is better than a Bible-believing Gentile.

Most Jews who intermarry value their Jewish identity. Their choice of a non-Jewish partner is not a rejection of their

Jewishness. It is merely an expression of their power to love people who share their ideas and values, even though their lovers are not Jews. Jewish identity is an important commitment. But it is not their *only* commitment nor their *chief* value. To elevate Jewish identity to a supreme position is to violate the basis of a humanistic ethics. It is to deprive the individual of personal identity and to narrow the exploration for personal dignity.

If the most important Jewish enterprise is the promotion of Jewish identity, then the ban on intermarriage is perfectly rational as a means to that end. If the most significant thing for a Jew to be is to be Jewish, then denouncing the immorality of outmarriage is a logical consequence.

If, on the other hand, the primary goal of life for all Jews is to secure their own happiness and dignity, then the ban on intermarriage is an unethical interference. If the purpose of a group, whether kinship, ethnic, religious, or professional, is to serve the welfare of its individual members, then the refusal of rabbis to place personal love above Jewish identity is a form of moral negligence.

Certainly, it would be wrong to pretend that rabbinic ethics is neutral to these options. As a group-oriented conventional morality, it makes the same demands on the individual that the morality of any insular minority makes. The rabbis of old would have found an individualistic ethic abhorrent and subversive of the divine will. A humanistic morality, which affirms the ultimate value of the individual, has never been a part of any national religion — least of all the rabbinic variety.

A consistent humanist maintains the right of individuals to pursue their own dignity in the way that their personal needs and temperament require, so long as they do not harm the dignity of others. The consistent humanist maintains the right of all Jews to marry whomever they choose and is happy to assist them in exercising this choice. Recognizing the value of personal love and respect to human happiness, the consistent humanist welcomes the fact that two people have discovered these positive experiences in their new relationship. If the value of Jewish identity for humanistic Jews lies in its message of human self-reliance, how can this value be maintained if Jewish identity is used to promote its very opposite?

The children of Jewish parents are Jews whether they want to do anything about their Jewish identity or do not. Since the Jewish connection is a kinship connection — especially in the eyes of the Gentile world — intermarriage does not deny this birthright to the child of a Jewish father or mother. The protests of the Rejectionists and some of the Ambivalents, who claim that a Jewish mother is necessary for Jewish identity, go against the practices of social reality.[6] Just as who is a black is determined not only by blacks but also by the majority whites, so who is a Jew is determined not only by Jews but also by the Gentile world. In the eyes of most Jews and Gentiles, Jewish descent becomes a sufficient reason for conferring Jewish identity. In fact, Jewish fathers, because they give their children Jewish surnames, are more powerful in determining the kinship labels of their descendants than Jewish mothers. If Cohen is not Jewish, he has to explain why.

Secular Gentiles who marry Jews may freely choose a secular Jewish identity for themselves if they are not treated as rejects. Unlike the demands of Rejectionist and Ambivalent Jews who insist on the public disavowal of past belief systems as the price of conversion, the approach of humanistic Jews is to make Jewishness an addition, not a repudiation. Since humanistic Gentiles are already humanistic, the assumption of Jewish identity does not negate what they believe. It merely reenforces it.

Nevertheless, humanistic Jews who do marry fundamentalist Christians have a serious problem. It is the same prob-

lem of incompatibility that they face when they marry fundamentalist Jews.

The Jewish people of the future will be different from the
Jewish people of the past. Except for a small minority, it will
be more open in an open society. Intermarriage will make
Jewish identity less intense. But it will also make it more
widespread and more significant to secular people in a
secular world.

This change is not unwelcome. The rabbinic segregation
that led to bigotry and to the rejection of the Gentile world is
subversive of the values which individual Jews should
cultivate in themselves.

The Jewish identity of the future will depend not only on
the children of Jewish mothers. It will also be a kinship option
for born Jews and for those who choose to marry Jews. Unless we want a Lubavitcher redoubt — where the saving
remnant lives in self-righteous isolation from the Gentile
world — the boundaries of the future between Jew and non-
Jew need to be less formidable and more accommodating.

BECOMING JEWISH

When a Gentile says, "I want to become a Jew," or "I
want to convert to Judaism," how should humanistic Jews
deal with these requests?

More conventional approaches to Judaism — the Rejectionists and the Ambivalents — have developed procedures of
formal admission to the Jewish people. The English word *conversion* is now generally used to describe this acceptance.

The Orthodox and Conservative converters tend to downplay affirmations of belief and to "upplay" non-verbal initiation behaviors like circumcision or ritual dunking. They also

tend to discourage conversion and to emphasize the hard-ships of Jewish identity.

Reformers, on the other hand, place great emphasis on verbal behavior, especially declarations of theological belief in the presence of witnesses. They also encourage conversion. In fact, their American leaders, frightened by the declining Jewish birthrate, have proposed that Reform Jews actively missionize the American Gentile population.

Since most of these conventional procedures are unrelated to a humanistic view of Jewish identity, human-istic Jews have to explore alternatives. These alternatives have to deal with certain realities.

Most potential converts to Judaism do not seek Jewish identity because they have suddenly seen the "light." Most theologies are busy work for clergymen and are of no interest to lay people. The petitioners arrive because they are involved in intermarriage and want to remove a barrier to the labeling of future children. Most conversions throughout his-tory have had very little to do with internal belief. They arise out of the necessity of changing membership from one group to another, either because of marriage or because of govern-ment decree.

Among the potential converts who are not involved in an intermarriage, most are attracted to Jews and to Jewish identity and not to a list of theological statements. They like Jewish people and want to be associated with them. Or they are fascinated by the special character of the Jewish his-torical experience. Oddly enough, it is the intellectual power and secular achievements of the modern Jew that makes Jewish identity attractive to many people.

Jewish identity is a kinship identity. The Jewish people antedate any system of theological belief. Even Orthodoxy recognizes that Jews are normally Jews because they are born of Jewish mothers. Even Gentiles usually identify Jews by checking their parents or their last names. In neither case does anyone assume that theological belief or ritual practice is essential to Jewishness. Like the authors of the Bible who identified the Hebrews as the descendants of Abraham, Isaac, and Jacob, most of the people of the world, including traditional authorities, view the Jewish connection as a kinship reality.

Christian identity (or Muslim identity) is different from Jewish identity. Christians all over the world do not share a bond of kinship and ethnic roots. And if they embrace secularism, they cease to be Christians. While most Christians derive their label through birth and not through choice, they are aware that their inherited religion began as a religion of choice and not as a tribal federation.

The word *conversion* is inappropriate to becoming a Jew because it implies a change in belief. Since we cannot choose to change our beliefs (in the same way that we choose to change our behavior), the cause of the transformation has to be some external compelling force such as "divine grace." *Conversion* is a word that fits the reality of Christianity and Islam, not the reality of Judaism. *Naturalization, affiliation,* or *adoption* are more accurate terms. Changing religions has more to do with changing family relations and cultural aspirations than with experiencing fundamental alterations of belief. Normal, stable people do not experience such quick massive breaks with their past views of life. If they move from religion to religion, they do so for reasons other than theological.

All national and religious communities have initiation ceremonies. The purpose of the ritual is clear. It allows the adoptee to receive what the native-born has already received in the childhood ceremony of naming, circumcision, or baptism: the public recognition of membership by the members of the new community. Joining a group without the consent of the group is an act of insanity. If nobody wants you, you cannot belong. Group adoption is a group affair. The adopted need the adopters. Even where there exists no formal ceremony, the group informally offers its acceptance by allowing the person to participate in the work of the group.

Since the Jewish community is presently divided and has no central authority to determine "naturalization," the decision-making has to be local. If Orthodox Jews do not wish to recognize Reform and Humanistic joiners as Jews, the rejected "can't care less." They are not excommunicants. They have their own Jewish communities, which accept them and give them a sense of belonging.

Although becoming Jewish is not urgent in the way that becoming a Christian is urgent to fundamentalists, many Gentile humanists may find Jewish identity convenient, attractive, or compelling. They may find it convenient because their husband or wife is Jewish. They may find it attractive because Jews, as a group, provide a ready-made community in which secularism and humanism comfortably thrive. They may find it compelling because Jewish history is a compelling testimony to the absurdity of the universe and the necessity for human self-reliance and they wish to identify with that history.

In the face of these realities, Humanistic Jews need to provide certain opportunities to potential adoptees.

They need to explain to the Gentile world the difference between their view of Jewish identity and that of conventional Judaism.

They need to invite Gentile humanists to adopt Jewish identity if these non-Jews want it.

They need to provide them with a training program in Jewish history and Jewish celebration from a humanistic perspective. Most native Humanistic Jews need the same training.

They need to provide an initiation ceremony, a joining ritual for those who want it. Some adoptees will find a formal ceremony either unnecessary or contrived. But many will want some public recognition of their choice. The Bar Mitzvah ceremony is a useful model for the adoption celebration. Just as the native-born confirm their membership in the community in late adolescence or in adulthood, so can new-comers at any age. The ceremony does not magically turn the non-Jew into a Jew. It simply allows the community to celebrate a decision already made.

HUMANISM

Humanistic Jews have two important identities. They are Jews, part of the Jewish people, members of an ancient kinship group, bound together by a social destiny with all other Jews. They are also connected to all other humanists — whatever their kinship attachments and whatever their ethnic origin. For some humanistic Jews, their Jewish identity is the strongest emotional bond. For other humanistic Jews, their intellectual and moral commitment to humanism is more powerful than their tie to Jewishness. Both groups value their Jewish identity — but in differing degrees. Humanistic Judaism has room for both commitments.

Humanistic Jews share a Jewish agenda with other Jews. Holidays, Israel, anti-Semitism, and the study of Jewish history are some of the items on this list of common activity. They also share a humanist agenda with other humanists. Humanist philosophy, ethical education, and the defense of the secular state are some of the items on this second list. Neither excludes the other. They are both necessary.

Gentile humanists, like Jewish humanists, generally have no formal ties to a humanist community. They are either "closet" humanists in established religious organizations or they are so hostile to the religious experiences of their childhood that they refuse to join any group with a formal structure. Some Gentile humanists are Unitarians (even though most Unitarians do not claim to be humanists). Some are members of the Ethical Culture movement established by Felix Adler. Others belong to a variety of small humanist societies or subscribe to publications that espouse humanism. Many are libertarian devotees of Ayn Rand or scientific agnostics or atheistic socialists.

The individualism of humanists and the absence of any well-established historic humanist community that transcends political and religious boundaries have made it difficult for humanists to feel humanistic in the same way that Jews feel Jewish. Ironically, the hostility of religious fundamentalism to secular humanism, especially in America today, has been a catalyst for self-awareness and group solidarity.

The humanist world, by its very nature, has too much variety and freedom to produce either a conformist unity or centralization. But it needs more solidarity than it presently has. Humanistic Jews need to participate in the development of that cooperation. The stronger humanism is, the easier it will be to present Jewish history in a humanistic way.

Gentile humanists have an important role to play in the lives of humanistic Jews. So long as they are committed to the procedures of liberal democracy (Marxists beware!), they are our natural allies.

CHAPTER XIX

Secular Religion

Jewish identity has been tied to religion for more than two thousand years. The rabbinic establishment found the value of Jewishness in the will of Yahveh and in the promise of supernatural help that Yahveh offered.

But a secular and humanistic approach to Jewish identity lacks the theology that most people associate with religion. In fact, it rejects it. What is secular seems clearly opposed to what is religious. Humanistic Judaism is certainly a philosophy of life. It is also secular.

But a secular religion? Is such a thing possible? Or is it a contradiction in terms, as it appears to be?

In one sense, the designation "secular religion" is a dramatic way of conveying the truth that Humanistic Judaism plays the same role in the lives of humanistic Jews that conventional Judaism plays in the lives of its adherents. It provides a world view and a basis for decision making. If we define religion as a philosophy of life, then humanists are religious.[1]

But everybody has a philosophy of life (whether articulated or not). And everybody, by this definition, would be religious. The consequence of this usage is to eliminate the normal distinction between the religious and the secular, the sacred and the profane. If all human belief is religious, then the word *religious* is itself trivial. It is only significant if it stands in contrast to other kinds of human commitment.

The problem with most discussions on religion is that the participants wrongly assume that religion is a set of ideas. They wrongly maintain that religion is either a set of ideas about God and the supernatural or a set of ideas about appropriate human values.[2] They reduce religion to an invisible belief system. On the contrary, religion is a form of behavior, visible and unique. To be religious is *not* to believe certain things. It is to do certain things.

Religious behavior is distinct from moral behavior. The person who helps a neighbor is an ethical person. But that person is not necessarily religious. Even if someone helps a neighbor because they believe that God has commanded them to do so, their action is not a religious action. It could just as easily be performed by a person who does not believe in God. The motivation may be theological. But the activity is neutral. Religious people may be nice to their neighbors. But being nice to their neighbors does not identify them as being religious.[3]

However, if people pray continually, we assume that they are religious. Even if they pray because they are afraid of adverse public opinion and not because they believe in God, their activity is still religious. Most people who behave in this religious way are unaware of the theological reasons which clergymen invent to justify this behavior. They pray out of childhood conditioning where prayer is rewarded by social approval and theology is an afterthought. People pray first. Then they find it socially approved. Then they discover some philosophic reason for continuing to pray.

Religious activity, like moral activity, may have a variety of motivations. But it does not cease to be religious because the practitioner does it for a "non-respectable" reason. A world of closet atheists in which citizens prayed out of an irrational fear of ancestral rejection would, for all practical purposes, still be a religious world.

There are three kinds of activities that are uniquely religious. One is worship. Another is prayer. And the third is resignation.

Worship is the most common form of religious activity. It is an act of appeasement, visibly similar to the actions which higher animals perform to reduce the anger of a more powerful adversary. Worshipers bow their heads, prostrate themselves, offer verbal flattery, open their hands in gestures of non-aggression, adopt obsequious poses, and provide sacrificial gifts. Worship is appropriate in a situation where the appeaser feels overwhelmed by the presence of a dangerous and irresistible power. Without the "fear of God," there is no worship response.[4]

Worship is unmistakably religious. Even when it is directed to visible kings or dictators, it is described as a religious act. Whenever a person, real or imagined, stimulates this act of appeasement, they assume the status of a sacred being. To be sacred is to be dangerous and, therefore, taboo.

The worship of the gods most likely derives from the worship of the dead — dead ancestors who have been elevated to immortality. The descendants and subjects of the dead leader continue to perform the same act of appeasement even when the visible presence of the ruler no longer exists. A symbol is substituted for the former living stimulus. It may be a statue, a book, or an abstract design. The symbol, by association, arouses the same fear and reverence as the human reality it replaced.

Worship, today, is mainly confined to invisible "supernatural" beings. Acts of appeasement are performed with nobody visibly present. The imagination of the worshiper has to complete the scene. From the outsider's point of view, the behavior seems bizarre, since nobody appears to be around provoking the ritual.

Worship behavior is a pessimistic appeasement ritual. It

lacks the confidence that the tables may be turned, the roles reversed, with the appeaser becoming the "appeasee." Its purpose is to hold the terrible force at bay, to keep it from advancing, not to master it.

Behavior that seeks to master dangerous powers is the stuff of magic. Magic lacks reverence. Its purpose is manipulative, a conscious attempt to use natural or supernatural power to serve human needs. The mood of magic is the same as the mood of science, a shameless desire to control the environment. Evil spirits are to the magician what bacteria are to the physician. Magic is different from science because it is confined to ritual and traditional behavior and lacks testing and experimentation. It is the ritual side of magic, as much as its concern with supernatural beings, that make it seem just like religion.

The second uniquely religious act is prayer. Objectively, prayer is the use of words to effect change. Prayer differs from conversation in that there is no visible listener to the words that are uttered. The person who prays may rationalize the act by affirming that there is an invisible god who hears their words and that their behavior is really part of a one-sided conversation. But reality features only the individuals and their words.

Prayer is distinct from worship although it may accompany it. It derives from a childhood fantasy and a childhood success. Helpless infants cry out for help and generally receive it. The act of saying "mama" or "papa" produces immediate "magical" results. When the infant grows up and becomes an adult, the memory of the early success remains. The adult irrationally assumes that the utterance of certain words will produce the desired change without any other intervening effort. Historically speaking, old and venerable verbal formulas that have been tested over the centuries are preferable to new and spontaneous prayers, the effectiveness of which is doubtful.

Because theology and God are not intrinsic to prayer, atheists often pray in times of crisis. This "slip" is not the result of a sudden rediscovery of the reality of God. It is the result of an infant conditioning that makes people use words as a way of changing their environment when all other techniques have been exhausted.

Prayer differs from worship because it started out as magic. It started out with more manipulation and less reverence, with a firm belief in the power of words to alter the environment. As verbal magic, it was bolder and better humored. When it was integrated into appeasement behavior, it became less confident, shifting from commanding to pleading. Prayer is now a begging behavior, quite distinct from the verbal magic that spawned it.

The third uniquely religious activity is resignation. Resignation is apathy. It is the bodily posture and mood that expresses futility. Resignation is distinct from despair. Despair is extreme fear and often involves hysterical attempts to alter an unpleasant situation. Apathy, on the other hand, is an extreme calm in the face of the inevitable.

Religious institutions have always provided reasons for resignation. It may be rationalized as *islam*, submission to the will of Allah — or *faith*, trust in the goodness of God in the presence of immutable disaster — or *kismet*, acceptance of a script already written by the stars. But, regardless of rationalization, the human action remains the same.

The apathy of resignation is distinct from the apathy of paralyzing fear. The first is a surrender behavior, one step beyond appeasement. The second is a survival behavior, an attempt to "freeze" the body into a motionless state so that the terrorizer will not notice the terrified.

It is by no mere coincidence that we regard pious people as the most accepting of what happens to them. Resignation is an obvious sign of religiosity. People who display this behavior, regardless of their stated theological beliefs, are viewed as religious. Even the angry Hebrew prophets, like Jeremiah, counseled resignation, stating that the punishments of Yahveh were just, inevitable, and unchangeable.

All three behaviors — worship, prayer, and resignation — share a common emotional theme, a sense of helplessness in the face of overwhelming power. God or Destiny will do what he will do, and there is very little that humans can do to stop it. As the gods grew more powerful and even omnipotent in the eyes of their devotees, magic became less effective and religion became more necessary. People are most religious when they feel most helpless.

Of these three forms of uniquely religious behavior, only *one* is appropriate to humanists and humanistic Jews.

Worship is inappropriate. An act of extreme appeasement is both dangerous and irrational. It is dangerous to treat any power as sacred and taboo, beyond human challenge and investigation. It is also irrational to treat any natural power as a personal being who requires obsequious honor and devotion. There are many forces in nature that are frightening and traumatizing. But they cannot be influenced by acts of appeasement.

Prayer is also inappropriate. The use of words in a magical way can be both diverting and wasteful. It can divert people in trouble from seeking realistic help. And it can waste time and energy that could be more constructively employed to conquer social and natural disasters. Occasional lapses into prayer are inevitable. But to build an institution around its regular recitation is an absurdity.

Resignation is the only religious behavior that *is* appropriate. A rational person knows that the universe is too big and too complex for ambitious humans to tame it to their needs. Rational people know that there are certain events that they can neither change nor avoid. Gravity will behave as it pleases. And so will the stars.

While it is theoretically possible for us to eliminate death through science, it is highly unlikely that, in the foreseeable future, this will be achieved. For all practical purposes, death is a persistent reality. It can be postponed but never avoided. Resignation in the face of one's inevitable death is both rational and desirable. To be angry about death in old age is a wasteful and unsuitable emotion. No matter how much anxiety is devoted to the fact, the fact remains.

Each of us is born with certain talents and certain limitations that the environment cannot correct. To set our ambitions beyond our abilities is to court eternal frustration. To tailor our desires to what we can become under the best of conditions is to taste success. Bitterness and despair over our unavoidable deficiencies is an exhausting exercise in useless self-pity. Resignation is more appropriate.

All of us make mistakes every day of our lives. Many of them cannot be corrected. All of us endure painful surprises. Many of them cannot be changed. As we all know, the past is not reversible. Its events are beyond our control and direction.

Many people devote their lives to the irrational effort of altering the past. They spend endless hours in expressing regret, in offering apologies, in asking forgiveness, in refusing responsibility, and in fantasizing about how it might have been different. All their obsessions are futile. Simple resignation would be much more sensible.

Sometimes resignation "to the unavoidable" is just plain common sense. And sometimes it is an aesthetic pleasure. If there is any kind of humanistic "mysticism," it is the experience of our connection with all other living things and with the universe as a whole. In the struggle for survival, nature becomes our adversary and keeps us on the alert. But in the act of philosophic contemplation, the world becomes an extension of our own being and fills us with a temporary calm. We feel our smallness before the overwhelming unconscious forces that control our lives.

Yet too much resignation is dangerous. Most of the events in the human environment are correctible and changeable. The appropriate response to these situations is action, not passivity. When a society, like the traditional Muslim world, becomes too religious, it becomes too apathetic. In such a milieu, social progress becomes impossible.

Humanists and humanistic Jews are a little bit religious, but never very religious. Avoiding worship and prayer, they sometimes indulge resignation when resignation is rational. Before death, genetic limitation, and the past, they are stoic and accepting. They do not waste their energies in futile activity.

But — in the face of all that they can change — humanistic Jews prefer morality to religion. They resist resignation. They assume responsibility for improving their lives and the lives of others. Defiance is their mood.

A secular religion is less religious than other religions. It accepts resignation as an appropriate human response to the human condition only when human effort is pointless. The rest of the time, it encourages people to discover their own power and to resist the excuse of helplessness.

Humanistic Judaism is a secular religion.

CHAPTER XX

Humanistic Judaism

Consistency is not "the hobgoblin of little minds." It is the sign of integrity and the friend of personal dignity. Ambivalence is charming when we are detached observers of the universe. It is less than charming when it persuades us to postpone decisions that need to be made. And it is graceless when it becomes the foundation of a philosophy of life.

Ambivalent feelings are unavoidable. Without absolute certainty, it is only sensible to find value on both sides of an issue. But ambivalent behavior is something different. It seeks to pursue two incompatible goals simultaneously. Obedience to God and personal autonomy become a single project. Religious tradition and science find reconciliation. Individual freedom and tribal segregation go hand in hand.

Humanistic Jews are tired of being timid. They are tired of mergers that do not work. They are fed up with using the theological language of their enemies and never saying clearly what they think and feel. They find no virtue in ambivalence.

There is a need in the Jewish world to take the Secular Revolution seriously and to provide a clear alternative to rabbinic Judaism. The Ambivalents do neither tradition nor humanism well because they are trying to do both.

Humanistic Jews want to bring their beliefs and their behavior together and to find their integrity. They are eager to affirm:

That they are disciples of the Secular Revolution.

That the Secular Revolution was good for the Jews.

That reason is the best method for the discovery of truth.

That morality derives from human needs and is the defense of human dignity.

That the universe is indifferent to the desires and aspirations of human beings.

That people must ultimately rely on people.

That Jewish history is a testimony to the absence of God and the necessity of human self-esteem.

That Jewish identity is valuable because it connects them to that history.

That Jewish personality flows from that history — and not from official texts that seek to describe it.

That Jewish identity serves individual dignity — and not the reverse.

That the Jewish people is an international family that has its center in Israel and its roots in the Diaspora.

That the humanistic Gentile has a positive role to play in the life of the Jewish people.

Humanistic Jews want to translate these affirmations and commitments into an effective life style — for themselves and for those who share their convictions. They need a community of believers to work with and to share with in this pioneering venture. They also need a cadre of trained leaders and spokespeople to provide scholarship and guidance along the way.

Having read this book you may have discovered that you are a Humanistic Jew. If so, now is the time to test your integrity.

AFTERWORD

In North America, Humanistic Judaism, as a movement, is represented by the Society for Humanistic Judaism, a world-wide organization of individuals, groups, and congregations. The Society publishes the quarterly journal *Humanistic Judaism*, commissions educational materials, and stimulates the growth of new groups and congregations. It works closely with its sister organization in Israel, the Israel Association for Secular Humanistic Judaism, the Institute for Secular Humanistic Judaism, and the Association of Humanistic Rabbis.

For information about Humanistic Judaism, contact:

The Society for Humanistic Judaism
28611 West Twelve Mile Road
Farmington Hills, Michigan 48018
(313) 478-7610

Notes

CHAPTER II

The Yahveh Story

1. Christianity became the official religion of the Roman Empire and included all the nations (with the exception of the Jews) who were part of that empire. Latins, Greeks, Syrians, Egyptians, and Kelts shared this new religion. Therefore, the ethnic base of Christianity was not national — confined to one nation, nor was it universal — embracing all nations. It was *imperial* — including a group of nations which were culturally related and politically united.

2. After the Jews lost their political independence in 586 B.C. and Hebrew was replaced by Aramaic as the language of the Jews, the preservation of Jewish identity was threatened. The theology of the Torah was perfected at that time by the Levitical priests and provided a reason for Jews to remain Jewish.

3. Only Noah and his family survived the Flood.

4. Genesis 13: 14-17. *"Yahveh said to Abram: Lift up your eyes and look from the place where you are northward and southward and eastward and westward. For all the land which you see I will give to you and to your descendants forever. I will make your descendants as the dust of the earth. So that if you can count the dust of the earth, your descendants also can be counted. Arise, walk through the length and the breadth of the land, for I will give it to you."*

5. Deuteronomy 12: 5-6. *"But you shall seek the place which Yahveh your God will choose out of all your tribes to put his name and make his habitation there. Thither you shall go and thither you shall bring your burnt offerings and your sacrifices."*

6. Daniel 12: 1-3. *"At that time shall arise Michael, the great prince who has charge of your people. And there shall be a time of trouble, such as never has been since there was a nation till that time. But, at that time, your people shall be delivered, every one whose name shall be found written in the book. And many of those who sleep in the dust of the earth shall awake, some to everlasting life and some to shame and everlasting contempt. And those who are wise shall shine like the brightness of the firmament; and those who turn many to righteousness, like the stars forever and ever."*

7. Rabbi Elazar Hakappar, *Sayings of the Fathers* 4:22. *"They that are born are destined to die; and the dead to be brought to life again; and the living to be judged, to know, to make known, and to be made conscious that He is God, He the Maker, He the Creator, He the Discerner, He the Judge, He the Witness, He the Complainant. He it is that will in future judge...Know also that everything is according to the reckoning; and let not your imagination give you hope that the grave will be a place of refuge for you."*

8. Sanhedrin 10:1. *"All Israelites have a share in the world to come...And these are they that have no share in the world to come: he that says that there is no resurrection of the dead prescribed in the Law, and he that says that the Law is not from Heaven, and an Epicurean."*

9. Siddur *(Shemoneh Esreh)*. *"Return in mercy to your city Jerusalem and dwell in it as you have promised. Rebuild it soon in our days as an everlasting structure and speedily establish in it the throne of David. Speedily cause the offspring of your servant David to flourish and let his glory be exalted by your help, for we hope for your deliverance all day."*

10. *Sayings of the Fathers* 1:1. *"Moses received the Torah on Sinai and handed it down to Joshua, Joshua to the elders, the elders to the prophets; and the prophets handed it down to the Men of the Great Assembly. They said three things: Be deliberate in judgment, raise up many disciples and make a fence around the Torah."*

Baba Metzia 59a. *"If one profane sacred things and despise the holy days, and put his fellow man to shame publicly and make void the covenant of Abraham our father, and cause the Torah to bear a meaning other than in accordance with traditional law, then, even though knowledge of the Torah and good deeds are his, he has no share in the world to come."*

Yehuda Halevi, *Sefer Ha-Kuzari*, 11th Century. *"For it is impossible to come close to God save by His directions; and it is impossible to know His commandments save through the tradition that merits credence."*

11. Isaiah 56: 6-7. *"The aliens that join themselves to Yahveh, to serve Him and to love the name of Yahveh...every man that keeps from profaning the*

Sabbath and holds fast by my covenant. . .even them will I (Yahveh) bring to
my holy mountain and make them joyful in my house of prayer."

12. Medieval *gezera* (rabbinic decree). *"Above all, do not question the*
justice of the Holy One, Blessed be He, and Blessed be His name. . .Happy
shall we be if we do His will and happy everyone who is slain and
slaughtered and dies for the sanctification of His name. Such a one is
destined for the World to Come and shall dwell in the same regions as those
righteous men, Rabbi Akiba and his companions, the pillars of the world,
who were slain for the sake of His name."

CHAPTER III

The Secular Revolution

1. Mordecai Kaplan, *Judaism as a Civilization*, 1934. *"Judaism is a*
problem mainly to those who find that they cannot be spiritually whole and
happy if they repudiate their Jewish heritage, and who, at the same time,
are fairly convinced that to expect that heritage to function in the manner in
which it did in the past is neither desirable nor practicable. The Jews who
represent the most vital and promising element in Jewry today are those to
whom Judaism is a problem."

CHAPTER IV

Faith and Reason

1. Epicurus (341-270 B.C.), *Principal Doctrines 12*. *"A man cannot*
dispel his fear about the most important matters if he does not know what is
the nature of the universe but suspects the truth of some mythical story. So
that without natural science it is not possible to attain our pleasures
unalloyed."

2. Bertrand Russell, *Faith of a Rationalist*, 1947. *"Veracity. . .consists*
broadly in believing according to evidence and not because a belief is
comfortable or a source of pleasure. In the absence of veracity, kindly feeling
will often be defeated by self-deception."

3. John Dewey, *The Quest for Certainty*, 1929. *"Science is not*
constituted by any particular body of subject-matter. It is constituted by a
method of changing beliefs by means of tested inquiry as well as of arriving
at them. It is its glory, not its condemnation, that its subject matter develops
as the method is improved. There is no special subject matter of belief that is

sacrosanct. The identification of science with a particular set of beliefs and ideas is itself a holdover of ancient and still current dogmatic habits of thought which are opposed to science in its actuality and which science is undermining."

4. Walter Kaufman, *Critique of Religion and Philosophy*, 1958. *"When I say that I know that a proposition is true, I say that I think that it is true; that, in fact, it is true; and that there is evidence sufficient to compel the assent of every reasonable person...Belief, in the narrow sense in which it is contrasted with knowledge, is distinguished by the lack of evidence sufficient to compel the assent of every reasonable person."*

5. See Marilyn Ferguson, *The Aquarian Conspiracy*, 1980.

6. Friedrich Nietzsche, *Beyond Good and Evil*, 1886. *"Man, in his highest and most noble capacities, is wholly nature and embodies its uncanny dual character. Those of his abilities which are awesome and considered inhuman are perhaps the fertile soil out of which alone all humanity can grow."*

"The man who would not belong in the mass needs only to cease being comfortable with himself. He should follow his conscience which shouts at him: Be yourself. You are not really all that which you do, think and desire now."

7. Bertrand Russell, *Our Knowledge of the External World*, 1929. *"But, in fact, the opposition of instinct and reason is mainly illusory. Instinct, intuition or insight is what first leads to the beliefs which subsequent reason confirms or confutes. But the confirmation, where it is possible, consists, in the last analysis, of agreement with other beliefs no less instinctive. Reason is a harmonizing controlling force rather than a creative one. Even in the most purely logical realms, it is insight that first arrives at what is new."*

8. Moses Maimonides, *Guide to the Perplexed* 1:57, 12th Century. *"[God is] existing but not in existence, living but not in life, knowing but not in knowledge, powerful but not with power, wise but not in wisdom...one, but not in unity..."*

9. Immanuel Kant, *Critique of Pure Reason, Transcendental Logic*, 1781. *"Now I maintain that all attempts of reason to establish a theology by the aid of speculation alone are fruitless, that the principles of reason as applied to nature do not conduct us to any theological truths — and, consequently, that a rational theology can have no existence..."*

10. C.E. Joad, *The Present and Future of Religion*, 1930. *"To say that there is a God is not to say anything more than that we need to think that there is, and the need is in no sense a guarantee of the existence of that which satisfies it. Thus the great religions of the world are not theology, but psychology; witnesses...to the inventive faculty of man."*

11. Anthony Flew, "Theology and Falsification," *New Essays in Philosophical Theology*, 1955. *"Once upon a time two explorers came upon a clearing in the jungle. In the clearing were growing many flowers and many weeds. One explorer says, 'Some gardener must tend this plot.' The other disagrees, 'There is no gardener.' So they pitch their tents and set a watch. No gardener is ever seen. But perhaps he is an invisible gardener. So they set up a barbed wire fence. They electrify it. They patrol with bloodhounds. But no shrieks ever suggest that some intruder has received a shock. No movement of the wire ever betrays an invisible climber. The bloodhounds never give cry. Yet still the Believer is not convinced. 'But there is a gardener, invisible, intangible, insensitive to electric shocks, a gardener who has no scent and makes no sound, a gardener who comes secretly to look after the garden he loves.' At last the Skeptic despairs. 'But what remains of your original assertion? Just how does what you call an invisible intangible eternally elusive gardener differ from an imaginary gardener or even no gardener at all?'"*

12. Bertrand Russell, *Why I Am Not a Christian*, 1957. *"I may say that when I was a young man and was debating these questions very seriously in my mind, I for a long time accepted the argument of the First Cause, until one day, at the age of eighteen, I read John Stuart Mill's Autobiography, and there I found this sentence: 'My father taught me that the question, Who made me? cannot be answered, since it immediately suggests the further question, Who made God?' That very simple sentence showed me, as I still think, the fallacy in the argument of the First Cause. If everything must have a cause, then God must have a cause. If there can be anything without a cause, it may just as well be the world as God, so that there cannot be any validity in that argument. It is exactly of the same nature as the Hindu's view, that the world rested upon an elephant and the elephant rested upon a tortoise; and when they said, 'How about the tortoise?' the Indian said, 'Suppose we change the subject.' The argument is really no better than that. There is no reason why the world could not have come into being without a cause; nor, on the other hand, is there any reason why it should not have always existed. There is no reason to suppose that the world had a beginning at all. The idea that things must have a beginning is really due to the poverty of our imagination."*

CHAPTER V

Ethics and Dignity

1. Walter Lippmann, *A Preface to Morals*, 1929. *"When men can no longer be theists they must, if they are civilized, become humanists. They must live by the premise that whatever is righteous is inherently desirable, because experience will demonstrate its desirability. They must live, therefore, in the belief that the duty of man is not to make his will to conform to the will of God, but to the surest knowledge of the conditions of human happiness."*

"But the teachers of humanism have no credentials. Their teaching is not certified. They have to prove their case by the test of mundane experience. They speak with no authority which can be scrutinized once and for all, and then forever accepted. They cannot command...They can only inquire, infer, and persuade. They have only human insight to guide them and those to whom they speak must in the end themselves accept the full responsibility for the consequences of any advice they choose to accept."

John Dewey, *A Quest for Certainty*, 1929. *"A moral law, like a law in physics, is not something to swear by and stick to at all hazards. It is a formula of the way to respond when specified conditions present themselves. Its soundness and pertinence are tested by what happens when it is acted upon. Its claim or authority rests finally upon the imperativeness of the situation that has to be dealt with, not upon its own intrinsic nature."*

2. Deuteronomy 5: 32-33. *"You shall be careful to do as Yahveh your God has commanded you; do not turn from it to the right or to the left. You must conform to all Yahveh your God commands you, if you would live and prosper and remain long in the land you are to occupy."*

3. Jacob Bronowski, *Science and Human Values*, 1953. *"A rational and coherent system of ethics must grow out of the exploration of the relations between man and society. It will not be a permanent system; it will not teach us what ought to be forever, any more than science teaches us what is forever. Both science and ethics are activities in which we explore relations which, though permanent in the larger sense, are also in constant evolution. This is the nature of the relations of man and society, that they must rest on what is permanently human and yet even this slowly changes and evolves. It is not man and society as they are now that we study, but all the potential which they carry within them by virtue of being human. The studies of a new rationalism are the potential of man in society, and society in man: most deeply, the fulfillment of man."*

4. Sigmund Freud. *Civilization and Its Discontents*, 1930. *"The urge for freedom, therefore, is directed against particular forms and demands of*

civilization or against civilization altogether. It does not seem as though any influence could induce a man to change his nature into that of termites. No doubt he will always defend his claim to individual liberty against the will of the group. A good part of the struggles of mankind center around the single task of finding an expedient accommodation — one, that is, that will bring happiness — between this claim of the individual and the cultural claims of the group; and one of the problems that touches the fate of humanity is whether such an accommodation can be reached by means of some particular form of civilization or whether this conflict is irreconcilable."

Sigmund Freud, *A General Introduction to Psychoanalysis,* 1935. *"We believe that civilization has been built up, under the pressure of the struggle for existence, by sacrifices in gratification of the primitive impulses, and that it is to a great extent forever being re-created, as each individual, successively joining the community, repeats the sacrifice of his instinctive pleasures for the common good. The sexual are amongst the most important of the instinctive forces thus utilized. They are in this way sublimated, that is to say, their energy is turned aside from its sexual goal and diverted towards other ends, no longer sexual and socially more valuable."*

5. Ayn Rand, *The Virtue of Being Selfish,* 1964. *"The egoist in the absolute sense, is not the man who sacrifices others. He is the man who stands above the need of using others in any manner. He does not function through them. He is not concerned with them in any primary matter. Not in his aim, not in his motive, not in his thinking, not in his desires, not in the source of his energy. He does not exist for any other man — and he asks no other man to exist for him. This is the only form of brotherhood and mutual respect possible between men."*

6. John Stuart Mill, *Utilitarianism,* 1863. *"Questions of ultimate ends are not amenable to direct proof. Whatever can be proved to be good must be so by being shown to be a means to something admitted to be good without proof...The art of music is good, for the reason among others, that it produces pleasure; but what proof is it possible to give that pleasure is good?"*

"The creed which accepts as the foundation of morals, Utility, or the Greatest Happiness Principle, holds that actions are right in proportion as they tend to promote happiness, wrong as they tend to produce the reverse of happiness. By happiness is intended pleasure and the absence of pain; by unhappiness, pain and the privation of pleasure."

7. Albert Camus, *The Rebel,* 1956. *"The aim of life can only be to increase the sum of freedom and responsibility to be found in every man and in the world. It cannot, under any circumstances, be to reduce or suppress that freedom, even temporarily."*

8. Konrad Lorenz, *On Aggression,* 1966. *"Undoubtedly the personal bond developed at that phase of evolution when, in aggressive animals, the cooperation of two or more individuals was necessary for a species-preserving purpose, usually brood tending. Doubtless the personal bond, love, arose in many cases from intra-specific aggression by way of ritualization of a redirected attack or threatening...This intra-specific aggression can certainly exist without its counterpart love, but conversely there is no love without aggression...A personal bond is found only in animals with highly developed intra-specific aggression. In fact, this bond is the firmer the more aggressive the particular animal is."*

9. Albert Camus, *The Rebel,* 1956. *"Rebellion is born of the spectacle of irrationality confronted with an unjust and incomprehensible condition. But its blind impulse is to demand order in the midst of chaos, and unity in the very heart of the ephemeral. It protests, it demands, it insists that the outrage be brought to an end, and that what has up to now been built upon shifting sands should henceforth be founded on rock. Man is the only creature who refuses to be what he is."*

Bertrand Russell, *A Free Man's Worship,* 1903. *"We want to stand upon our own feet and look fair and square at the world — its good facts, its bad facts, its beauties and its ugliness; see the world as it is and not be afraid of it. Conquer the world by intelligence and not merely by being slavishly subdued by the terror that comes from it...We ought to stand up and look the world frankly in the face. We ought to make the best we can of the world. A good world needs...a fearless outlook and a free intelligence. It needs hope for the future, not looking back all the time toward a past that is dead."*

10. Robert Ingersoll, *The Works of Ingersoll,* 1909. *"I feel as though I could exist without God just as well as he could exist without me. And I also feel that if there must be an orthodox God in Heaven, I am in favor of electing him ourselves."*

"We are not endeavoring to chain the future, but to free the present. We are not forging fetters for our children, but we are breaking those our fathers made for us. We are the advocates of inquiry, of investigation and thought...Philosophy has not the egotism of faith. While superstition builds walls and creates obstructions, science opens all the highways of thought. We do not pretend to have circumnavigated everything and to have solved all difficulties, but we do believe that it is better to love men than to fear gods; that it is grander and nobler to think and investigate for yourself than to repeat a creed. We are satisfied that there can be but little liberty on earth while men worship a tyrant in heaven."

Thomas Huxley, *Collected Essays,* 1898. *"The practice of that which is ethically best — what we call goodness or virtue — involves a course of conduct which, in all respects, is opposed to that which leads to success in the cosmic struggle for existence. In place of ruthless self-assertions, it demands self-restraint. In place of thrusting aside or treading down all competitors, it requires that the individual shall not merely respect but shall help his fellows...Let us understand, once for all, that the ethical progress of society depends not on imitating the cosmic process, still less in running away from it, but in combating it."*

11. Walter Lippmann, *A Preface to Morals*, 1929. *"When men do not outgrow their childish desires, they seek to repress them. The ascetic discipline, if it is successful, is a form of education."*

12. Erich Fromm, *The Art of Loving*, 1951. *"Giving is more joyous than receiving, not because it is a deprivation, but because, in the act of giving, lies the expression of my aliveness."*

13. Bruno Bettelheim. *"I have no use for saints. They are impossible people; they destroy everything around them. The sooner they go to heaven the better, because that is where they belong."*

14. John Stuart Mill, *On Liberty*, 1859. *"The only part of the conduct of anyone for which he (the individual) is amenable to society is that which concerns others. In the part which merely concerns himself, his independence is, of right, absolute. Over himself, over his own body and mind, the individual is sovereign."*

15. Sigmund Freud, *The Future of an Illusion*, 1927. *"It seems not to be true that there is a power in the universe which watches over the well-being of every individual with parental care and brings all his concerns to a happy ending. On the contrary, the destinies of man are incompatible with a universal principle of benevolence or with — what is to some degree contradictory — a universal principle of justice. Earthquakes, floods and fires do not differentiate between the good and devout man and the sinner and unbeliever. And, even if we leave inanimate nature out of the account and consider the destinies of individual men in so far as they depend on their relations with others of their own kind, it is by no means the rule that virtue is rewarded and wickedness punished, but it happens often enough that the violent, the crafty and the unprincipled seize the desirable goods of the earth for themselves, while the pious go empty away. Dark, unfeeling and unloving powers determine human destiny."*

CHAPTER VI

The Rejectionists

1. French National Assembly, *Declaration of Human Rights*, August, 1789. *"Men are born equal and remain free and with equal rights. All citizens are equal before the law. No one may be molested for his opinions, not even his religious views."*

2. The final impetus to the formation of *Agudat Yisrael* was given when the Tenth Zionist Congress decided to include cultural activities in its program, thereby recognizing a secular Jewish culture co-existent with the religious. Some members of the *Mizrachi* (Religious Zionist) party left the Zionist movement and joined the founders of *Agudat Yisrael* in an assembly held in May, 1912, at Kattowitz in Upper Silesia.

CHAPTER VII

The Ambivalents

1. The Reconstructionists do not officially endorse Halakhic reasoning. But they resurrect much of its behavior pattern under the guise of folk-religion. Both as devotees of the Torah system and as the most radical of the Ambivalents, they have difficulty developing a consistent approach to Halakha. While they do not like many Halakhic conclusions, they are reluctant to repudiate the Halakha, lest they be indistinguishable from Reform.

2. It is difficult to find any important Conservative ideologue who is ardently supernaturalist. Few Conservative rabbis would survive in their pulpits if they sought to motivate their congregations to be Jewish through frequent sermons on the after-life, the resurrection of the dead, and faith healing. However, it would be very important for them to demonstrate that female liberation and the "essence" of the Halakha are compatible.

3. Most of the establishment congregations in Western Europe, especially England and France, are Modern Orthodox. In North America, the Jewish Theological Seminary originally served as the center of this approach. But with the coming of Solomon Schecter and mixed seating, the Seminary drifted into official Conservatism. The seminaries of the Yeshiva University in New York and the Hebrew Theological College in Chicago replaced it as the place to train religious leaders for Modern Orthodox congregations. In recent years, the word *Traditional* has become fashionable as a designation for this commitment. The line between Modern Orthodoxy and official Conservatism is fuzzy, with many Modern Orthodox congregations and rabbis accepting mixed seating and moving into official Conservatism. Ironically, at the same time, the facilities of the training institutions are becoming more Rejectionist.

4. Zacharias Frankel. *Proceedings*, Rabbinical Conference, Frankfort, Germany, 1845. "*The reform of Judaism, furthermore, is not a reform of faith but of practices demanded by law. These still live within the people and*

exercise their power. It is not our task to weaken this influence but rather to strengthen it as much as possible. We need pay no attention to those individual few who do not practice the customs. We are not a party, but ours is the task to care for the needs of the whole people. We must maintain their true sanctuary and prevent any schism in Israel."

Solomon Schecter, *Studies in Judaism,* 1908. *"Another consequence of this conception of Tradition is that it is neither Scripture nor primitive Judaism but general custom which forms the real rule of practice. Holy Writ, as well as history, Zunz tells us, teaches that the law of Moses was never fully and absolutely put in practice. Liberty was always given to the great teachers of every generation to make modifications and innovations in harmony with the spirit of existing institutions. Hence a return to Mosaism would be illegal, pernicious and indeed impossible. The norm, as well as the sanction of Judaism, is the practice actually in vogue."*

5. There is a new vogue in Ambivalent circles for women to dress up in the costume of Traditional males. Donning the *kipa* and the *tallit,* as well as the *tefillin,* they wish to demonstrate that they are entitled to all the privileges of traditional men. The procedure is ironic. The women display their liberation by using the very symbols of the old male supremacy and their own historic subjection. The prayer system attached to these symbols includes such marvelous theological goodies as *"Praised are You, Yahveh our God, . . . who has not made me a woman."*

6. John Dewey, *A Common Faith,* 1934. *"Suppose for the moment that the word God means the ideal ends that at a given time and place one acknowledges as having authority over his volition and emotion, the values to which one is supremely devoted, as far as these ends, through imagination, take on unity. If we make this supposition, the issue will stand out clearly in contrast with the doctrine of religions that God designates some kind of Being having prior and therefore non-ideal existence."*

7. Emile Durkheim, *The Elementary Forms of Religious Life,* 1912. *"Thus there is something eternal in religion which is destined to survive all the particular symbols in which religious thought has successively enveloped itself. There can be no society which does not feel the need of upholding and reaffirming at regular intervals the collective sentimentality and the collective ideas which make its unity and its personality. Now this moral remaking cannot be achieved except by the means of reunions, assemblies and meetings where the individuals, being closely united to one another, reaffirm in common their common sentiments. Hence come ceremonies which do not differ from regular religions, either in their object, the results which they produce, or the processes employed to attain these results. What*

*essential difference is there between an assembly of Christians celebrating
the principal dates of the life of Christ, or of Jews remembering the exodus
from Egypt or the promulgation of the Decalogue, and a reunion of citizens
commemorating the promulgation of a new moral or legal system or some
great event in the national life?"*

8. Mordecai Kaplan, *Judaism as Civilization*, 1934. *"A religion is not a
philosophical doctrine originating in the mind of an individual and
communicated by him to his fellows. It is a product of a people's life, the soul
of its civilization. The essence of a religion is the effort to discover what
makes life worthwhile, and to bring life into conformity with those laws on
which the achievement of a worthwhile life depends. A religion is thus a
social institution, a product of man's social life, of his efforts to achieve his
salvation through whatever tribe, nation, people or church to which he
belongs.*

    *"Different religions result from the fact that every civilization iden-
tifies the more important elements of its life as* sancta, *i.e., as media
through which its people can achieve salvation or self-fulfillment...In
Jewish religion such* sancta *are, among others, the Torah, Eretz Israel, the
synagogue, Sabbaths and holy days, the Hebrew language, Moses and the
Patriarchs.*

    *"Thus arise formulas of tabu, religious beliefs, ethical standards and
national ideals which give coherence and continuity to a civilization. These
constitute what may be termed 'folk ideology,' insofar as they are ideas
which are not only subscribed to by the entire folk, but refer to the interests
and the welfare of the entire folk. These ideas express in articulate form why
certain places, objects, persons, events, laws, customs, are important. The
adjective in folk ideology that corresponds to 'important' is 'sacred.' The
attitudes that anything important or sacred evokes are awe, reverence, fear,
love, and devotion."*

9. *Pittsburgh Platform*, 1885. The *Pittsburgh Platform* was the unofficial
manifesto of the American Reform Movement until 1937.

    *"The modern era heralds the approach of Israel's great Messianic hope
for the establishment of the kingdom of truth, justice and peace among all
men. We consider ourselves no longer a nation, but a religious community,
and therefore expect neither a return to Palestine, nor the restoration of a
sacrificial worship under the sons of Aaron, or of any of the laws concerning
the Jewish state."*

10. Samuel Holdheim, *The Ceremonial Law in the Messianic Era*, 1845.
Samuel Holdheim (1806-1860) was the principal exponent of radical reform
in Germany.

"It is an unpardonable weakness. Reform must avoid as much as possible to press the banner of progress into the rigid hands of the Talmud. The time has to come when one feels strong enough vis-a-vis the Talmud to oppose it, in the knowledge of having gone far beyond it. One must not with every forward step drag along the heavy tomes, and, without even opening them, wait for some innocent remark, therewith to prove the foundations of progress. Incidentally, the Talmud has found its own nemesis. For exactly what the Talmud once did with the Bible, the rabbis of today now do with it."

11. S.L. Steinheim, *Vom Bleibenden und Verganglichen*, 1935. *"Thus, when it came to divine things, the most primitive Jewish lad was master over the most educated and thinking Greek. What the latter was not capable of grasping was the Jew's property, a gift from heaven which he accepted unconsciously, without realizing or appreciating it fully, without recognizing its value and its difference from heathendom. This great and most unique endowment of the mind, this holy treasure was his universal possession, even as it was the people's inner flame. It was this element which formed the nation."*

Samuel Holdheim, *Neue Sammlung Juedischer Predigten*, 1852. *"It is the destiny of Judaism to pour the light of its thoughts, the fire of its sentiments, the fervor of its feelings upon all souls and hearts on earth. Then all of these peoples and nations, each according to its soil and historic characteristics, will, by accepting our teachings, kindle their own lights, which will then shine independently and warm their souls. Judaism shall be the seed-bed of the nations filled with the blessing and promise, but not a fully grown matured tree with roots and trunk, crowned with branches and twigs, with blossoms and fruit — a tree which is merely to be transplanted into a foreign soil."*

12. Julius Wellhausen, *Prolegomena to the History of Ancient Israel*, 1878. Wellhausen (1844-1918) was one of the founders of Biblical Higher Criticism.

"For the Law, if by that word, we understand the entire Pentateuch, is no literary unity, and no simple historical quantity. Since the days of Peyrerius and Spinoza, criticism has acknowledged the complex character of that remarkable literary production, and from Jean Astruc onwards has labored, not without success, at disentangling its original elements."

13. The Biblical Prophets generally assumed that Yahveh spoke to them alone and not to their rivals. Only *they* were the voice of God.

Jeremiah 23: 25-26. *"I have heard what the prophets say, the prophets who speak lies in my name and cry, 'I have had a dream, a dream!' How long will it be til they change their tune, these prophets who prophesy lies and give voice to their own inventions?"*

Jeremiah 27: 15-17. *"Then Jeremiah said to Hananiah, 'Listen, Hananiah. Yahveh has not sent you, and you have led this nation to trust in false prophecies. Therefore, these are the words of Yahveh: Beware, I will remove you from the face of the earth; you shall die within the year, because you have preached rebellion against Yahveh.'"*

The prophets held a very dim view of a society in which there was diversity of life style and the freedoms of an urban culture, including freedom of religion.

Isaiah 3: 16-17. *"Then Yahveh said: 'Because the women of Zion hold themselves high and walk with necks outstretched and wanton glances, moving with mincing gait and jingling feet, Yahveh will give the women of Zion bald heads. Yahveh will strip the hair from their foreheads.'"*

Jeremiah 7: 17-18. *"Do you not see what is going on in the cities of Judah and in the streets of Jerusalem? Children are gathering wood, fathers lighting fires, women kneading dough to make crescent cakes in honor of the queen of heaven; and drink offerings are poured out to other gods to hurt me."*

Hosea 7: 15-16. *"Though I support them, though I give them strength of arm, they plot evil against me. Like a bow gone slack, they relapse into the worship of their high god. Their talk is all lies, and so their princes shall fall by the sword."*

The Prophets spent an inordinate amount of time describing the violent punishments that people would suffer for their failure to conform to the moral standards of the Prophets. The punishments were collective, not individual.

Jeremiah 5: 15-17. *"I will bring against you, Israel, a nation from afar, an ancient people established long ago, says Yahveh, a people whose language you do not know, whose speech you will not understand. They are all mighty warriors, their jaws are a grave, wide open to devour your harvest and your bread, to devour your sons and your daughters, to devour your flocks and your herds, to devour your vines and your fig-trees. They shall batter down the cities in which you trust."*

Hosea 9: 13-14. *"As lion cubs emerge only to be hunted, so must Ephraim bring out his children for slaughter. Give them Yahveh, — what will you give them — give them a womb that miscarries and dry breasts."*

Amos 9: 1. *"I saw Yahveh standing by the altar and He said: 'Strike the capitals so that the whole porch is shaken. I will smash them all into pieces and I will kill them to the last man with the sword. No fugitive shall escape, no survivor find safety.'"*

Micah 7: 7-10. *"But I will look for Yahveh. I will wait for God my savior. My God will hear me. O, my enemies, do not exalt over me. I have fallen, but I shall rise again. Though I dwell in darkness, Yahveh is my light. I will bear the anger of Yahveh, for I have sinned against Him, until He takes up my cause and gives judgment for me, until He brings me out into light, and I see His justice. Then may my enemies see and be abashed, those who said to me, 'Where is Yahveh your God?' Then shall they be trampled like mud in the streets. I shall gloat over them."*

14. There was very little connection between the flowery missionary vocabulary of the Reform ideologues and the secularized attitudes and behavior of Reform adherents. It was quite obvious that the motivation for joining a Reform congregation had very little to do with missionary zeal.

CHAPTER VIII

The Enthusiasts

1. The ethnicity of Jews always made them vulnerable to accusations of dual loyalty. In bourgeois circles, Jews saw themselves as safer if they had some kind of religious affiliation.

2. Edouard Drumont, the author of *La France Juive,* and Housten Stewart Chamberlain, the author of *The Foundation of the Nineteenth Century,* were the intellectual fathers of the new racial anti-Semitism.

3. The Bund was the common Yiddish name of the Jewish social democratic workers' organization in Russia, Poland, and Lithuania. It was founded in 1897. The Bund opposed the Tsarist regime in Russia. In Jewish life, it claimed the right of the Jewish people to national cultural autonomy wherever they lived. The Bund opposed Zionism and proclaimed Yiddish to be the national language of the Jewish people. It demanded that the government support Yiddish schools and established numerous Yiddish cultural institutions and clubs for the Jewish masses. Following the Bolshevik revolution, most of the Bundists became staunch opponents of communism because the communists envisioned the ultimate elimination of Jewish identity.

4. The famous promoter of Jewish communal autonomy in the midst of a majority non-Jewish culture was Simon Dubnow (1860-1941). Dubnow maintained that Jewish existence does not depend on culture and religion alone, but also on communal organization in the Diaspora. He did not think that Jewish unity depends upon a national territory or an independent

state. He declared that Jewish minority groups, wherever found, should be considered as national groups entitled to cultural and communal autonomy.

5. David Ben Gurion, *The Imperatives of the Jewish Revolution*, 1944. *"What, therefore, is the meaning of our contemporary Jewish revolution — the revolt against destiny which the vanguard of the Jewish national renaissance has been cultivating in this small country for the last three generations? Our entire history in the Galut has represented a resistance of fate — what, therefore, is new in the content of our contemporary revolution? There is one fundamental difference. In the Galut the Jewish people knew the courage of non-surrender, even in the face of the noose and the auto-da-fe, even, as in our day, in the face of being buried alive by the tens of thousands. But the makers of the contemporary Jewish revolution have asserted: Resisting fate is not enough.* We must master our fate. We must take our destiny into our own hands. *This is the doctrine of the Jewish revolution — not non-surrender to the Galut but making an end of it."*

6. Vladimir Jabotinsky, before the Palestine Commission, 1937. *". . . try what has never been tried — try re-establishing the Jewish regiment as part and parcel of the permanent garrison. Try legalizing Jewish self-defense. It is anyway almost inevitable. Jewish self-defense is 'practically' legalized today . . ."*

7. Ber Borochov, *Our Platform*, 1906. *"Political territorial autonomy in Palestine is the ultimate aim of Zionism. For proletarian Zionists, this is also a step toward socialism."*

8. In the *Pittsburgh Platform* (1885) of the American Reform Movement, the Reformers stated clearly: *"We consider ourselves no longer a nation, but a religious community, and therefore expect neither a return to Palestine nor a sacrificial worship under the administration of the sons of Aaron, nor the restoration of any of the laws concerning the Jewish state."*

But in the *Columbus Platform* (1937), after the rise of Hitler to power, the Reformers reversed their former position and declared: *"We affirm the obligation of all Jewry to aid in its* [Israel's] *upbuilding as a Jewish homeland by endeavoring to make it not only a haven of refuge for the oppressed but also a center of Jewish culture and spiritual life."*

9. Thomas Hobbes, *De Corpore*, 1655. *"The world is corporeal, that is to say, body; and has the dimensions of magnitude, namely, length, breadth and depth. Also every part of body is likewise body and has the like dimensions. And consequently every part of the universe is body, and that*

which is not body, is no part of the universe. And because the universe is all, that which is no part of it is nothing and, consequently, no where."

10. Aaron David Gordon, *People and Labor*, 1911. *"The Jewish people has been completely cut off from nature and imprisoned within city walls these two thousand years. We have become accustomed to every form of life, except a life of labor — of labor done at our behest and for its own sake. It will require the greatest effort of will for such a people to become normal again. We lack the principal ingredient for national life. We lack the habit of labor — not labor performed out of external compulsion, but labor to which one is attached in a natural and organic way. This kind of labor binds a people to its soil and to its national culture, which in turn is an outgrowth of the people's soil and the people's labor."*

11. Theodore Herzl (1860-1904), *The Jewish State*, 1896. *"And what glory awaits the selfless fighters for the cause! Therefore I believe that a wondrous breed of Jews will spring up from the earth. The Maccabees will rise again. Let me repeat once more my opening words: The Jews who will it shall achieve their State. We shall live at last as free men on our own soil, and in our own homes peacefully die. The world will be liberated by our freedom, enriched by our wealth, magnified by our greatness. And whatever we attempt there for our own benefit will rebound mightily and beneficially to the good of all mankind."*

12. Asher Ginsberg (Ahad Ha-Am) (1856-1927), *The Jewish State and the Jewish Problem*, 1897. *"The secret of our people's persistence is...that at a very early period the Prophets taught it to respect only the power of the spirit and not to worship material power. Therefore, unlike the other nations of antiquity, the Jewish people never reached the point of losing its self-respect in the face of more powerful armies. As long as we remain faithful to this principle, our existence has a secure basis, and we shall not lose our self-respect..."*

CHAPTER IX

Jewish Identity

1. Brother Daniel was a Polish Jew who was baptized as a Catholic during the war but who was persecuted as a Jew. When he immigrated to Israel after the war, he saw no conflict between his Jewishness and his Catholicism. His Jewish identity was a cultural national identity to which he was deeply attached and for which he had personally suffered.

Although, by traditional law, he was a Jew because his mother was Jewish, the Israeli High Court declared that he was not Jewish because he had formally joined a Christian church. It seemed ironic that a Jewish state, which was established on the Zionist principle that the Jews were a nation, not a religious denomination, would exclude from membership in the Jewish people a person who was passionately nationalistic. Jewish atheists were obviously acceptable. Jewish Catholics were not.

2. Menahem Schneerson, leader of the Lubavitcher Hasidim. *"Every Jew, regardless of his status and station, is essentially willing to do all that is commanded to do by our Torah...When, therefore, the Jewish court compels a Jew to do something, it is not with a view of creating in him a new desire, but rather to release him from the compulsion which had paralyzed his desire, thus enabling him to express his true self...The conscious state of a Jew can be affected by external factors to the extent of inducing states of mind and even behavior which is contrary to his subconscious, which is the Jew's essential nature. When the external pressures are removed, it does not constitute a change of transformation of his essential nature, but, on the contrary, merely the reassertion of his innate and true character."*

3. In the traditional conversion process, the convert is given a "new" ancestry. Converts are designated children of Abraham and Sarah so that their connection with the Jewish people is not only religious, but especially familial.

4. Exodus 7: 2-5. *"You must tell your brother Aaron all I bid you say, and he will tell Pharaoh, and Pharaoh will let the Israelites go out of his country. But I will make him stubborn. Then will I show sign after sign and portent after portent in the land of Egypt. But Pharaoh will not listen to you, so I will assert my power in Egypt, and with mighty acts of judgment I will bring my people, the Israelites, out of Egypt in their tribal hosts. When I put forth my power against the Egyptians and bring the Israelites out from them, then Egypt will know that I am Yahveh."*

5. Exodus 14: 15-18. *"Yahveh said to Moses, 'What is the meaning of this clamor? Tell the Israelites to strike camp. And you shall raise high your staff, stretch out your hand over the sea and cleave it in two, so that the Israelites can pass through the sea on dry ground. For my part I will make the Egyptians obstinate and they will come after you. Thus will I win glory for myself at the expense of Pharaoh and his army, chariots and cavalry all together. The Egyptians will know that I am Yahveh when I win glory for myself at the expense of their Pharaoh, his chariots and cavalry.'"*

6. Jeremiah 27: 12-14. *"I have said all this to Zedekiah king of Judah: If you will submit to the yoke of the king of Babylon and serve him and his people, then you shall save your lives. Why should you and your people die by sword, famine and pestilence, the fate with which Yahveh has threatened any nation which does not serve the king of Babylon?"*

7. Isaiah 45: 1-3. *"Thus says Yahveh to Cyrus his anointed, Cyrus whom he has taken by the hand to subdue the nations before him and undo the might of kings; before whom gates shall be opened and no doors be shut: 'I will go before you and level the swelling hills...that you may know that I am Yahveh, Israel's God who calls you by name.'"*

8. 2 Kings 17: 6-7. *"Then he [Shalmaneser] invaded the whole country and, reaching Samaria, besieged it for three years. In the ninth year of Hoshea he captured Samaria and deported its people to Assyria and settled them in Halah and on the Hobor, the river of Goran, and in the cities of Media. All this happened to the Israelites because they had sinned against Yahveh their God who brought them up from Egypt."*

9. Job 1: 9-12. *"Satan answered Yahveh: 'Has not Job good reason to be God-fearing? Have you not hedged him round on every side with your protection, him and his family and all his possessions?...But stretch out your hand and touch all that he has, and then he will curse you to your face?' Then Yahveh said to Satan, 'So be it. All that he has is in your hands...'"*

10. Isaiah 53: 12. *"Therefore I will allot him a portion with the great and he shall share the spoil with the mighty, because he exposed himself to face death and was reckoned among the transgressors, because he bore the sin of many and interceded for their transgressions."*

11. Numbers 14: 11-16. *"Then Yahveh said to Moses: 'How much longer will this people treat me with contempt? How much longer will they refuse to trust me in spite of all the signs I have shown among them? I will strike them with pestilence. I will deny them their heritage, and you and your descendants I will make into a nation greater and more numerous than they.' But Moses assured Yahveh, 'What if the Egyptians hear of it? It was you who brought the people out of Egypt by your strength. What if they tell the inhabitants of the land? They too have heard of you, Yahveh, that you are with this people and are seen face to face, that your cloud stays over them, and you go before them in a pillar of cloud by day and a pillar of fire by night. If then you do put them to death with one blow, the nations who have heard these tales of you will say, "Yahveh could not bring this people into the land which he promised them by oath." ' "*

12. Isaiah 51: 4-5. *"Pay heed to me, my people, and hear me, O my nation. For my law shall shine forth and I will flash the light of my judgment over the nations."*

13. Christianity picked up on the Jewish misfortune to prove its own point. Jewish suffering was indeed a sign of Yahveh's presence and Yahveh's justice. The Jews who were given the first opportunity to embrace Yahveh's son and failed to do so were now getting what they deserved. They had rejected Yahveh. And Yahveh, in turn, had rejected them.

John 15: 22-25. *"If I had not come and spoken to them, they would not be guilty of sin. But now they have no excuse for their sin. He who hates me hates my Father. If I had not worked among them and accomplished what no other man has done, they would not be guilty of sin. But now they have both seen and hated both me and my Father. However, this text in their Law had to come true: 'They hated me without reason.' "*

14. John Cuddihy, *The Ordeal of Civility,* 1974. *"The 'final triumph' of Marxism is Marx's refusal to give a remedial and apologetic reading of the economic behavior of the Jews, describing it with unembarrassed bluntness, only to turn around and make this crude* Judentum *the very stuff of the bourgeois civilization of the* goyim.

"The famous Jewish social 'impudence'...works at once to destroy aggressively the artificiality of Western 'passing' and to restore the old familiarity of the pre-Emancipation shtetl *Jew...It is the Jewish conviction of the unreconstructed 'Yid' beneath the civil appearance of Jews who are 'passing' that Freud turns into a science. In psychoanalysis the 'id' is the functional equivalent of the 'Yid' in social intercourse. (Sigmund Freud: Because I was a Jew I found myself free from many prejudices which restricted others in the use of their intellect; and as a Jew I was prepared to join the opposition, and to do without agreement with the 'compact majority.')"*

15. Erich Fromm, *You Shall Be As Gods,* 1966. *"The logical consequence of Jewish monotheism is the absurdity of theology. If God has no name there is nothing to talk about. However, any talk about God...implies using God's name in vain. In fact, it brings one close to the danger of idolatry... Although there is no place for theology, I suggest that there is a place and a need for 'idology.' "*

16. Establishment ideology persuaded Jews to accept what was unaccept- able, to praise what deserved no praise, and to thank what deserved no

thanks. These excuses for defeat robbed the Jews of their dignity by exchanging illusion for reality.

17. *Protocols of the Elders of Zion,* an anonymous work created by Russian anti-Semites who identified the Jews as the center of a vicious world conspiracy: *"The principal object of our (the Jews) directorate is this: to debilitate the public mind by criticism; to lead it away from serious reflections calculated to arouse resistance; to distract the forces of the mind towards a sham fight of empty eloquence...In order to put public opinion in our own hands we must bring it into a state of bewilderment, by giving expression from all sides to so many contradictory opinions and for such length of time as will suffice to make the Goyim lose their heads in the labyrinth."*

18. Haim Nahman Bialik, *On the Slaughter,* 1903, written at the time of the Kishinev pogrom:

> *Heaven, beg mercy for me!*
>
> *If there is a God in you, and a pathway through you*
>
> *to this God — which I have not discovered —*
>
> *then pray for me!*
>
> *For my heart is dead, no longer is there prayer on my life.*
>
> *All strength is gone and hope is no more.*
>
> *Until when, how much longer, until when?*
>
> *And if there is justice — let it show itself at once!*
>
> *But if justice shows itself after I have been blotted out from*
>
> > *beneath the skies —*
>
> *Let its throne be hurled down forever.*

19. Sidney Hook, *Out of Step: A Life in the Twentieth Century,* 1984. *"To bring my point home to a pious Jewish audience that prayed to a God who is both all powerful, just and merciful, I asked: 'In the light of the shattering revelations about the Nazi holocaust, how can you still believe that our destinies are governed by an omnipotent and benevolent God?' No sooner had I finished and turned away from the podium than Rabbi Jung sprang from his chair, strode to the front of the platform and, pointing an accusing finger at me, said in loud, withering tones: 'Just listen to the man! He blames God for the Holocaust. It was Roosevelt's fault!'...My interjection, 'But isn't God stronger than Roosevelt?' was lost in the tumultuous applause that greeted Rabbi Jung's devastating retort to me."*

CHAPTER X

Jewish History

1. Since the days of Baruch Spinoza, the idea that the Bible is of divine dictation has been open to question. A scientific criticism of Scripture arose to challenge the traditional view. The foundation of that criticism is that all the sacred literature has a human context and human motivation.

2. If the supernatural exists only in the human imagination, and if the human imagination is controlled by human desire, then the stories about the supernatural arise from human need.

3. The Ten Commandments are part of the *D* document, which the higher scientific critics trace to the reign of King Josiah of Judah around 620 B.C. An earlier version of the Ten Commandments, with a different set of commandments, appears in Exodus 34.

Theophile Meek, in his book *Hebrew Origins* (1936), maintains that the Jews and Israelites, as two distinct nations, arrived at different times in Canaan. The Israelites under Joshua arrived first around 1500 B.C. The Jews under Moses arrived second around 1200 B.C. In the Torah story, edited by the Jews, Moses is given first billing, and the Israelites are incorporated into the Jewish exodus story.

Abraham, Isaac, and Jacob — as the "fathers" of an entire nation — are less likely to be individuals and more likely to be symbols of clans and tribes. They probably symbolize three Semitic invasions of Canaan, the last one of which (Jacob) went down to Egypt.

4. In the oldest historical record of the Hanukka story, the First Book of Maccabees, no mention is made of the miracle of lights. Only centuries later did a Talmudic legend discuss it. There are two *real* reasons why the holiday lasted for eight days. Seasonal festivals, like Sukkot and Pesakh, last for seven or eight days. Hanukka was the renamed winter festival. Also, dedications of the Temple took eight days, as is evidenced in the story of the dedication of Solomon's Temple.

As for the Mishnah, the second Torah of Rabbinic Judaism, the Hebrew of the basic laws would preclude a Mosaic origin.

5. The pre-exilic prophets make almost no reference to Moses, a startling avoidance if Moses is viewed as the great founding prophet of Jewish law. This avoidance is evidence of the fact that, during Davidic times, both Moses and the House of Moses were not seen to be supremely important. Only after the destruction of Jerusalem and the royal House of

David did the House of Moses (the Levitical Zadokites) come to power. It was they who wrote the Torah and who projected the origins of the Law into Mosaic times. In their rivalry with the memory of the House of David, they designed a story in which Moses became the divine vehicle for the creation of the national religion.

6. Since the viewpoint of Jeremiah was the viewpoint of the Biblical editors, his response to the Chaldean invasion of Judah is designated patriotic and divine. But, in reality, there was a legitimate dispute going on between Jeremiah and his prophetic opponents. Jeremiah advocated surrender to the Chaldeans. His enemies advocated resistance. Jeremiah justified his advice by claiming that the Jews deserved to be punished for their sins and that Nebuchadnezzar, the king of the Chaldeans, was the instrument of the divine wrath. His opponents rejected both the analysis and the masochism.

Both contending sides claimed that their opponents were false prophets. They revealed, by their controversy, that ordinary citizens had no easy time trying to figure out what Yahveh wanted them to do.

7. Before the destruction of the Second Temple, two religious parties vied for allegiance of the Jewish public. The larger was the Pharisees, whose leaders were the rabbis. The smaller was the Sadducees, whose leaders were the priests. The main contention between the two was the refusal of the Sadducees to recognize the authority of the rabbinic "second Torah," a tradition of oral laws which the rabbis traced back to Moses. Ultimately, this Oral Law was written down and became the Mishnah, the beginning of the Talmud.

8. Writings contrary to rabbinic doctrine were banned by the rabbis. The most familiar example are the banned books of the Bible, the Apocrypha in Greek, which were denied scriptural standing at the Council of Yavne (*circa* 90). These books were suppressed in Palestine, but were rescued by Greek Jews. They ultimately found their way into the Catholic version of the Old Testament. Among the Apocrypha is the First Book of Maccabees, the only semi-reliable history of the Hanukka story. Since the Maccabees were despised by the Mishnaic rabbis, the book was suppressed.

9. Yahveh emerges as the supreme god of the world at a time when victorious Near Eastern nations were turning their gods into universal rulers. Mazda of Persia was also viewed as god of gods in the same way that his ethnic patron was designated king of kings. In the end, the lesser gods were simply seen as manifestations of a single divine intelligence, as among the Greek philosophers, or they were demoted to the status of angels and devils, as among the Jews and the Persians.

What made Jewish monotheism unique was not the notion of a unique supreme world commander, but the insistence that Yahveh was his name and that no other name would do for invoking his presence and assistance. It was an ungracious denial of the possibility that he could be called by many national names and still be God. Insisting that only the Jewish god was the god of the world had a bizarre parochial edge to it.

10. Today, almost all the Jews of the world live in large cities. Even in Israel, most Jews live in the urban crescent of Haifa, Tel Aviv, and Jerusalem. No other ethnic group — with the possible exception of the Parsees in Bombay — is so heavily citified.

11. Aaron David Gordon (1856-1922), *People and Labor*, 1911. See Chapter VIII, Note 10.

12. In the Bible, the superiority of the past is demonstrated by the age of the first people. There is a descending order of longevity from Noah to David. The first humans possess the character of demi-gods. Methuselah with his one thousand years, Abraham with his two hundred, and Moses with his 120 seem more than human. The figures of the past have a divine character. They are symbols of a golden age, now vanished, when people were superior to what they are now.

Even the generation of Moses was special because it was privileged to hear the divine voice and to witness divine miracles. The Jews who followed the prophets did not have that privilege. In modern times, the reverence for the rabbinic fathers prevents traditional rabbis from altering the most innocuous customs of the past.

13. The prophecy attributed to Amos (Amos 9: 9-12) was most likely not authored by Amos, but its insertion "kosherized" his prophecies by fitting them into Messianic expectations: *"On that day I [Yahveh] will restore David's fallen house. I will repair its gaping walls and restore its ruins. I will rebuild it as it was long ago, that they may possess what is left of Edom, and all the nations who were once named mine."*

For the compilers of the Bible the social message of the prophets was less important than the imagined predictions of national salvation (many of which were simply insertions by later writers). As prophecies of consolation, they were preserved and used as the ritual readings of the early synagogue.

14. The glorification of Moses in the Torah also includes his relatives, the Levitical priests. The story served their vested interests and enhanced their power.

The glorification of David in the Book of Samuel, especially in his relationship to his supposed persecutor Saul, justifies his assumption of power and legitimizes the rule of his descendants.

CHAPTER XI

Anti-Semitism

1. Tacitus, *Histories, circa* 100. As you can see, anti-Semitism preceded Christianity.

"The customs of the Jews are base and abominable, and owe their persistence to their depravity. Jews are extremely loyal towards one another, and always ready to show compassion, but toward every other people they feel only hate and enmity. As a race they are prone to lust. Among themselves nothing is unlawful."

"The Jews reveal a stubborn attachment to one another, an active commiseration which contrasts with their implacable hatred for the rest of mankind. They sit apart at meals. They sleep apart. And, though, as a nation, they are singularly prone to debauchery, they abstain from intercourse with foreign women."

2. *New York Morning Post*, August 7, 1971. *"The Jews are a great nation, emphatically a nation, and the able statecraft of their secret rulers has kept them a nation through forty centuries of the world's history. In their heads lies the traditional knowledge of the whole earth, and there are no State secrets of any nation but are shared also by the secret rulers of Jewry."*

3. John Cuddihy, *The Ordeal of Civility*, 1974. *"Freud's campaign... was not for truth and against lies. It was for shocking truth and against 'decorous lies.' An important feature of Freud's thought was its shocking content."*

4. Leo Pinsker (1821-1891), *Auto-Emancipation*, 1882. *"In the life of peoples, as in the life of individuals, there are important moments which do not often recur, and which, depending on whether they are utilized or not utilized, exercise a decisive influence upon the future of the people as upon that of the individual, whether for weal or for woe. We are now passing through such a moment. The consciousness of the people is awake. The great ideas of the eighteenth and nineteenth centuries have not passed by our people without leaving a trace. We feel not only as Jews, we feel as men. As men, we, too, wish to live like other men and be a nation like the others. And if we seriously desire that, we must first of all throw off the old yoke of*

oppression and rise manfully to our full height. We must first of all desire
to help ourselves...*Only, then, will the help of others, as well, be sure to
come."*

5. The Jews were replaced as bankers in Western Europe by the Italian
Lombards. The Lombards had several advantages. They were Christians.
They had access to new and powerful resources. They enabled the debtors
to repudiate their debts to the Jews without fear of retaliation.

CHAPTER XII

Evolution of the Holidays

1. Alvin Reines, *Questions and Answers on Polydoxy*, 1979. *"What
changes in the celebration dates of holidays have been presented as options to
Polydox Jews?...It is an evident value for all Jews to celebrate holidays on
the same dates. When it becomes quite clear, however, that the dates on
which certain holidays fall in the present Jewish calendar result either in
the holiday going without celebration or in a celebration of vastly
diminished relevance and meaning, then the option of a different celebration
date is made available...A person may celebrate Chanukah for eight days
beginning on the twenty-fifth day of Kislev in the present Jewish calendar.
Others choose to celebrate Chanukah for eight days, beginning on the winter
solstice, December 21, 22."*

2. During the period of the Davidic kings the harvest festivals of Sukkot
and *Matsot* (later combined with Pesakh) had no connection with the story
of the Jewish exodus and the leadership primacy of Moses. But the Torah,
the supreme document of the Levitical priests, connects both major
festivals with Moses. Pesakh comes to commemorate the miraculous departure of the Hebrews from Egypt under the leadership of Moses. Sukkot
ends up commemorating the dwelling of the Jews for forty years in the
desert in huts. The tracing of two agricultural festivals to a wilderness of
nomads is a dramatic example of theological *hutspa*.

CHAPTER XIII

The Jewish Calendar

1. The original mood of the Shabbat was not restful. It corresponded to
the Babylonian *Shabbatum*, which fell on the full moon and was regarded as
an unlucky day when abstinence from activity was indispensable to

survival. The concepts of *danger* and *holiness* often go together. When, in the priestly period, the seventh day of the week was declared a Shabbat, the abstinence from activity followed. In the historic documents that were authored in the pre-Exilic period, there is very little reference to a seventh day Sabbath.

2. Genesis 2: 1-3. *"Thus heaven and earth were completed with all their mighty throng. On the sixth day God completed all the work He had been doing and on the seventh day He ceased from all his work. God blessed the seventh day and made it holy, because on that day He ceased from all the work He had set Himself to do."*

Isaiah 56: 1-2. *"These are the words of Yahveh: Maintain justice, do the right! For my deliverance is close at hand, and my righteousness will show itself victorious. Happy is the man who follows these precepts, happy is the mortal who holds them fast, who keeps the Sabbath undefiled, who refrains from all wrong-doing."* (The Sabbath here is elevated to the status of the major sign of allegiance to Yahveh.)

3. Isaiah 56: 6-7. *"So too with the foreigners who give their allegiance to me, Yahveh, to minister to me and love my name and to become my servants. All who keep the Sabbath undefiled and hold fast to my covenant* [circumcision], *them will I bring to my holy hill and give them joy in my house of prayer."*

4. Originally Rosh Hashana was an *atseret,* a closing day of the fall (Sukkot) festival. Shemini Atseret, the eighth day of the Sukkot celebration, still retains repentance features reminiscent of the New Year. And the annual cycle of the Torah reading does not begin again on Rosh Hashana, but on Shemini Atseret (Simhat Torah).

5. The moving of Rosh Hashana from the end of Sukkot to the first day of the seventh month destroyed the logical sequence of the holidays. Yom Kippur (the day of purification) which should precede Rosh Hashana (the day of judgment) now followed it. Ultimately, the rabbis rationalized the discrepancy by inventing a nine day hold on the divine judgment before it became final.

6. Leviticus 23: 41-43. *"It is a rule binding for all time on your descendants. In the seventh month you shall hold this pilgrim feast. You shall live in arbors for seven days, all who are native Israelites, so that your decendants may be reminded how I made the Israelites live in huts when I brought them out of Egypt. I am Yahveh your God."*

7. Fire and human survival evolutionarily go together. Fire is a symbol of human continuity and safety. The maintenance of sacred fires and the lighting of new fires on special occasions are important duties in almost all cultures.

The connection between the *Hanukkiya* (the flat board of eight lights) and the *Menorah* (the Temple candelabra of seven lights) is dubious. The lighting of fires in increasing numbers over an eight day period does not follow logically from the legend about sacred lights that burned miraculously for eight days. Kindling seven fires for eight days would be more consistent with the story. The actual practice fits more comfortably into a magical procedure to increase the intensity of the sun's fire.

8. Having captured Jerusalem in September, Judah Maccabee chose the next convenient festival for the eight day dedication of the altar *(Hanukkat Ha-Mizbeakh)* in the Temple. The Maccabeans transformed *Nayrot* into a Maccabean festival, touting Maccabean virtues. Ultimately, the new name *Hanukka* replaced the old.

"Moreover Judah and his brothers, with the whole congregation of Israel, ordained that the days of the dedication of the altar should be kept in their season from year to year by the space of eight days, from the 25th day of the month of Kislev, with mirth and gladness." (I Maccabees 4: 59.)

9. In the Mishnah, the second Torah of rabbinic Judaism, no mention is made of Hanukka. Only in the Gemara commentary of later centuries do sparse references emerge, including the legend of the holy oil.

Purim was a folk holiday which the rabbis viewed suspiciously, since it seemed to be clearly of Mesopotamian and Persian origin and since the Book of Esther (the admission of which to Holy Scriptures was hotly debated) makes no reference to Yahveh.

Only the necessity of suppressing a hated Maccabean holiday finally convinced the rabbis to support Purim.

Nicanor's Day, which was the major patriotic celebration of the Maccabean period and which commemorated the decisive victory of the Maccabees over the Greek general Nicanor, fell on the 13th day of Adar. Purim fell on the 14th.

The rabbis suppressed the Nicanor's Day celebration by declaring the day to be a fast day (Fast of Esther) preceding Purim.

10. Despite all the new "pizzazz," Hanukka has a hard time competing with Christmas in America. First, the story of a minor Jewish military victory pales before the story of a god's incarnation and birth.

Second, Christmas in secular America is so tied up with the end of year New Year celebration that the worlds of media and commerce give it continuous attention.

11. In many respects the Maccabees were no different from Antiochus. Each adversary was committed to the absolute validity of his position and to the necessity of destroying all opposition. The Hellenists fared no better under the Maccabees than the pious did under Antiochus. "Toleration" was not one of the bywords of that struggle. Ultimately, John Maccabee, through his conquest of Samaria and Galilee, sought to impose Jewish identity on the newly conquered. As a Jewish Antiochus, he combined imperialism with religious conformity.

National liberation is distinct from personal liberation and personal freedom. It is a struggle for what many perceive to be dignity — the right of ethnic groups to be governed by members of their own race. What the Maccabees achieved for the Jews was not religious freedom or personal independence. What they conferred upon the Jews was a government of Jews who were not the puppets of outside powers. The high priests in the Persian period were the agents of the Persians. But the Maccabees were their own agents. In so far as they were independent, the nation was independent.

12. Phallic pillars were associated with Baal. And sacred trees (and groves) were identified with his consort in fertility, Asherah. The priests and priestesses of Asherah (Ashtarot) were tree worshipers very much like the Keltic Druids.

The Yahveh prophets denounced the pillars and trees and insisted on their removal.

13. In rabbinic Judaism, the holiday was "purified." All non-Yahvistic associations were removed. As the New Year of the Trees, it received Talmudic sanction and remained a very minor innocuous festival until Zionism resurrected it.

14. While Yom Haatsmaut (Iyar 5), which commemorates the achievement of Israeli independence, is more dramatically identified with the new Jewish state, there are no "rituals" which compellingly involve Diaspora Jews. Buying trees for planting in Israel, which Tu Bi-Shevat makes important, has become a very widespread constructive "ritual" among Diaspora Jews. In the end, Tu Bi-Shevat has more to offer as an Israel Day than its showier rival.

15. In Mesopotamia, where Purim originated and where the aristocratic priestly exiles of Judah imbibed the local culture, Purim was a Mardi Gras-type festival where the victory of life over death was dramatically re-enacted.

16. The Book of Esther, on the surface, makes no reference to God and supernatural intervention. But, of course, this surprising absence is the result of rabbinic censorship. The Babylonian gods are turned into people to make them acceptable to a Jewish audience.

But, for the rabbis, a story with no reference to Yahveh — even though enormously appealing to the masses — was highly suspect. If it were not for the fact that the rabbis needed Purim to erase the memory of the Maccabees, the Book of Esther would never have been accepted into Holy Scriptures.

17. The Torah refers to *two* spring holidays. *Hag Ha-Matsot* (the Feast of Unleavened Bread) often appears with no reference to Pesakh (Exodus 34: 18). Like the eight lights of *Nayrot* (Hanukka) which were lit by Jews for many centuries before the Maccabees emerged, the matsa was part of the spring celebration long before it was attached to the Exodus story. The spring grain harvest of barley and wheat was the grand celebration. And the flat bread from new grain became the symbol of the harvest.

18. The *pesakh* or "passover" may refer either to a skipping dance or to the passing over of the omnipresent evil spirits who are always abundant around the full moon (Nissan 15).

Using blood to hold back death-bearing supernatural powers is part of the folk practices in many cultures. Even the angel of death is driven away from Jewish homes by the blood of the sacrificial lamb.

Among shepherd Jews, marking the doorplate with lamb's blood at Pesakh time preceded the formulation of the Exodus story. The story of the Egyptian first-born is a rationalization of an existing practice.

19. The scientific criticism of the Bible reveals that the Torah is composed of four documents which have been merged by priestly editors. In chronological order they are designated *J, E, D* and *P*. In *J* and *E, Pesakh* and *Matsot* are separate and distinct. In *D*, they have been united.

D refers to the basic style which pervades the books of Deuteronomy, Judges, Samuel, and Kings. It was most likely created around 620 B.C. during the reign of King Josiah of Judah, who sought to reunite the two Hebrew kingdoms of Judah and Israel (Samaria).

The *new* Pesakh was developed around a new great national epic, the Exodus from Egypt. What had been only the experience of the Jews was now made the experience of all the Hebrews. The spring holidays of both farmer and shepherd were subordinated to this epic. All their historic rituals were tied to Exodus explanations.

Josiah imagined that the enlarged Pesakh festival, with its epic story of national origins, would help to bind Jews and Samaritans. But the unexpected arrival of the hostile Chaldeans shattered his ambition.

20. The Exodus story that now appears in the Torah had an important political meaning. The exaltation of the Levitical Moses gave prestige and legitimacy to the Levitical priests. The exaltation of Yahveh made them essential to Jewish survival, since they alone possessed the means to appease Yahveh.

21. Theophile Meek, *Hebrew Origins*, 1936. According to Theophile Meek, only the Levites, the priestly tribe of the Jews, made the "exodus" from Egypt. Most Hebrews had never lived in Egypt. Nor did they have Moses as their leader.

"The more the records are studied, the clearer it is that there are two cycles of traditions concerning the Hebrew entry into Palestine. According to one, the entry was from the east across the Jordan and in this Joshua is the leading figure. The tribes are Israelites. And the conquests are in the north. According to the other, the entry was from the south and it is associated with Judah, Simeon, Caleb, Othmiel and other related tribes, with Moses as the leading figure. The first invasion was manifestly Israelite, and the second Judean. The Old Testament narrative, as we have it now in its later nationalized form, has dovetailed the two conquests into each other as the work of a single people, resulting naturally in a good deal of confusion and inconsistency."

22. The great song of the ghetto fighters affirms their defiance in the face of desperation:

Never say that you are on your final road,

Though overhead dark skies of lead may death forbode.

The long-awaited hour's surely drawing near,

When with a roar our steps will thunder we are here.

(translated from the Yiddish)

CHAPTER XIV

Passages

1. The original significance of circumcision is reflected in one of the oldest passages from the Torah (Exodus 4: 24-26): *"And it came to pass on the way to the lodging place that Yahveh met him [the son of Moses] and sought to kill him. Then Zipporah took a flint and cut off the foreskin of her son and cast it at his feet. And she said: 'Surely a bridegroom of blood are you to me.' So He [Yahveh] let him alone. Then she said: 'A bridegroom of blood in regard of the circumcision.' "*

2. The authors of the Torah made infant circumcision the chief sign of Jewish identity and divine protection.

Genesis 17: 9-14. *"God said to Abraham, 'For your part you must keep my covenant, you and your descendants after you, generation by generation. This is how you shall keep my covenant between myself and you and your descendants after you. Circumcize yourselves, every male among you. You shall circumcize the flesh of your foreskin, and it shall be the sign of the covenant between us. Every male among you, in every generation, shall be circumcized on the eighth day, both those born in your house and any foreigner, not of your blood but bought with your money. Circumcize both those born in your house and those bought with your money. Thus shall my covenant be marked in your flesh as an everlasting covenant. Every uncircumcized male, everyone who has not had the flesh of his foreskin circumcized, shall be cut off from the kin of his father. He has broken my covenant!' "*

3. Among most Semitic peoples, including the Arabs, circumcision took place at the onset of puberty. It was part of the tribal rite of passage that permitted young males to enter adult society. Even today, among the Arabs, circumcision is performed somewhere between infancy and puberty.

4. Hayyim Schauss, *The Lifetime of a Jew*, 1950. *"No ceremonial to celebrate the attainment of majority could have evolved in Talmudic and early medieval times because, according to the Talmud, a minor was permitted to participate in all religious observances as soon as he was considered mentally fit...Gradually, during the later Middle Ages this situation underwent a change. The religious rights which the Talmud accorded to the minor were now restricted. He was deprived of the right to be 'called up' to the reading of the Torah. He was no longer permitted to wear t'fillin (two black boxes tied to the head and the left arm). The attainment of majority gained new importance as an attainment of new religious rights*

and the ground was prepared for a ceremonial around the bar mitzva as a boy thirteen years old was beginning to be called...The attainment of religious majority signified the attainment of the right to witness the reading of the Torah on the bima and to recite the benediction over it."

5. See Chapter XIII, pp. 169 f. The criteria of a humanistic Jewish hero are laid out in the description of Purim as Hero Day.

6. The ring formula is recited only by the groom and is quite male chauvinistic. *"Behold, you are consecrated to me* [made my possession] *with this ring in accordance with the law of Moses and Israel."*

7. In the minds of many people, the removal of the body would also involve the quick removal of the attached spirit. Since the spirits of the dead were either angry or jealous, they might prove dangerous if they remained in the area.

8. For parents, mourning lasts one year. For "lesser" relatives, a month will do, with one week of intense mourning.

CHAPTER XV

The Bible and Humanistic Judaism

1. Exodus 10: 1-2. *"Then Yahveh said to Moses, 'Go into Pharaoh's presence. I have made him and his courtiers obdurate, so that I may show these my signs among them, and so that you can tell your children and grandchildren the story: how I made sport of the Egyptians, and what signs I showed among them. Thus you will know that I am Yahveh.'"*

2. Genesis 1 and 2 are mutually incompatible. In the first creation story, God made the animals first and then man. In the second creation story, God made man first and then the animals.

Exodus 20: 5. *("I Yahveh, your God, am a jealous God. I punish the children for the sins of the fathers to the third and fourth generations of those who hate me.")* and Deuteronomy 24: 16 *("Fathers shall not be put to death for their children, nor children for their fathers. A man shall be put to death only for his own sin.")* are incompatible. Individual and collective guilt are opposing ideas.

Mesopotamia may have suffered a massive flood. But the whole world did not.

The Hebrew of the Torah comes from the Hebrew of the later royal period and the priestly period, many centuries after Moses lived. In fact, there are at least four distinct Hebrew styles in the Torah.

The documentary theory of Julius Wellhausen (a nineteenth century German Biblical scholar whose ideas became the basis of modern scientific Biblical criticism) was an attempt to account for these and numerous other contradictions and puzzlements. Wellhausen proposed that the Torah was a composite book. Four separate documents had been merged to make one. In the merger, the priestly editors failed to eliminate all contradictions and repetitions.

The four documents are generally labelled *J, E, D* and *P. J* comes from the Hebrew kingdom of Judah and the ninth century. *E* comes from the Hebrew kingdom of Israel and the eighth century. *D* comes from the time of Josiah, the king of the Jews who reigned around 620 B.C. And *P*, the most important, comes from the Jerusalem priesthood, the family of the Zadokites and the fifth century. The authors of *P* edited the final Torah.

3. Both Sabbath observance and honesty are given equal status in the Decalogue. In fact, the punishment for Sabbath violation is more severe than that for stealing: *"Whoever works on that day shall be put to death."* (Exodus 35: 2.)

4. Eve is punished for seducing her husband: *"You shall be eager for your husband and he shall be your master."* (Genesis 3: 16.)

The Canaanites, the neighbors of the Hebrews, are declared the descendants of the wicked Ham, the abuser of his father Noah, and are condemned to eternal slavery: *"Cursed be Canaan, slave of slaves shall he be to his brothers."* (Genesis 9: 25.)

5. Abraham Geiger, the leading ideologue of nineteenth century Reform Judaism, viewed the Torah as one step in the continuing revelation of God's will through the ages. The ethics of the Torah were an anticipation of the more sophisticated morality of later centuries.

6. Isaiah 3: 8. *"Jerusalem is stricken and Judah fallen because they have spoken and acted against Yahveh, rebelling against the glance of his glorious eye."*

Isaiah 10: 4. *"So the anger of Yahveh is roused against his people. He has stretched out his hand against them and struck them down. The mountains trembled, and their corpses lay like offal in the streets."*

Jeremiah 9: 11.*"I will make Jerusalem a heap of ruins, a haunt of wolves, and the cities of Judah unpeopled waste."*

Micah 5: 14-15. *"I will pull down the sacred poles in your land, and demolish your blood-spattered altars. In anger and fury will I take vengeance on all nations who disobey me."*

7. Jeremiah 37: 17-18. *"These are the words of Yahveh, the God of Hosts, the God of Israel: 'If you go out and surrender to the officers of the king of Babylon, you shall live and this city shall not be burnt down. You and your family shall live. But if you do not surrender to the officers of the king of Babylon, the city shall fall into the hands of the Chaldeans, and they shall burn it down, and you will not escape them.' "*

8. The four prophetic books (Isaiah, Jeremiah, Ezekiel and The Twelve) are dominated by the ideas of divine judgment and divine forgiveness. In the end, Yahveh will restore the Jews to their fortunes, and they will live happily ever after.

Isaiah 40: 1-2. *"Comfort, comfort my people. It is the voice of your God. Speak tenderly to Jerusalem and tell her this — that she has fulfilled her term of bondage, that her penalty is paid. She has received at Yahveh's hand double measure for all her sins."*

Without this message of hope, the other messages of the prophets would never have been preserved.

9. The prophets whose words are recorded in the Bible were not the *only* prophets. There were many other prophets of Yahveh in the land who disagreed with the men favored by the Biblical editors.

When Amaziah, the priest of Bethel, ordered Amos to depart his temple (Amos 7: 10-17), he firmly believed that the Temple ritual which Amos denounced was commanded by Yahveh and was the *right* thing to do. In his eyes, Amos was the blasphemer.

When Hananiah, the prophet of Jerusalem, denounced Jeremiah because Jeremiah recommended that Jews surrender to their Chaldean enemies, he firmly believed that surrender was *evil* and that Jeremiah was a *false* prophet (Jeremiah 28: 1-11.)

The Biblical authors do not do justice to the prophecies and arguments of the opposition. They prefer to denounce them.

10. One of the great dangers is to project modern reasoning into the past. The dietary laws are a perfect example of the difficulty. Given the nature of slaughter and food preservation in ancient times, eating mutton was as dangerous as eating pork. Even if you maintain that the avoidance of pork was to prevent trichinosis, how do you account for the fact that such lovely insects as grasshoppers and crickets were declared kosher? *All* the dietary

laws do not sustain the governing principle of health maintained by many
modern "rational" traditionalists.

CHAPTER XVI

The Alternative Literature

The following books and essays by Jewish writers are candidates for
the beginning of a "classic" Humanistic Jewish literature.

Hannah Arendt (1906-1975), *Anti-Semitism (The Origins of Totalitar-
ianism)*, 1951.

David Ben Gurion (1886-1973), *The Imperatives of the Jewish Revolution*,
1944.

Micah Berdichevsky (1865-1921), *Wrecking and Building*, 1900.

Isaiah Berlin (1909-   ), *The Age of Enlightenment*, 1956, *The Concepts of
Liberty*, 1958.

Franz Boas (1858-1942), *Race, Language and Culture*, 1940.

Joseph Brenner (1881-1921), *Self-Criticism*, 1914.

Jacob Bronowski (1908-1974), *Science and Human Values*, 1953.

Simon Dubnow (1860-1941), *World History of the Jewish People*, 1923.

Emile Durkheim (1858-1917), *The Elementary Forms of the Religious Life*,
1912.

Albert Einstein (1879-1955), *Out of My Later Years*, 1950.

Howard Fast (1914-   ), *The Jews*, 1968.

Sigmund Freud (1856-1939), *The Future of an Illusion*, 1927.

Erich Fromm (1900-1980), *The Art of Loving*, 1951.

Theodore Gaster (1906-   ), *Customs and Folkways of Jewish Life*, 1955,
Festivals of the Jewish Year, 1952.

Emma Goldman, (1869-1940), *Living My Life,* 1931.

Aaron David Gordon (1856-1922), *People and Labor,* 1911.

Theodore Herzl (1860-1904), *The Jewish State,* 1896.

Horace Kallen (1882-1974), *Judaism at Bay,* 1932.

Berl Katzenelson (1887-1944), *Revolution and Tradition,* 1934.

Abraham Maslow (1908-1970), *Towards a Psychology of Being,* 1962.

Albert Memmi (1920-   ), *Portrait of a Jew,* 1962.

Max Nordau (1849-1923), *The Conventional Lies of Our Civilization,* 1883, *Morals and the Evolution of Man,* 1921.

Hayyim Schauss (1884-1953), *The Jewish Festivals,* 1938, *Lifetime of the Jew,* 1950.

Peretz Smolenskin (1842-1885), *It Is Time to Plant,* 1877.

Chaim Zhitlowsky (1865-1943), *The Development of Philosophy,* 1910.

CHAPTER XVII

Israel

1. In America, where the Israelis are viewed as allies, dual loyalty presents few problems. But in the Soviet Union, where Israel is seen as an enemy satellite of the United States, dual loyalty provides a scenario of incompatible goals.

So long as nation states remain the highest political reality, the Jews, as an international people, will not be easily accommodated. Only in a world where it is accepted that individual citizens may have loyalties and commitments that transcend national boundaries will Jews be truly comfortable.

2. David Ben Gurion, *The Imperatives of the Jewish Revolution,* 1944. *"Galut (Diaspora) means dependence — material, political, spiritual, cultural and intellectual dependence — because we are aliens, a minority bereft of a homeland, rootless and separated from the soil, from labor, and*

from basic industry. Our task is to break radically with this dependence and to become masters of our own fate — in a word, to achieve independence."

Jacob Klatzkin (1882-1948), *Boundaries*, 1914-1922. Klatzkin was the most devastating anti-traditionalist of all the rebels within Zionism.

"Galut Jewry cannot survive and all our efforts to keep it alive can have only a temporary success. But let us by no means disparage such a success. Such a temporary life has a great function, if it serves the purpose of a lasting life, of the upbuilding of our nation in its homeland. Galut Jewry cannot survive and all our efforts to keep it alive are simply an act of coercion, the maintenance of an unnatural existence."

3. Aaron David Gordon (1856-1922), *Our Tasks Ahead,* 1920. Gordon was Zionism's secular mystic and saint.

"Jewish life in the Diaspora lacks this cosmic element of national identity. It is sustained by the historic element alone, which keeps us alive and will not let us die, but it cannot provide us with a full national life."

4. The "Canaanites" wanted the Hebrew state to be "normal." To be a Hebrew was to live in the Hebrew homeland and to speak Hebrew — in the same way that to be French was to live in France and to speak French. If a Palestinian Arab Muslim adopted Hebrew as his personal language, he would be more of a Hebrew than the non-Hebrew speaking Jew of the Diaspora.

5. There are two nations living within the state of Israel — a Hebrew-speaking Jewish nation and an Arabic-speaking Palestinian nation. If you include the "Occupied Territories" of the West Bank and Gaza, two out of every five inhabitants of Israel is a Palestinian Arab. The presence of the Arabs in Israel is certainly as dramatic as that of the French in Canada.

CHAPTER XVIII

Intermarriage and Conversion

1. The Central Conference of American Rabbis adopted a resolution in 1909 that stated *"that mixed marriage is contrary to the Jewish tradition and should be discouraged."* But they never declared their opposition to Reform rabbis officiating at intermarriage ceremonies.

2. In 1973, in Atlanta, the Central Conference of American Rabbis passed a strong resolution condemning Reform rabbis who officiated at

intermarriage ceremonies. It declared its *"opposition to participation by its members in any ceremony which solemnizes a mixed marriage."*

3. Deuteronomy 7: 1-4. *"When Yahveh your God brings you into the land which you are entering to occupy and drives out many nations before you...you must put them to death. You must not make any treaty with them or spare them. You must not intermarry with them, neither giving your daughters to their sons nor taking their daughters for your sons. If you do they will draw your sons away from Yahveh and make them worship other gods."*

4. Nehemiah 13: 23-27. *"In those days also I* [Nehemiah, the colleague of Ezra] *saw that some Jews had married women from Ashdod, Ammon and Moab. Half their children spoke the language of Ashdod or of the other peoples and could not speak the language of the Jews. I argued with them and reviled them. I beat them and tore out their hair. And I made them swear in the name of God: 'We will not marry our daughters to their sons, or take any of their daughters in marriage for our sons or for ourselves.'"*

5. Emil Fackenheim, *Quest for Past and Future,* 1968. Fackenheim is a Canadian Jewish philosopher who derives much of his theology from the Holocaust experience.

"We have lived in this contradiction for twenty years without being able to face it. Unless I am mistaken, we are now beginning to face it, however fragmentarily and inconclusively. And from this beginning confrontation there emerges what I will boldly term a 614th commandment: the authentic Jew of today is forbidden to hand Hitler yet another posthumous victory."

6. In popular culture, children of Jewish fathers are regarded as half-Jews (a tribute to the perception of the Jews as an ethnic group). Certainly, in a culture dominated by surnames, fathers are more powerful at determining the social identities of their children than are mothers. A child with a Gentile mother and the surname *Cohen* is more likely to be regarded as Jewish by both Jews and Gentiles than a child born of a Jewish mother with the last name of *Murphy.*

CHAPTER XIX

Secular Religion

1. John Stuart Mill, *The Utility of Religion,* 1874. *"The essence of religion is the strong and earnest direction of the emotions and desires*

toward an ideal object, recognized as of the highest excellence, and as rightfully paramount over all selfish objects of desire. This condition is fulfilled by the Religion of Humanity in as eminent a degree and in as high a sense as by the supernatural religions even in their best manifestations, and far more so than in any of their others."

2. Alfred North Whitehead, *Science and the Modern World*, 1925. Whitehead was a liberal theist who is enjoying a new vogue in liberal theological circles.

"Religion is the vision of something which stands beyond, behind and within the passing flux of immediate things; something which is real and yet waiting to be realized; something that gives meaning to all that passes, and yet eludes apprehension; something whose possession is the final good and yet is beyond all reach; something which is the ultimate ideal and the hopeless quest."

3. Attempts to equate religion and morality — like those of Felix Adler and Matthew Arnold — raise the question of redundancy. If religion is no more than ethics, then why the word *religion*? Similarly, liberal attempts to equate religion with the "meaning of life" — like those of Gordon Allport and Paul Tillich — pose similar problems. Is religion only a synonym for the search for meaning?

Allport, one of America's most prominent psychologists of the religious experience, seeks to make any behavior religious so long as there is the appropriate internal disposition: *"Shall we then define the mature religious sentiment as a disposition, built up through experience, to respond favorably and in certain habitual ways to conceptual objects and principles that the individual regards as of ultimate importance in his own life and as having to do with what he regards as permanent or central in the nature of things."*

4. Desmond Morris, *Manwatching*, 1977. *"We are forced to the conclusion that, in a behavioral sense, religious activities consist of the coming together of large groups of people to perform repeated and prolonged submissive displays to appease a dominant individual...The submissive responses to it may consist of closing the eyes, lowering the head, clasping the hands together in a begging gesture, kneeling, kissing the ground or even extreme prostration, with the frequent accompaniment of wailing or chanting vocalizations. The dominant individual is usually, but not always, referred to as a god."*